BLACK ON BOTH SIDES

Also by C. Riley Snorton
Nobody Is Supposed to Know: Black Sexuality on the Down Low

BLACK

A Racial History of

ON BOTH

Trans Identity

SIDES

C. RILEY SNORTON

University of Minnesota Press | Minneapolis | London

Lyrics in chapter 5 were previously published as "The Father, Son, and Unholy Ghosts," in Essex Hemphill, *Tongues Untied: Poems by Dirg Aaab-Richards, Craig G. Harris, Essex Hemphill, Isaac Jackson, Assotto Sainte* (London: GMP, 1987). Reprinted with permission of the Frances Goldin Literary Agency, Inc.

Published by the University of Minnesota Press
111 Third Avenue South, Suite 290
Minneapolis, MN 55401-2520
http://www.upress.umn.edu

ISBN 978-1-5179-0172-1 (hc)
ISBN 978-1-5179-0173-8 (pb)
A Cataloging-in-Publication record for this book is available from the Library of Congress.

Printed in the United States of America on acid-free paper

The University of Minnesota is an equal-opportunity educator and employer.

22 21 20 19 18 17   10 9 8 7 6 5 4 3 2 1

CONTENTS

PREFACE   vii

INTRODUCTION   I

Part I. Blacken

1. Anatomically Speaking: Ungendered Flesh and the
   Science of Sex   17

2. Trans Capable: Fungibility, Fugitivity, and the
   Matter of Being   55

Part II. Transit

3. Reading the "Trans-" in Transatlantic Literature:
   On the "Female" within *Three Negro Classics*   101

Part III. Blackout

4. A Nightmarish Silhouette: Racialization and the
   Long Exposure of Transition   139

5. DeVine's Cut: Public Memory and the
   Politics of Martyrdom   177

ACKNOWLEDGMENTS   199

NOTES   205

INDEX   245

PREFACE

The problem considered here is one of time.

—**FRANTZ FANON**, *Black Skin, White Masks*

IN 2015, WHILE GARNERING PUBLICITY for the feature film *Grandma* in a live interview with Robin Roberts on *Good Morning America*, actress, artist, and advocate Laverne Cox expressed a public grief:

> We in the transgender community right now are reeling. Just yesterday we found out another trans woman was murdered—Tamara Dominguez, and that makes a total seventeen known transgender women who have been murdered in 2015 alone. It really is a state of emergency. Your life should not be in danger simply for being who you are. We have to say these people's names. I think the reasons why trans women experience so much violence has to do with employment, housing, health care, etcetera, so we need to make sure that trans lives matter.[1]

Tamara Dominguez died on Monday, August 17, 2015, in a Missouri hospital after sustaining injuries from being struck repeatedly with a sports-utility vehicle in a church parking lot in northeast Kansas City. According to her boyfriend, "She had been living as a woman in the United States for at least seven years . . . after leaving her native Mexico to escape discrimination for being transgender."[2] "She had a lot of dreams," the unidentified boyfriend told the *Kansas City Star*, invoking a familiar mythology of the hopes, dreams, and promises of different experiential modes of freedom possible in the United States.[3] The framing of her death in such terms underscores the failed promise of the nation-state, as it also calls attention to what Enoch Page and Matt Richardson describe as a state technique of "racialized gender" that produces "gender-variant social formations as an excluded caste."[4]

According to an article published on Advocate.com under the headline "Victim Number 17: Trans Woman of Color Murdered in Missouri," information regarding Dominguez's death came on the heels of news about "three African-American trans women [Amber Monroe of Detroit, Michigan; Kandis Capri of Phoenix, Arizona; and Elisha Walker of Smithfield, North Carolina] . . . reported murdered just in the past few days."[5] The recurrent practice of enumerating the dead in mass and social media seems to conform to the logics of accumulation that structure racial capitalism, in which the quantified abstraction of black and trans deaths reveals the calculated value of black and trans lives through states' grammars of deficit and debt. As Katherine McKittrick explains about the *longue durée* of slavery, "This is where we begin, this is where historic blackness comes from: the list, the breathless numbers, the absolutely economic, the mathematics of unliving."[6] This mode of accounting, of expressing the arithmetic violence of black and trans death, as it also refers to antiblack, antiqueer, and antitrans forms of slow and imminent death, finds additional elaboration in what Dagmawi Woubshet refers to as a "poetics of compounding loss," which he defines as "a leitmotif of inventory taking; the reconceptualization of relentless serial losses not as cumulative, but as compounding . . . with the subject's loss both object and subject, past and prospective, memory and immediate threat."[7]

From this vantage point, consider how Cox's designation of a "state of emergency" to refer to the killings of trans women, most of whom were black and brown, sharpens the distinction between the state's rhetorical use of that phrase and the *real* state of emergency that surfaces as a matter of history. As Walter Benjamin writes in his eighth tenet in "Theses on the Philosophy of History," "[T]he tradition of the oppressed teaches us that the 'state of emergency' in which we live is not the exception but the rule." Benjamin continues: "We must attain a conception of history that is in keeping with this insight. Then we shall clearly realize that it is our task to bring about a *real* state of emergency, and this will improve our position in the struggle against Fascism."[8] To put it differently, a *real* state of emergency occurs as a rupture in history to reveal, as Homi Bhabha has written in his foreword to Fanon's *Black Skin, White Masks,* that "the state of emergency is also always a state *of emergence,*" in which the event of struggle challenges the "historicist 'idea' of time as a progressive, ordered whole."[9] As such, Cox's gesture toward the numerous structural factors and institutional practices of racialized gender that delimit black and brown trans women's life chances expresses territories of violence, sites of vulnerability and precarity, and scenes of slow death to which one might read into the "et cetera" the prison system, asylums, and detention centers. These institutions and their emplacement within current biopolitical and necropolitical orders bear upon the problem of history as a mode of organizing time according to antiblack and antitrans "rule." They perpetuate racialized gender as the norm and as the necessary and naturalized consequence of the current order of things, the experience of which Kara Keeling describes as a spatiotemporal concern, as that "intolerable yet quotidian violence" that functions as "the historical index . . . [of] belonging to our time."[10]

Cox's comment, which emerges as an interruption in the flow of entertainment news to inhere within the disruptive temporality of mourning, is articulated within the persistent tense of the present, as another indication of its break with teleological time. Her articulation of loss on behalf of the transgender community intimates an understanding of what Frantz Fanon wrote, in relation to the colonial state of emergency that produces black alienation (black grief), was more than mere individual concern, and into that political and epistemological aporia famously expressed that "besides phylogeny and ontogeny stands sociogeny."[11] As Keeling explains, "Fanon's own interest [is] in exploding the temporality of the colonial mode of representation of otherness and in revealing a temporality that raises the possibility of impossibility within colonial rule, black liberation."[12] The sliding indexicality of Cox's "we" seems also to gesture toward the temporality of sociogenesis, in the form of a plea (or, better yet, a prayer) for a different future to begin now. The named "we" of the transgender community that opens Cox's expression feels different from the undesignated "we" in the concluding flourish, which invents an intersubjective community called forth by the urgency of "trans life matters," in which one can hear as an echo from the future what Cathy Cohen carefully elaborated in a question about the "radical potential" of a queer politic based on analyses of power rather than a fraught sense of shared identity.[13] This, too, is what Kai M. Green and Treva Ellison describe as "tranifesting" as a politic and epistemic operation that attempts to bring forth "forms of collective life that can enliven and sustain us in a future worth living."[14] It is in this sense that Cox's final rhetorical flourish—"we need to make sure that trans lives matter," which indexes without citation the Movement for Black Lives—does not sound wholly appropriative and becomes an opportunity to hear that there is no absolute distinction between black lives' mattering and trans lives' mattering within the rubrics of racialized gender.[15]

I think a lot about Blake Brockington, a black trans man who garnered national attention in 2014 as the "first out trans homecoming king in . . . North Carolina."[16] He was nominated by his classmates at East Meck- lenburg High School in Charlotte, but he also earned his title by raising money ($2,555.55 out of the total $3,203.22 collected) for the school's selected charity, Mothering across Continents, a Charlotte-based non- profit that focuses on youth development in South Sudan, Haiti, South Africa, and Mexico.[17] Before moving to Charlotte to live with his father, Brockington grew up in the coastal city of Charleston, South Carolina. I grew up in inland South Carolina, near the state capital, Columbia. By the time he was made king, Brockington had already moved in with a foster family. Life with his father and stepmother became untenable after he came out as trans, in the tenth grade. In an interview with the *Charlotte Observer*, he explained, "My family feels like this is a decision I made. . . . They think, 'You're already black, why would you want to draw more attention to yourself?' But it's not a decision. It is who I am. I wouldn't wish this on my worst enemy."[18] Suffice to say that I under- stand his family's reaction. The sensibilities expressed by Brockington's family, particularly in the use of "already black," underscore how black- ness and transness are tethered in the contemporary landscape in terms of visibility, in which the form of "attention" directed at black and trans people is frequently articulated through policies, such as House Bill 2 (HB2), which passed on the one-year anniversary of Brockington's death, on March 23, 2016. Sometimes referred to as the "transgender bathroom bill," HB2 prohibits city municipalities from defining LGBT people as a protected class while simultaneously eliminating any state modes of redress for workplace discrimination based on the narrowly prescribed rubrics of difference (race, religion, color, national origin, age, handicap, or biological sex) it purportedly protects.[19] Media focus on transgender people's abilities to use the bathroom of their choice obscures a more urgent conversation about what modes of dispossession are possible under the ruse of state inclusion.

Brockington, however, described the attention he received after his homecoming win as the hardest part of his trans journey: "Really hateful things were said on the Internet. It was hard. I saw how narrow-minded the world really is."[20] He elaborated in the short documentary *BrocKINGton*: "I've had people call me a tranny, a dyke. I've had people call me he-she, it, thing. You know, they called me homecoming thing and called me a pervert and an abomination. Different things, I've gotten a lot of different things."[21] The list of "different things" echoes what Hortense Spillers has described as "a meeting ground of investments and privations in the national treasury of rhetorical wealth," in which the preponderance of terminology is a testament to the need of the nation-state and national culture to invent such a thing into being.[22] This list also expresses the imbrications of antiblack and antitrans animus, as each entry materializes a history of racialized gender denigration. As Spillers writes in reference to the "particular figuration[s]" of the "black woman,"

> Embedded in a bizarre axiological ground, they demonstrate a sort of telegraphic coding; they are markers so loaded with mythical prepossession that there is no easy way for the agents buried beneath them to come clean. In that regard, the names by which I am called in the public place render an example of signifying property plus. In order for me to speak a truer word concerning myself, I must strip down through layers of attenuated meanings, made in excess over time, assigned by a particular historical order, and there await whatever marvels of my own inventiveness. The personal pronouns are offered in the service of a collective function.[23]

For Brockington, that "truer word" seems to have been "human," against its biocentric determinism or ethnocentric overrepresentation as "Man" and in all of the richness of meaning that Sylvia Wynter has imbued to the term, as a form of praxis.[24] In an interview, Brockington related, "I'm still a person . . . [and] trans people are still people. Our bodies just don't match what's up [in our heads]. We need support, not people looking down at us or degrading us or overlooking us. We are still human."[25] The frequency with which he availed himself of interviews and participated in Black Lives Matter rallies and events associated with Transgender Days of Remembrance is perhaps the evidence of an impetus to replace one collective function with another. In one of a number of photographs taken at a rally in late November 2014, Brockington is positioned between two signs, which read "I have the right to be alive" and "I am not a criminal." The photograph occurs as an afterimage, what Kimberly Juanita Brown defines as "an ocular residue, a visual duplication as well as an alteration," in a riff on Audre Lorde.[26] Dressed in all black, Brockington wears a shirt that bears a list of names conjoined by ampersands and "finished" with an ellipsis: "Emmett&Amadou&Sean& Oscar&Trayvon&Jordan&Eric&Mike&Ezell& . . ." A few months later, his own name occupied the elliptical space.

An article published on Advocate.com on March 24, 2015, the day after Brockington's death, notes that "Brockington's death [was] the sixth reported suicide of a trans youth in the U.S. [that] year, in an 'epidemic' that trans advocates say sees far more casualties than are noted by the media."[27] In an online search for "Blake Brockington," one finds that his *Wikipedia* entry appears under the heading "Death of Blake Brockington."[28] Its first line narrates the international media coverage of his suicide. The international circulation of news of Brockington's death reiterates what Jin Haritaworn and I have raised elsewhere as "the need to think transgender both transnationally and intersectionally" in the "current globalization of hate crime activism," antidiscrimination advocacy, and other modes of organizing for state-based inclusion projects.[29] There, we asked, "What are the seductions for a trans activism for [which] traumatized citizenship is more than merely an identitarian pitfall . . . , and is rather a key condition of its own emergence . . . ?," and, "What would a trans politics and theory look like that refuses such 'murderous inclusion'?"[30] To emphasize a dimension of our initial critique, I would add a reformulation based on another thinker and artist whose work on the mathematics of black life has framed much of my thinking here. On his track "Mathematics," from the 1999 album *Black on Both Sides*,

Blake Brockington at a Black Lives Matter rally in Charlotte, North Carolina, in late November 2014. Copyright 2014 Alvin C. Jacobs Jr. for To Speak No Evil. All rights reserved. www.tospeaknoevil.com.

Yasiin Bey explains, "Numbers is hard and real and they never have feelings / But you push too hard, even numbers got limits."[31] In relation to matters of black trans life, I read Bey's description as an invitation to consider the theories and politics that emerge at the limits of current operations for making biopolitical and necropolitical sense of black and trans death.

In the introduction to her award-winning memoir *Redefining Realness: My Path to Womanhood, Identity, Love, and So Much More,* Janet Mock explains that some of the impetus to write her story came from living with survivor's guilt.[32] I feel that, too—deeply—and, as it relates to Blake Brockington, it moves me to consider the conditions in which he would be understood according to his self-definition. Keeling is again helpful here, as she distinguishes the politics of "looking after" from the politics of "looking for" in an analysis attuned to the temporalities of emergence, articulated as a question that I bring to the figures in this book as when they might be—a question that suspends ontological assumptions—rather than where they were and are.[33] From this view, the connections within blackness and transness gesture to what Fanon described as the "real *leap* . . . [of] introducing invention into existence" that constitutes being to the degree that it exceeds it.[34] This book is principally concerned with the mechanics of invention, by which I mean that I am seeking to understand the conditions of emergence of things and beings that may not yet exist; to imagine temporalities in which saying their names—Tamara&Amber&Kandis&Elisha&Blake& . . .—occur as ways to destroy the meanings those names have been accorded by states' grammars. Against and pressing beyond the instrumental materiality of black and trans death, *Black on Both Sides* is an attempt to find a vocabulary for black and trans life. In this sense, it works to do more than provide a "shadow history" of blackness in trans studies or transness in black studies. For many, it will not be understood as history at all, but, as with Fanon, the problem under review here is time.

INTRODUCTION

[T]he *history* of black counter-historical projects is one of failure,
precisely because these accounts have never been able to install
themselves as history, but rather are insurgent, disruptive narratives
that are marginalized and derailed before they ever gain a footing.

—SAIDIYA HARTMAN, "Venus in Two Acts"

UNDER THE DISPLAY GLASS, assembled along with other materials on queer and trans performance, appeared an image with the following description: "French cross-dressing couple. Hand-colored postcard, ca. 1900." A part of the *Speaking of Sex* exhibit, which commemorated the twenty-fifth anniversary of Cornell University Library's Human Sexuality Collection, the postcard was a promotional image associated with a music-hall act. According to the longer description provided in the digital exhibition, it was "exceptionally rare" and "the only image featuring black performers" among the library's collection of more than two hundred French postcards portraying "female and male impersonators between 1900 and 1925."[1] In a conversation with the arts dealer who first acquired the postcard, I was told that white French audiences would have read the figures' clothes and embellishments as garish, a perception predisposed by colonial relationalities that would have indicated that the performers were probably from the Caribbean.[2] The image's title, "[Black couple]"—a nomenclature produced in the archival process—provides a grammar lesson on its black subject matter. The use of brackets delineates typographically how blackness is set apart from its context, making

1

concrete through a mode of punctuation one sense of what Saidiya Hartman explains about the derailment of black counterhistorical projects in this chapter's epigraph.[3] In both the material and digital displays, the image purportedly portrayed two male performers. However, to my eye, the sex/gender of both figures is uncertain. One figure, in formal men's attire, holds a "lady's fan" and gives a sideways glance to a slightly taller figure, who is gathering the skirt of a dress in one hand and holding a pale blue top hat in the other. The stature and fullness of the tuxedo shirt across the first figure's torso signal that one should not readily imagine that gender, in this instance (or any, for that matter), can be adjudicated by making recourse to the visual. The interchange of gendered accessories amplifies the sense of gender indefiniteness. The backdrop is similarly enigmatic, as the figures stand before a rush of swirls that connect and ambiguously render the ocean and the sky.

The ambiguity in the postcard provides a visual key for deciphering this book's title, *Black on Both Sides: A Racial History of Trans Identity*. Although the perception that "race" and "gender" are fixed and knowable terms is the dominant logic of identity, in this book "trans" is more about a movement with no clear origin and no point of arrival, and "blackness" signifies upon an enveloping environment and condition of possibility. Here, trans—in each of its permutations—finds expression and continuous circulation within blackness, and blackness is transected by embodied procedures that fall under the sign of gender.

The emphasis on movement found in this study is also present in the image. The postures and positions of the figures signal that they are in motion; perhaps the postcard depicts the pair in the downbeat of the cakewalk, which by the late nineteenth century was a highly anticipated and customary grand finale for minstrel acts touring North America and Europe. In an account of its complex genealogy, Daphne Brooks describes how cakewalking featured "black performers imitating white performers who, in turn, were believed to have been imitating African Americans."[4] Though frequently regarded as a distinctive cultural form emerging from African America, cakewalking also traffics particular meanings in the anglophone Caribbean, including, for example, in Guyana, where it was "much favoured by middle-class 'coloured' people, especially at church functions," or in Saint Kitts, where it was understood as "a feature of masquerading, popular at Christmas."[5] As

Black couple, circa 1900. French transvestite postcards, #7778 Card 81, Human Sexuality Collection. Division of Rare and Manuscript Collections, Cornell University Library.

described by the unnamed narrator in *The Autobiography of an Ex-Colored Man,* cakewalking is an itinerant form:

> The couples did not walk round in a circle, but in a square, with the men on the inside. The fine points to be considered were the bearing of the men, the precision with which they turned the corners, the grace of the women, and the ease with which they swung around the pivots. The men walked with stately and soldierly step, and the women with considerable grace. . . . This was the cake-walk in its original form, and it is what the colored performers on the theatrical stage developed into the prancing movements now known all over the world, and which some Parisian critics pronounced the acme of poetic motion.[6]

Exhibiting a repertoire of gestures and poses that belong, as Brooks notes, "to the discourse of camp" that makes "visible camp's black genealogical roots," cakewalking "served as a performance of travel that literally walked the color line of identity politics."[7] The imbrications of black performance and queer gesture that contextualize cakewalking's transnational circulation are visually amplified in the modes of trans embodiment imaged in the French postcard. Audiences attending their music-hall act circa 1900 might have heard at the couple's performance the interplay of two prophetic utterances that would reiterate across the twentieth century (and resound in the present) in what W. E. B. Du Bois declared at the First Pan-African Conference in London, in 1900, as "the problem of the color-line," and in what Havelock Ellis and John Addington Symonds described as "a chief problem for solution" in the 1897 publication of *Sexual Inversion*, namely, "the question of sex—with the racial question that rests on it."[8] Although *Sexual Inversion* has been regarded as the first sustained study of sexuality in the English language, the imbrications of gender and sexual aberrance require that one does not read "the question of sex" as exclusively concerned with sexual acts or object choice but as also indicative of gendering practices and trans ways of being.

In one sense, the postcard portrays what Nadia Ellis describes as the "queer elsewhere of black diaspora," displaying—in a staged choreography of figures and forms—the "places and people of black identification that are most lively as horizons of possibility, a call from afar that one keeps trying and trying to answer."[9] Certainly the postcard raises a number of questions, the answers to which are seemingly interred in a discarded archive. By whom, when, and why was it photographed and painted? What were the conditions of its production? What was its initial viewership, and how did the postcard correspond with the performance it was conceived to promote? Are the figures African American or Caribbean or from another node in the black diaspora? Are they queer or trans or both or neither? And how would possessing a definitive answer on these matters matter? Upon each encounter with the postcard in the archive, I became increasingly aware of feeling transfixed and transposed by what Fred Moten describes as the "elsewhere and elsewhen" of a thing that one already inhabits but must also keep learning to desire.[10] Another line of inquiry emerges: What can the image reveal about the histories of blackness, transness, and sexual cultures? about their indefinities and irreducibilities? about their temporalities of emergence? The postcard, as it depicts the transitivity and transversality of blackness and transness, represents not an origin but an entry point for these questions.

Transitivity/Transversality

In resisting the impetus to nominalize "trans" as a category of gender, sex, or species, Claire Colebrook argues for the primacy of transitivity, defining "trans" as "a not-yet differentiated singularity from *which* distinct genders, race[s], species, sexes, and sexualities are generated in a form of relative stability."[11] For Colebrook, transitivity "is the condition for what becomes known as *the* human," as "trans" expresses primordial being from which difference is formed.[12] Rather than reading race as a secondary order of difference, which would presume that race is principally a biologized form (and consequence of reproduction), I propose that "blackness" is in apposition to Colebrook's formulation of "trans"— that is, that they overlap in referentiality—inasmuch as blackness is a condition of possibility for the modern world and insofar as blackness articulates the paradox of nonbeing, as expressed in its deployment as appositional flesh. Such a view necessitates drawing on multiple meanings of "transitive," not only as a term that articulates the quality of "passing into another condition, changeable, changeful; passing away, transient, transitory," but also in terms of the mechanics of grammar, in which the transitive refers to the expression of an action that requires a direct object to complete its sense of meaning.[13] As a grammar, the transitive provides critical insight into the transubstantiation of things, and this study begins by tracing the circulation of "black" and "trans" as they are brought into the same frame by the various ways they have been constituted as fungible, thingified, and interchangeable, particularly within the logics of transatlantic exchange. As Bill Brown has argued, the process by which an object becomes a thing tells a "story of how the thing really names less an object than a particular subject-object *relation*."[14] Thing theory, then, could be regarded as a grammatical expression of (at least) capital, power, and knowledge. Thingliness, in turn, denotes transitive modes of differentiation in which difference is neither absolute nor binaristic but changeable.

Exchange becomes a critical frame for understanding transitivity's multiple meanings, functioning as a rubric that situates blackness and transness as within the "order of things" that produce and maintain an androcentric European ethnoclass of Man as the pinnacle of being.[15] Reading the transitivities of blackness and transness within the logics of exchange offers a way to think about the intersubjectivity of subjection and subjectification within racial capitalism in which exchange rarely expresses an idealized reciprocity but articulates a logic of accumulation and interchangeability, which is another way to express "passing into another condition." Reading "black" and "trans" in transitive relation, then, requires that one become acquainted with the social life of things, which is also to consider how one's relationship to things and as a thing entails a confrontation and rethinking of the past as it has been rendered into History. According to Nancy Farriss, an attention to the social life of things necessitates a view of the past "as more [than an] undifferentiated prelude to the ethnographic present," and an understanding of history as more than "merely a source of facts."[16] As Frantz Fanon identified, when one is compelled to be a body of history, then time itself is the problem.[17] Organized around a series of events that provide occasions for bringing both signs—blackness and transness— into the same frame, *Black on Both Sides* is not a history per se so much as it is a set of political propositions, theories of history, and writerly experiments.

Just as "transitive" invokes a number of concepts that denote imper-manence, it also names the materials that constitute this book's archive: partial and ephemeral, subject to change, and altered by changing con-ditions. Like the postcard, they occur "through negation," or what José Muñoz described as "a process of erasure that redoubles and marks [a] systemic erasure."[18] The figures explored here are likewise transitory, per-ceived through glimpses and furtive glances, by fictive traces and fugi-tive moves. *Black on Both Sides* is a meditation on an eclectic collection of materials, including mid-nineteenth- and twentieth-century medical illustrations, pickup notices, fugitive-slave narratives, Afromodernist lit-erature, twentieth-century journalistic accounts of black people "exposed" as living in/as different genders, true-crime books, documentary film, and poetry. As with any archive or historiographical project, its organization is political. The assemblage of materials and my readings are deeply in-fluenced by Sylvia Wynter's thinking on the transformative potential of sociogenesis, about which she has written as a call to arms: "The true leap, Fanon wrote at the end of his *Black Skin, White Masks,* consists in intro-ducing invention into existence. The buck stops with us."[19] Heeding her call, my analysis here is particularly attentive to the possibilities of valorizing—without necessarily redeeming—different ways of knowing and being, as it is also invested in reviving and inventing strategies for inhabiting unlivable worlds.[20] It is an attempt to think more precisely about the connections within blackness and transness in the midst of ongoing black and trans death and against the backdrop of the rapid institutionalization of trans studies.

This book proceeds with a series of questions: What pasts have been submerged and discarded to solidify—or, more precisely, indemnify—a set of procedures that would render blackness and transness as dis-tinct categories of social valuation? Relatedly, what insights are yielded in a reading of "black" and "trans" that do not regard these as social markers that are manifestly transparent? Throughout the book, I eschew binaristic logic that might reify a distinction between transgender and cisgender, black and white, disabled and abled, and so on, in an effort to think expansively about how blackness and black studies, and trans-ness and trans studies, yield insights that surpass an additive logic. Crit-ically engaging black feminist thought, queer- and trans-of-color critique, visual-culture studies, and disability theory, among other fields of inquiry,

Black on Both Sides explains how the condensation of transness into the category of transgender is a racial narrative, as it also attends to how blackness finds articulation within transness.

As Susan Stryker, Paisley Currah, and Lisa Jean Moore argue, "neither '-gender' nor any of the other suffixes of 'trans-' can be understood in isolation."[21] In their reading of "trans-" as a concept that encompasses "categorical crossings, leakages, and slips of all sorts," Stryker, Currah, and Moore offer the notion of "doubly trans-" to describe certain modes of inquiry that, while referencing "transgender," move "beyond the narrow politics of gender identity."[22] Although the concept of "doubly trans-" seems to recast and redouble "trans-" in spatial terms, that is, as a formulation that gestures toward modes of thought that move *beyond* matters of gender, "doubly trans-" also names the double relation (transitive and transversal) under examination in this study, wherein blackness and transness, with few exceptions, have been expressed in terms of a disavowal, which Neil Roberts explains as a "*double movement*: an acknowledgement *and* a denial" that "locates an event and then rejects its relevance, knowing full well that it occurred."[23] This maneuver brings to the fore another two-part formulation, which Du Bois named "double-consciousness" to refer to the "peculiar sensation" of "always looking at one's self through the eyes of others, of measuring one's soul by the tape of a world that looks on in amused contempt and pity."[24] Double consciousness as the expression of "two souls, two thoughts, [and] two un-reconciled strivings" simultaneously articulates the feelings that emerge for blacks in America and throughout the diaspora and provides a way to perceive how race and gender are inextricably linked yet irreconcilable and irreducible projects.[25] To feel black in the diaspora, then, might be a trans experience.

If, as Tavia Nyong'o has argued, "race is a theory of history"— an explanation for why things happened the way they did—then one might also consider that race is a history of theory that functions to express what is un/thinkable across complex temporalities.[26] In each formulation, history becomes less a program for examining change over time and more an examination of disruptions in linear time. Race, then, becomes a way of thinking history doubly, or of thinking about the history of historicity, wherein one transitive relation within blackness and transness expresses what Fanon described as "the real *leap* . . . [of]

introducing invention into existence."[27] This is to confirm that this book fails at writing history, sometimes unintentionally but also intentionally, for, as David Marriott explains, "there is no invention without a leap, and no leap without unsettling the borders of self and history[;] for history to be meaningful it can never be completed, and precisely because truth is itself an event of endless revision and recovery."[28] In the chapters that follow, I focus on the transitive connections within blackness and transness that emerge in moments of transition: from slavery to emancipation and the free market; from civil rights to the Black Power movement; from World War II to the Cold War; and from analog to digital, emblematized by the rise in popular use of the Internet in the 1990s. Although "transition" helps to frame the set of flashpoints of analysis in this study, my use of the word here and throughout *Black on Both Sides* does not align with the ways "transition" is deployed for organizing time according to a linear or teleological formulation of progress. That is because the connections within blackness and transness are also transversal.

Deriving the term from his clinical practice, Félix Guattari makes use of "transversality" as an aesthetic, ethical, and political operation that calls "into question disciplinary boundaries" and traverses "the solipsistic closure of Universes of value."[29] For Guattari, as Troy Rhoades and Christoph Brunner explain, "[t]ransversality as a field of expression provides the *milieu* for a creative emergence from disparate forces. . . . Transversality never links. It crafts, shifts, and relates."[30] Figuring a condition of possibility for emergence, transversality's aesthetic takes the shape of what Dionne Brand has described as a "tear in the world," "a rupture in history, a rupture in the quality of being."[31] For the transitivity and transversality of blackness and transness exist prior to their articulation, which is to say that the connections within these concepts occur in the formal anterior to their various calcifications of meaning or territorializations or permutative nominalizations. In one sense, the relations between blackness and transness have been forged in and by way of what Nyong'o calls a "hollow of the circum-Atlantic fold,"[32] which, like the promotional image of the performers, contravenes hegemonic common sense about a body or a national body politic. This is in keeping with Édouard Glissant's use of the term in *Caribbean Discourse: Selected Essays,* in which he describes transversality as a consequence of "all of

those Africans weighed down with ball and chain and thrown over-
board . . . [who] *sowed in the depths the seeds of an invisible presence.*"[33]
According to Glissant, these depths are not the "abyss of neurosis but
primarily the site of multiple converging paths." Constituting the Caribbean by crosscurrents, undercurrents, and "submarine roots" that are
"floating free, not fixed in one position . . . but extending in all direc-
tions," transversality articulates submerged forms of relationalities that
need not be visible to have effects.[34]

Glissant comes to transversality in a phenomenology of the abyss,
and his theorization offers a different schema for genealogical practice.
Here, transversality expresses the interior, nonlinear, and asymmetrical
spaces that could constitute "a map to the door of no return," which
Brand describes as "not mere physicality" but a "spiritual location" and
"psychic destination" for which there is "no way in; no return."[35] Reading Glissant and Brand together offers a way to perceive how transversality refers to a "collateral genealogy" in which encounters with the past
necessarily contend with myriad forms of collateral damage produced
in the Middle Passage and lived in the present in the "afterlives of slavery."[36] It also names how the narratives in this study do not occur as if
they properly belong in the past. Tarrying with the unfixed, submerged,
and frequently disavowed connections within blackness and transness
requires that both author and reader suspend a demand for transparency,
which is also, as Glissant suggests, to forgo a methodological operation
that seeks to bring the submerged to the surface. As he maintains, one
must agree "not merely to the right to difference, but, carrying this further, agree also to the right to opacity that is not enclosure within an im-
penetrable autarchy but subsistence within an irreducible singularity."[37]
A transversal approach to history, then, becomes a way to perceive how
difference can take transitive form, expressed in shifting modalities of
time and meaning from within the abyss. Transversality also describes
this study's treatment of submerged thought, naming its propensity to
linger in the depths of discarded theories for what they can and cannot
say about their temporalities of emergence.

As Rizvanna Bradley and Damien-Adia Marassa argue, "From the
point of having been thrown into the abyss, another horizon for language and for writing can be glimpsed."[38] Drawing on Glissant, Hortense
Spillers, and Jacques Derrida to underscore writing's "double gesture"

"whose conditions of inscription reveal the limits of geography and of texts," Bradley and Marassa indicate one way to read this book's title, in which "black on both sides" refers to the temporal, spatial, and semantic concerns that are multiplicatively redoubled—between, beside, within, and across themselves—in transitive and transversal relation.[39] *Black on Both Sides*, then, is an attempt to write in and about what Spillers describes in "Interstices: A Small Drama of Words" as "the historical moment[s] when language ceases to speak, the historical moment[s] at which hierarchies of power . . . simply run out of terms."[40] In the sense that an abyss is also an interstice, transversality's alternate meaning as a "deviation [and] digression" comes into view as a way to articulate lines of thought and ways of being that exceed capture in language, history, or metaphysics.[41]

Collateral Genealogies

Black on Both Sides does not attempt to be exhaustive or even fully explanatory. This is in part due to the nature of the archives, but it is also a consequence of a scholarly gambit to replace certain aspects of what is commonly regarded as methodological rigor with a political and ethical imperative to the right to opacity. As L. H. Stallings writes, "If transgender and transsexual history and culture depend upon what has been published, visible, legible, and authorized enough to be archived, then we might query what has been omitted as a result of the conditions of illiteracy, criminalization, or poverty."[42] The circumstances for omission that Stallings identifies are the conditions of possibility for this black and trans historiographical project. Black study, as that which exceeds its institutional formation, provides numerous examples for how to proceed. Through a "combination of foraging and disfiguration" and with an attentiveness to the "interstitial spaces" in the archives, this book continues an ongoing examination of racialized gender.[43] It re/asks the question, perhaps with a slightly different inflection, What does it mean to have a body that has been made into a grammar for whole worlds of meaning?

This book is told in three parts. The first section, "Blacken," traces how flesh figures one route into the proverbial question of how matter matters. In these first two chapters, Spillers's notion of "female flesh ungendered" guides my analysis of sex and gender as racial arrangements wherein the fungibility of captive flesh produced a critical context for understanding sex and gender as mutable and subject to rearrangement in the arenas of medicine and law. Chapter 1, "Anatomically Speaking," considers the founding of American gynecology and the archives of J. Marion Sims as narratives that underscore the transitive instrumentalities of flesh. Sims's three and one-half years of experiments on female captives—Anarcha, Betsey, Lucy, and several unnamed others—precipitates a view of sex as an effect of flesh and gender as a discourse indebted to racial slavery's political and visual economy. In its companion chapter, "Trans Capable," I discuss flesh's collateral genealogy, suggesting that the recurrence of "cross-dressing" and cross-gender modes of escape in fugitive-slave narratives engenders a way of seeing fungible flesh as a mode for fugitive action. Just as "gender," under captivity, refers not to a binary system of classification but rather to what Spillers describes as a "territory of cultural and political maneuver," this chapter looks at how fungibility and fugitivity occur within the narrative plots of *Incidents in the Life of a Slave Girl* (1861) and *Running a Thousand Miles for Freedom* (1860). "Trans Capable" also attends to how articulations of personal sovereignty for blacks living in the antebellum North were mapped visually and discursively in terms of "cross-dressing" and theft.

Part II, "Transit," serves as a point of transit within temporalities, genders, and geopolitics of racial blackness. Examining texts that initially emerged at the turn of the twentieth century and were later grouped together, in 1965, as *Three Negro Classics,* chapter 3 takes up the trans/gender implications of Booker T. Washington's *Up from Slavery,* W. E. B. Du Bois's *The Souls of Black Folk,* and James Weldon Johnson's *Autobiography of an Ex-Colored Man.* The production and reception of these works as expressions of what Du Bois referred to as "manhood rights" necessitated a symbolic rearrangement of black women's figurations.[44] Through this process, "black modernity" would indicate the ways that black gender is, as Christina Sharpe has articulated, "anagrammatical," which is to say, open to (at least literary) manipulation and rearrangement.[45] The association between being black and having a black mother was critical to maintaining the biopolitical ordering of slavery and continued as a question for consideration and redefinition throughout and in the wake of Reconstruction. In light of this interrelation, one could re-pose Du Bois's declaration about the problem of the color line in terms of social re/production, such that one substitutes the question of how it feels to be a problem with what it means to have a black mother. This metonymic move—which is also a play on how the logics of synecdoche and substitution structure the racial real—organizes this chapter along a series of meditations on what Spillers calls the unique heritage of men in the black diaspora to express the "'female' within."[46]

Part III, "Blackout," focuses on the negation of blackness, which gives rise to a transgender subject rendered legible by transnormativity. In chapter 4, "A Nightmarish Silhouette," I situate the ascendance of Christine Jorgensen, dubbed America's first transsexual celebrity, alongside myriad projects of U.S. imperial conquest and various forms of violent racist suppression at home. Focusing on the media narratives of Lucy Hicks Anderson, Georgia Black, Carlett Brown, James McHarris / Annie Lee Grant, and Ava Betty Brown that emerged in the black press, this chapter offers other ways to narrate trans embodiment in the postwar, early Cold War period, as their stories reflect upon the violent and volatile intimacies of darker to lighter bodies precipitated by the global dispersal of refugees following World War II, decolonial struggles throughout the "global South," and contestations of Jim Crow in the United States. The narratives of Hicks Anderson, Black, the Browns, and McHarris/Grant also indicate how black trans figures were mobilized to meditate on intramural black life, not simply as it related to matters of gender and sexuality but also as it pertained to shifting notions of human valuation.

Chapter 5, "DeVine's Cut," turns to the murders of Lisa Lambert, Brandon Teena, and Phillip DeVine on New Year's Eve in Humboldt, Nebraska, in 1993. Although much of the scholarship in trans and media studies has focused on the implications of Teena's death and cinematic portrayals of the case, this chapter, as the title alludes, narrates the Humboldt killings from the perspective of DeVine. His death is often figured as an instance of "wrong place, wrong time"—an explanation that casts him as a casualty of a more concentrated aggression aimed at Teena. Ungeographical and untimely, DeVine appears within a rhetorical maneuver that situates his existence in the Brandon archive by evacuating his constitutive presence from and place within the archive's construction. Considering DeVine becomes an occasion for considering the imbrications of antiblack and antitrans animus that bear upon the contemporary landscape of black and trans death. This chapter does

not construct DeVine's death as a psychic place for those who are understood within other identificatory rubrics to imagine, through his dying,
different modes of freedom and vitality. Rather, it enacts, in language,
a key transitivity of blackness and transness—in the form of invention—to construct DeVine's life with the referent of the Humboldt killings, which are themselves a necessarily unfinished geography of human
praxis.[47] "DeVine's Cut" confirms how the archives under review here
are all products of invention. What is necessary, then, are theoretical and
historical trajectories that further imaginative capacities to construct more
livable black and trans worlds.

PART I
BLACKEN

Those black and blackened bodies become the bearers (through violence, regulation, transmission, etc.) of the knowledge of certain subjection as well as the placeholders of freedom for those who would claim freedom as their rightful yield.

—CHRISTINA SHARPE, *Monstrous Intimacies: Making Post-slavery Subjects*

1

ANATOMICALLY SPEAKING
UNGENDERED FLESH AND THE SCIENCE OF SEX

> The profitable "atomizing" of the captive body provides another angle on the divided flesh: we lose any hint or suggestion of a dimension of ethics, of relatedness between human personality and its anatomical features, between one human personality and another, between human personality and cultural institutions. To that extent, the procedures adopted for the captive flesh demarcate a total objectification, as the entire captive community becomes a living laboratory.
>
> —HORTENSE SPILLERS, "Mama's Baby, Papa's Maybe:
> An American Grammar Book"

ON NOVEMBER 18, 1857, before an audience of the New York Academy of Medicine at the newly erected New-York Historical Society Building on Second Avenue and Eleventh Street, James Marion Sims delivered a speech on the importance of silver sutures in surgery. In his address to fellow physicians, Sims focused primarily on the three and one-half years of experiments performed on chattel women named Anarcha, Betsey, and Lucy, as well as several unnamed captives, which led to his career-making cure for vesicovaginal fistula (VVF).[1] Sims described this genital malady by making reference to a verse from the book of Genesis: "In sorrow and suffering shalt thou bring forth children."[2] The full verse contains the complete judgment God meted out on the nameless woman who would later be called Eve, which, in addition to an intensification of pain associated with childbirth, included a further imposition: "[T]hy desire shall be to thy husband, and he shall rule over thee" (Genesis 3:16 [King James Version]). Whereas Adam would be rendered mortal according to the parable of the fall of Man, Eve was, according to literal interpretation, conscripted to submission. Sims's inclusion of this biblical citation provides a key for reading his medical corpus, which constitutes the primary material under review in this chapter. On the one hand, his work signals how suffering and dominion transitively articulated the formation of gynecology. On the other, Sims's archive and the narratives of the named and unnamed experimentees indicate a transversal link between the metaphysical and the material, given expression in and as "flesh."

In the same speech, Sims described the experiments as part of a mission, which he imagined was, "if not of a Divine character, at least . . . of Divine origin": to relieve "the loveliest of all God's creation of one of the most loathsome maladies."[3] His repeated invocations of God did more than intimate how Sims was a man of faith; they constructed a grammar for methodological (medical and scientific) evaluation by way of a theopolitical justification for mechanisms of pain and control. As Achille Mbembe has argued, "[M]onotheism is a special way of formulating knowledge about final ends. . . . [H]ow truth and final ends are to be determined is . . . a political question."[4] This unethical grammar of suffering would dominantly express how Anarcha, Betsey, Lucy, and the unnamed others would function as a living laboratory within a political economy wherein their atomized flesh took on an adjunctive function in the production and reproduction of a series of proprietary instruments and procedures.[5]

Far from replacing God with science, Sims's professions evinced how the imbrication of race and species was given expression through the concept of value and, more precisely, its groundlessness, which, as Lindon Barrett has argued, is "marked, however surreptitiously, by forms of violence."[6] The encoding of value, like the naming of God, occurred in this instance through the violation of captive flesh, wherein the cause and cure of VVF signified upon the condition of captivity. As Hortense Spillers notes, divided flesh not only constituted a grammar of value devoid of "any hint or suggestion of a dimension of ethics" but also produced an onto-epistemological framework premised on the fungibility of captive bodies, wherein their flesh functioned as a disarticulation of human form from its anatomical features and their claims to humanity were controverted in favor of the production and perpetuation of cultural institutions.[7] Sims confessed as much in his speech before the New York Academy of Medicine when he told his colleagues that throughout the numerous failed surgical experiments, he found resolve "by feelings of national pride, as well as by a desire to advance our glorious profession."[8]

The international acclaim Sims received for his treatment of VVF generates a number of questions about the transubstantiation of things, as it relates to the life of flesh that resides in the series of instruments and procedures, including Sims's speculum, catheter, and sutures, and also in terms of what VVF and its cure reveal about the relationship between sex and ungendered flesh.[9] A vesicovaginal fistula is a breach in the vaginal wall that opens into the urinary tract and produces continuous involuntary discharge of urine. As L. L. Wall explains, VVFs "are the result of a massive crush injury to the soft tissues of the pelvis."[10] According to Durrenda Ojanuga, chattel persons were particularly at risk for VVF, because of "poor nutrition, lack of prenatal care, and births at an early age."[11] Yet the pelvis was also a critical site for producing racial hierarchies among nineteenth-century anatomists and sexologists intent on finding bodily "proof" of black inferiority. For example, sexologist Havelock Ellis, in his *Studies of the Psychology of Sex*, volume 2, argued that the average size of black women's buttocks (seen as larger than white women's) served a compensatory function for their smaller (read: inferior) average pelvic size.[12] Attending to a genealogy of nineteenth-century thinkers who would influence Ellis's work, Sander Gilman explains that the pelvis in racial science acted "in an intermediary role, as both a secondary and primary sexual sign" in theories of species differentiation.[13] In addition, and as another indication of how physicians viewed cases of VVF among chattel persons as further evidence of their racial inferiority, occurrences of VVF were frequently attributed to the ignorance of "midwives of their own color."[14] Though Sims would recursively euphemize the condition as an "accident," vesicovaginal fistula functioned as a sign of slavery, as signifier and signified in a chain of meaning, to give expression to what Saidiya Hartman described as the "erasure or disavowal of sexual violence [that] engendered black femaleness as a condition of unredressed injury."[15]

Sims's archive serves as a "materialized scene of female flesh 'ungendered,'" which, as Hortense Spillers notes, "offers a praxis and a theory, a text for living and for dying, and a method for reading both through diverse mediations."[16] His more than three years of experiments on named and unnamed chattel persons for the treatment of VVF served as "proof" of black females' genital exceptionalism (as nonreproductive, inverted, unfeminine), even as the procedures also produced an erasure of chattel slavery's effect on black female genitalia in the state of exception. The founding of the field of American gynecology thus raises a number of questions, including how race constructs biology, and whether sex is possible without flesh. Following an exposition of Sims's experiments, this chapter takes up multiple trajectories of/in the flesh: in the series of woodcuts that accompanied Sims's medical publications; in his illustrious medical career in New York City, in parts of Europe, and over his prolonged residency in Paris; and in the description of Sims as the "father of modern gynecology" and of Anarcha as the field's mother. These divergent paths provide a series of object lessons on flesh as a condition of possibility for the science and symbolics of modern sex. The final section examines key figures and images in gynecology's visual culture, focusing on a particular illustration by Max Brödel in Howard Kelly's *Medical Gynecology* (1912) and Robert Thom's *J. Marion Sims: Gynecologic Surgeon* (1961) to discuss sex and gender as the transoriented effects of flesh, anarranged in time, place, and meaning. This chapter and its companion, "Trans Capable" (chapter 2), trace collateral genealogies of blackness and transness in which captive and divided flesh functions as malleable matter for mediating and remaking sex and gender as matters of human categorization and personal definition.

Sims's Laboratory

According to J. Marion Sims's posthumously published autobiography, *The Story of My Life,* a fellow physician asked Sims to travel with him about a mile from Montgomery, Alabama, in order to attend to a "case of labor which had lasted three days and the child not yet born" in June 1845.[17] Sims related his first encounter with the "case," Anarcha, in some detail, describing her as "a young colored woman, about seventeen years of age, [and] well developed." Attending to the delivery, Sims wrote that it "was evident that matters could not long remain in this condition without the system becoming exhausted, and without the pressure producing a sloughing of the soft parts of the mother." (227).

Five days later, Sims's colleague, Dr. Henry, confirmed that there had been "an extensive sloughing of the soft parts, the mother having lost control of both the bladder and the rectum." In response, Sims opined, "Of course, aside from death, this was about the worst accident that could have happened to the poor young girl" (227). His use of "accident" here to describe Anarcha's condition disavows chattel slavery's transitive and transversal relations with death and the various ways VVF was a symptom of captivity. Sims described the case as "hopelessly incurable," and informed Anarcha's enslaver, Mr. Wescott, "to take good care of her," as she was unfit to work (227).

Within a month, Sims consulted on another fistula case at the request of a fellow physician. Describing his first examination of Betsey, "a young woman seventeen or eighteen years old," Sims related that again he found the condition incurable and sent her back to the owner: "The base of the bladder was destroyed, and her case was certainly a miserable one. I kept her a day or two in Montgomery and then sent her home, writing a note to the doctor, giving him my opinion of the case and its incurability" (228). Lucy, the third person named in Sims's autobiography in conjunction with the fistula experiments, came soon thereafter to live in his "little hospital [designated] . . . for taking care of . . . negro patients and for negro surgical cases." Arriving at a similar conclusion as he did with Anarcha and Betsey, Sims wrote, "I told her that I was unable to do anything for her, and I said, 'Tomorrow afternoon I shall have to send you home'" (230). Sims, however, contravened his initial plan. Having treated a white woman who he believed was suffering from a dislocated uterus in the intervening hours between his pronouncement to Lucy and the time of her planned departure, Sims explained in his autobiography, "Then, said I to myself, if I can place the patient in that position, and distend the vagina by the pressure of air, so as to produce such a wonderful result as this, why can I not take the incurable case of vesico-vaginal fistula, which seems now to be so incomprehensible, and put the girl in this position and see exactly what are the relations of the surrounding tissues?" (234).

Sims immediately went to his office and ordered his two apprentices to accompany him to the makeshift hospital, where he kept those he personally enslaved and where Lucy remained. Sims provides a lengthy account in his autobiography:

Dr. Sims Home in Montgomery, Ala. before he went to New York in 1853.

Office of Dr Marion Sims, in Montgomery, Ala. from 1840 to 1853. "I had a little hospital of eight beds, built in a corner of the yard, for taking care of my negro patients and for negro surgical cases; and so when Lucy came I gave her a bed. Here Lucy, Betsey and Anarcha were the first patients experimented upon and cured." — STORY OF MY LIFE.

Dr. Sims home at Mt. Meigs, Ala., before he moved to Montgomery in 1840. The small building in the rear is where he had his office.

Originally published in Seale Harris's biography *Woman's Surgeon: The Life Story of J. Marion Sims* [New York: Macmillan Company, 1950], these three photographs show Sims's home and office in Mount Megis and Montgomery, Alabama. Courtesy of the Alabama State Archives.

> Arriving there, I said, "Betsey, I told you that I would send you home this afternoon, but before you go I want to make one more examination of your case." She willingly consented. I got a table about three feet long, and put a coverlet upon it, and mounted her on the table, on her knees, with her head resting on the palms of her hands. I placed the two students one on each side of the pelvis and they laid hold of the nates [buttocks], and pulled them open. Before I could get the bent spoon-handle into the vagina, the air rushed in with a puffing noise, dilating the vagina to its fullest extent. Introducing the bent handle of the spoon I saw everything, as no man had ever seen before. (234)

The substitution of Betsey's name for Lucy's provides another view of how chattel slavery was a critical context for VVF and its cure, wherein the logics of fungibility gave rise to Lucy's nominal interchangeability with Betsey's. The elaborate description of procedures for turning slave quarters into a medical examination room articulates what Marie Jenkins

Schwartz called the "medical plantation," a model for medical knowledge in which life and death were "to be managed according to the wishes of slaveholders."[18] Here, the medical plantation rhetorically transverses the frontier, as the language of discovery that envelops the passage becomes an aperture with which to perceive how divided flesh was defined by its characteristic accessibility, its availability for viewing, exploration, and other modes of unrelenting, unmitigated apprehension. Sims's description corresponds with what he must have learned in medical school about the *nègre* and Hottentots whose nates and pelvises were dissected and copiously referred to in sexological and anatomical literature as "sufficiently well marked to distinguish [them] . . . from those of any of the ordinary varieties of the human species."[19] As Andrew Curran notes, the *nègre* of the eighteenth century played a constitutive role in providing a basis for racial difference: the "shift of the locus of race from the exterior to the interior . . . had been taking place since the late 1760s."[20] Sims's archive requires a reading that draws together, even before his account of the unanesthetized procedures performed on Lucy, Betsey, Anarcha, and the unnamed others, what Petra Kuppers describes as "themes of slavery and its justification, issues of degeneracy and the decline of the West, and other racist and eugenic stories."[21]

Sims's archive, however, does not provide a way to understand what the young woman called Lucy must have thought when she was addressed as Betsey and told to mount the three-foot table. Enslaved, surrounded by three white men, misnamed, and bent across a table, Lucy, whose "consent" Sims describes, endured conditions that call attention to how such a concept was unavailable to her (or Betsey, or Anarcha, or the unnamed others) under the law. Should one imagine the substitution of Betsey for Lucy in the preceding passage as the result of mere error or authorial oversight, the subsequent pages in Sims's autobiography reveal how this moment named—through misnaming—the way fungibility would suture medical "insight" to the rationalization of human captivity. Sims continued:

> I did not send Lucy home, and I wrote to her master that I would
> retain her there, and he must come and see me again. I saw Mr.
> Wescott, and I told him . . . that I would like to have him send
> Anarcha back to my hospital. I also wrote to Dr. Harris, saying
> that I had changed my mind in regard to Betsey, and for him to

send her back again. I ransacked the country for cases, told the doctors what had happened and what I had done, and it ended in my finding six or seven cases of vesico-vaginal fistula that had been hidden away for years in the country because they had been pronounced incurable. I went to work to put another story on my hospital, and this gave me sixteen beds; four beds for servants, and twelve for the patients. Then I made this proposition to the owners of the negroes: If you will give me Anarcha and Betsey for experiment; I agree to perform no experiment or operation on either of them to endanger their lives, and will not charge a cent for keeping them.[22]

In addition to confirming that it was Lucy rather than Betsey that he detained and wished to retain further, his description of plans for experimentation here indicate that enslavement was a necessary condition for his test subjects. As Harriet Washington explains, "Sims's writings often utilized imprisonment for the control he saw as key to restoring a woman's health. His enslaved experimental subjects were the ultimate in controllable patients."[23] Moreover, their collective status as slaves organized a way of encountering their bodies, as test subjects that were immanently analgesic or congenitally impervious to pain, and, by the very condition of slavery, inexhaustibly available through their interchangeability. The proposition made to their enslavers—the only binding agreement, which is to say, the only request that legally required and recognized "consent"— made rhetorical use of Anarcha and Betsey as stand-ins for the imprecise number of captives who would come to live among those Sims personally enslaved.

According to his 1857 lecture before the New York Academy of Medicine, Sims was unable to operate between December 9, 1845, and January 10, 1846: "[H]aving no proper instruments and no instrument maker, dentists, jewelers and blacksmiths were lade under contribution, and soon rude instruments were made" for the purposes of his experiments.[24] Soon thereafter, and in front of an audience of approximately a dozen doctors, Lucy was the first to go under Sims's knife. Sims later described her case as "very simple," causing him to believe that he would produce in front of his peers "at once a magical cure."[25] Sims's biographer Seale Harris provides a caricatured account of Lucy's experience that day: "Lucy . . . spent a whole hour crouched on her knees and elbows, [fortified] only by opium and hope against the searing, racking, operative pain. . . . Through all the attendant pain and hemorrhage Lucy bore up admirably, flinching only slightly; for this was, she knew, part of the price she had to pay for being made again a normal woman."[26] There is a discrepancy between the accounts as to whether Lucy received any kind of numbing agent, as Sims noted in his autobiography that these were "before the days of anaesthetics."[27] Where Harris's and Sims's versions do find congruence is in their estimation of Lucy's ability to endure pain. Whether as an emblem of her heroism or bravery, as in Sims's account, or as an indication of her hope for a restoration of feminine "normalcy," Lucy's stoic suffering is made to recast a theater of torture into a medical scene. Although the archive does not allow one to decipher whether Lucy believed that the spectacle of experimentation would ensure relief from pain, it is fairly certain that the restorative effects of these procedures would be physical rather than social, as the possibility of "being made again a normal woman" would not be available to her as a slave.

Sims's experimental operation nearly killed Lucy. According to Harris's account, "Five days after the operation Lucy became seriously ill, with high fever, rapid pulse, and all the indications of blood poisoning."[28] After removing a sponge from her urethra, which had calcified and conjoined with her urethral tissue, Sims placed Lucy on a postoperative program that included high doses of morphine, and crackers as a primary source of nutrition, and which required that she lie on her back until she recovered from his experiment. Sims would continue his experiments with other captives before Lucy's complete revival, some three months later; after arranging a substitute for the sponge, he operated on Betsey. Neither Sims's nor Harris's account describes Betsey's procedure. The opacity in the archive on this matter leaves room to imagine how Betsey might have somehow resisted the performance of stoic bravery or willing subjectivity that she was compelled to produce. Sims discusses Betsey's operation in terms of his development of proprietary medical knowledge. Though he failed to close the fistula opening, he narrates his success with devising a catheter that could be attached directly to the urethra.

Sims turned to Anarcha as his next case, and in this instance his narrative spends considerable time describing her state of injury, which remained unredressed in his first twenty-nine experiments. Of Anarcha, Sims writes,

> This woman had the very worst form of vesico-vaginal fistula. The urine was running day and night, saturating the bedding and cloth-ing, and producing an inflammation of the external parts wher-ever it came in contact with the person, almost similar to confluent small-pox, with constant pain and burning. The odor from this saturation permeated everything, and every corner of the room; and, of course, her life was one of suffering and disgust. Death would have been preferable. But patients of this kind never die; they must live and suffer.[29]

The description of Anarcha's life as one of "suffering and disgust" says as much about her condition in captivity as it does about her particu-larly grievous case of vesicovaginal fistula. As William Ian Miller explains, the sense of smell in the human sensorium "plays a motivating and con-firming role," in which disgust figures prominently in the process of social ranking to organize "people and things in a kind of cosmic order-ing."[30] According to Miller, within anti-Semitic, antiblack, and bourgeois societies, "Jews, blacks or workers smelled as a matter of principle," yet because of "context-sensitive rules that suspended the[ir] stench in par-ticular settings," they tended to smell more or less in relation to their proximity to others in a social hierarchy, such that "[w]hen out of place they smell[ed]; when safely in place they [did] not."[31] Harris's account underscores the transversal relations between geography and sensation, which find expression in the aesthetics of disgust: "Anarcha . . . seemed doomed to be forever as disgusting an object to herself as she was to everyone who came near her."[32] The copious attention paid to Anar-cha's smell in the literature speaks to the embedded nature of medical knowledge within slavery's sensorium, wherein her fistula was not the only cause of her apparent stench.

There are, however, other trajectories of thought precipitated by smell. L. H. Stallings's work on black funk is instructive here for per-ceiving how Anarcha's stench functioned as a disruptive force to slav-ery's ocular enterprise.[33] As Stallings argues, odor provides a way to think about bodily inhabitation "outside of the designs of ocularity," wherein "kinetic energy and smell express interiority . . . beyond the limits of what it means to be socially fabricated as black and human."[34] The discourse of disgust registers Anarcha's stench within the conjoined necropolitical and biopolitical logics of slavery and medicine, yet the recurrent descriptor of Anarcha's body odor also provides an opening to imagine what modicums of protection might have been afforded one by smelling noxious to one's enslaver. As a sign of a disability that made one unfit for work—reproductive or otherwise—smelling badly signals an unruly body within plantation economies. This also provides another dimension to Sims's quest for a cure to VVF, as his dependence on disabled captives became another mode for putting their bodies to work as flesh.

Disgust, both as a frequent descriptor of Anarcha's disability and in its animation of slavery's caste system at the level of sensorium, provides a requisite context for reading the racial connotations and significance of Sims's final descriptive lines about Anarcha's condition: "Death would have been preferable. But patients of this kind never die; they must live and suffer." As medical historians have noted, the prognosis of VVF as incurable frequently coincided with severe depression and suicide, particularly among middle-class European and European American women.[35] Deborah Kuhn McGregor also suggests that during this period, "[vesicovaginal] fistulas joined with childbearing to create an image of 'suffering womanhood,'" frequently contributing to "an image of universal femininity" that in practice was highly differentiated based on a person's social and political location.[36] Unable to adjust to their newly and contingently assumed status as objects of disgust, some white women opted for death before a cure was conceived. If being an object of disgust is allegorical to the status of the disabled slave, it is particularly meaningful that "patients" like Anarcha "never die" in the context of captivity, as they "must live and suffer" to create and reproduce the boundary between being and object, which is to say, to produce the possibility of distinction in the form of gynecology as a distinct field of medical inquiry.[37]

Sims's quest for a cure for VVF was situated in a scientific milieu that had yet to reconcile the interchangeability of race and species; scientists and doctors would continue to debate whether blacks were human or otherwise long after Sims published his career-making article on the treatment of VVF. Yet the uncertainty over the matter (in the flesh) of difference that blackness produced (in the social realm, in captivity, and as a matter of ontology) would critically animate the construction and reception of Sims's eventual "success," as he produced a reproducible treatment through the repeated subjection of Anarcha and the named and unnamed others. Sims would come to operate on Anarcha thirty times. Harris explains: "After Anarcha came the other patients who had been assembled from the countryside, and after them came Lucy and Betsy [*sic*] and Anarcha again—and again—and again—and again."[38]

Sims's audience of fellow doctors quickly diminished over the course of his experiments. In 1848, three years into the series of failed experiments, Sims's brother-in-law and fellow physician Rush Jones advised him to "resign the whole subject and give it up," citing the impact his obsession was having on Sims's family and the cost associated with providing for (usually in the form of crackers, morphine, and tea) at least half a dozen captives in addition to those whom Sims personally enslaved.[39] This visit from Jones coincided with increased talk of Alabama's possible secession from the Union over the matter of slavery, demonstrated in the passage of the 1848 Alabama Platform, which came on the heels of the first Code of Medical Ethics established by the American Medical Association (AMA), in 1847. With regard to the AMA's newly developed Code of Ethics, Harris writes, "Sims, engrossed as he was in his struggle with the riddle of vesicovaginal fistula, paid but slight attention to [the Code of Ethics] . . . not anticipating that the time might come when he would find himself in sharp conflict with some of its pontifical edicts."[40] Although there is no mention of slavery in the code, there is a passage that sheds partial light on the conversation between Sims and Jones. According to the first article of chapter 1, paragraph 7, the text stipulates that should a physician's patients suffer "under the consequences of vicious conduct," his peers should offer counsel "or even remonstrances . . . if they be proffered with politeness, and evince a genuine love of virtue, accompanied by a sincere interest in the welfare of the person to whom they are addressed."[41] The emphasis on civility between physicians evinces, at least in part, the manner with which the AMA conceptualized the role of medical practice as a form of civilizing work not incompatible with slavery's regime of sovereign biopower. Jones's remonstrances over the experiments stemmed from his concern for the financial strain they placed on his sister, figuring the "consequences" of the experiments for the one physician who intervened.

Taking the form of a series of gentlemen's agreements, the AMA's Code of Ethics was ill equipped to address Anarcha, Betsey, Lucy, and the unnamed others who were both Sims's "patients" and his surgical attendants.[42] Harris notes, "His medical friends who at first had been so anxious to be present at the making of history now usually managed to find themselves busy on the days of his vesico-vaginal fistula operations."[43] After two years of failed experiments, Sims could no longer depend on other doctors, and began to instruct the named and unnamed "patients" to assist him in surgeries by "holding the speculum in place for him, handing him his instruments as he needed them, restraining the patient on the table, shifting the reflecting mirror at his direction, doing all the many things which once upon a time the medical men had vied to do."[44] From the perspective of his captive experimentees, this training and their subsequent practice might have been regarded as a further imposition, a multiplicative form of emotional abuse that accompanied being coerced into facilitating the physical torture of others.

However, there are multiple ways to read this detail about the experiments, precipitating questions about authorship that situate Sims's chattel "patients" as the subjects—in addition to the objects—of medical knowledge and as the holders of expertise that exceed medicine's institutionalizing frame. It also points to other aspects of the narrative that were overlooked or underwritten in the historical record, chief among them the relations Lucy, Betsey, Anarcha, and the unnamed others forged and sustained with and among each other. If initially one pictures Sims's "hospital" as a site of racial containment and suffering, being both the domicile of those whom Sims personally enslaved and the structure that housed his "patients," it is also necessary to think about what other modes of relation occurred there without being overseen. What other modes of nourishment and care did they provide for one another? How did those whom Sims personally enslaved look after Sims's experimentees? And although their role as attendants was described as being totally under Sims's direction, what adjustments did Lucy, Betsey, Anarcha, and the unnamed others make when holding the instruments—perhaps an imperceptible twist of the wrist or an ever so slight change in pressure administered in response to each other's pain?

Sims ignored the AMA's Code of Ethics and Jones's counsel, continuing for another year, until May or June 1849, when he placed

Anarcha on his operation table after her thirtieth procedure only to find that "there was no inflammation . . . no tumefaction, nothing unnatural, and a very perfect union of the little fistula."[45] According to his autobiography, "In the course of two weeks more, Lucy and Betsey were both cured by the same means. . . . Then I realized the fact that, at last, my efforts had been blessed with success, and that I had made, perhaps, one of the most important discoveries of the age for the relief of suffering humanity."[46] After applying his fistula procedures, as a counterpoint to his apocryphal description of the discovery as being "for the relief of suffering humanity," Sims sent all of the named and unnamed captives back to their enslavers.

Object Lessons on Flesh

Almost immediately after concluding the experiments, Sims fell ill. Although he would live for another thirty years, Sims described writing his VVF article as a "last free-will offering to the medical profession."[47] Issued in the *American Journal of the Medical Sciences* in January 1852, "On the Treatment of Vesico-vaginal Fistula" makes claim to three original and proprietary contributions to medical knowledge: "the discovery of a method by which the vagina can be thoroughly explored, and the operation easily performed," "the introduction of a new suture apparatus," and "the invention of a self-retaining catheter."[48] Unlike his previous essays, which included at least a brief description of his patients, this article is symptomatically devoid of any identifying characteristics of Anarcha, Betsey, Lucy, or the unnamed others.[49] Sims does include that "[a]t the first, I had three cases, upon which I operated about forty times, but failed in every instance to effect a perfect cure, though succeeding so far as to encourage me to persevere."[50] As a pronouncement that bespeaks a set of subject-object relations, Sims's discussion of personal triumph, determination, and curiosity—qualities that would afford his status in the field of gynecology—works in tandem with the suppression of the conditions in which his knowledge was procured. The focus on proprietary instruments and procedures and the oblique references to his "patients," who are also invoked in terms of "the peculiarities of individual cases," finds visual reinforcement in the series of twenty-two woodcuts, printed from diagrams Sims drew himself, that organize the essay's prose.[51] As object lessons, the accompanying images provide a way to understand flesh as an expression of power's "polyvalent mobilities": here, there are no bodies (except, tacitly, Sims's), because his "patients" were nobodies according to the precepts of law and medicine.[52]

The first set of illustrations depicts two instruments: one is sparsely outlined, which Sims describes as "a small, slightly convex spatula" designed to supplement the figure on its left, which would later be referred to as Sims's speculum.[53] Of Latin origin, "speculum" roughly translates as a tool (*-ulum*) for looking (*specere*) and refers to a surgical instrument used for dilating orifices or to "a mirror used for scientific purpose."[54] Embellished with texture, Sims's speculum—although composed from German silver—appears to be hewn from the wood from which the images were made. Analogously to contemporaneous print-making practices, Sims suggests that the speculum should be reproduced with "two or three of different sizes, so as to be prepared for any case."[55] Each letter printed along the perimeter of the drawing corresponds to an instruction about the instrument's design. As Sims describes in the article, "The one ordinarily used by me is about 2½ inches from *a*, where it supports the sphincter, to its terminal extremity at *b*. . . . Its breadth from *d* to *e* is about ⅞ths of an inch, widening a little as it approaches the end."[56] The lettering not only maps the spatial coordinates of the speculum but also presents a topological relation between Sims's instrument and the instrumentality of flesh and its capacity for expansion and inspection. Reminiscent of another verse from the Christian Bible, in which the word was made flesh, the lettering here indicates at least two relations forged through flesh, as Anarcha, Betsey, Lucy, and the unnamed others were reiteratively put to use to develop the instrument's design, rendering the woodcut image itself a map of word to flesh.

It is perhaps unsurprising that an object that expressed the directive to look would perform an instrumental role in the narrative emergence of gynecology in the United States. Investitures in the visual in the making of racial slavery meant organizing life according to who was doing the seeing and who or what was being over/seen. In addition, the field of gynecology was developed according to a Manichean logic, what Maria Lugones refers to as the "dark" and "light side" of "the colonial/modern gender system," which as a "cognitive production of modernity . . . understood race as gendered and gender as raced in particularly differential

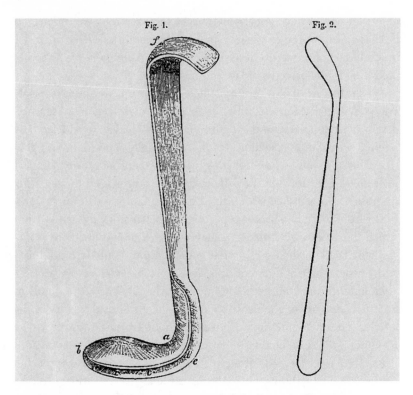

Sims's speculum and "slightly convex spatula," the first pair of woodcut illustrations in "On the Treatment of Vesico-vaginal Fistula," in the *American Journal of the Medical Sciences*, January 1852.

ways for Europeans/'whites' and colonized/'non-white' peoples."[57] Harris narrates gynecology's emergence in similar terms, suggesting that "in the field of women's diseases physicians were blind men, working in the dark." He continues: "Just how much in the dark they were is revealed by nineteenth century woodcuts portraying physicians examining their female patients. A picture of a lady on her medical adviser's table shows the patient not only fully clothed . . . but with hat and gloves thrown in for good measure, while over her rear, from waist to feet, is draped a sheet, beneath which the unseeing physician extends his groping hands, struggling manfully to solve the mystery of her ailments."[58] More than anecdotal, this passage exemplifies the instantiating rhetoric of gynecology, in which the coupling of sex and gender occurs as a racial arrangement.

The reference to the double bind of blindness while "working in the dark" that characterized the field at its genesis seems to figure the other side of Du Bois's "double-consciousness," in which the visualizing rhetoric of race (à la the veil) transverses gender's constitution (beneath the sheet). Here, Harris's description illustrates how, on the one hand, white femininity is conferred in relation to an unwillingness to view white female genitalia, that is, to look upon white women as flesh. On the other hand, the unrelenting scopic availability that defined blackness within the visual economy of racial slavery becomes the necessary context for producing a field of sex/gender knowledge. From this vantage point, one could consider the various ways "gender" functions as an effect of plantation visuality, wherein captive flesh expressed an ungendered position that defines race as the sine qua non of sex. In this arrangement, gender socially constructs sex, and captive flesh becomes the material and metaphorical ground for unsettling a view of sex and gender as neatly divided according to each term's relation to medicoscientific knowledge.

Elaine Scarry notes how the concepts of "body and voice (or in the language of the Christian scriptures, flesh and word)" emerge "as explanatory rubrics in early moments of creating, or when there is some problem in the relation between maker and made thing that carries us back to the original moment of making."[59] Supposing that the "problem" is an ethical one, the woodcut images of Sims's inventions in "On the Treatment of Vesico-vaginal Fistula," although not directly indicating chattel slavery as the necessary condition for VVF's cure, indicate how gynecology materialized a series of subject-object relations according to what Foucault described as "a type of power . . . that can only function thanks to the formation of a knowledge that is both its effect and also a condition of its exercise."[60]

Throughout the article, Sims describes the images according to the instruments or procedures he aims to highlight. Depictions invariably feature the penetration of flesh by objects, recursively imaging the etymology of his other proprietary contribution, the catheter, whose name, roughly translated from ancient Greek, refers to the letting down of something after an initial act of incursion.[61] The procedure for producing Sims's catheter is described over five drawings, depicting successive failures in design until the fifth iteration, whose illustration Sims describes as "a correct representation of the self-retaining catheter," with "exactly the size and shape that is most generally required."[62] Alongside the preceding images of discarded tools, Sims describes in pornotropic detail "the shreds of mucous membrane (some an inch long) hanging from each orifice on the under and lateral surfaces of the catheter" while making oblique references to the impact on the "patient," writing, "The injury done to the part, and the pain inflicted on the patient, may very well be imagined."[63]

Although the context for their development was left to his readers' imaginations, the erect form of the instruments in the article's accompanying illustrations—pictured as if they were sitting for a portrait—functioned as another sign of what Spillers describes in the epigraph to this chapter as procedures of "total objectification" that produced subjectified objects of flesh. Whereas penetrated flesh indexed the named and unnamed "patients," the totality of images represented the "hand" of Sims, both in the proprietary relationship between author and imaged objects and also by way of an implied movement of the instruments in several of the illustrations. Drawings aiming to depict the body reinforce this logic, alternately featuring bisected bodies, interior vaginal tissue, or a series of concentric oblong shapes composed of smooth or dotted lines meant to represent a fistula. As representations of flesh, the images figure flesh as blackness in abstraction, desubjectified and material, the substance of method and mode. As such, the woodcuts serve as illustrations

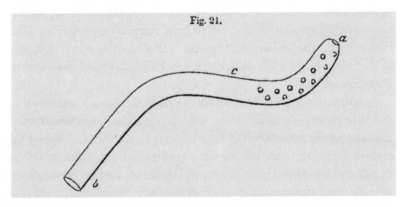

Fig. 21.

The fifth and final depiction of Sims's self-retaining catheter, which his article "On the Treatment of Vesico-vaginal Fistula" notes is "exactly the size and shape that is most generally required."

of the instrumentality of flesh, of flesh as a first order of instrumentation and of the creation of additional instruments of and for flesh.

In subsequent years, Sims wrote follow-up articles on VVF, including "Two Cases of Vesico-vaginal Fistula, Cured," which appeared in January 1854 in the *New-York Medical Gazette and Journal of Health* on the two-year anniversary of the initial article. By then, Sims was a practicing physician in New York City, having moved north for health reasons, and his articles frequently announced the author's relatively

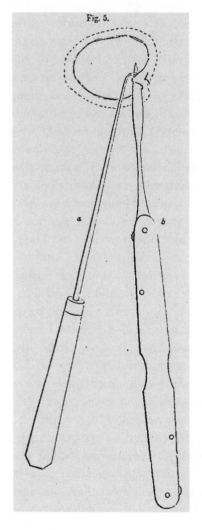

Woodcut in "On the Treatment of Vesico-vaginal Fistula" illustrating the tools and procedure for closing a fistula.

recent change of address. In "Two Cases," Sims casts the cure for VVF in proverbial terms, writing, "experiment, properly directed, could alone accomplish anything."[64] Relaying another variation of the experimental trials, Sims tells his readers that he "was fortunate in having three young healthy colored girls given to me by their owners," while also noting that he performed "no operation without the full consent of the patients."[65] As the title portends, in "Two Cases," Sims forwent the "truly interesting" history of "these three cases"—collapsing the nearly half dozen chattel experimentees—to address a question about the necessary duration of sutures for recovering patients. Sims introduces the first of the two cases with a brief biographical sketch of Amy McRee, who was the first case "cured by a single operation" and of whom Sims writes the following report: "black, aged but 16 years, very small, weighing no more than 90 pounds."[66] In his exposition of her condition and his procedures, Sims explains that in this instance the catheter had to be cast smaller because of the size of McRee's urethra, and his meticulous description of her size and physical under/development was further indication of McRee's enslavement.[67] Producing copious notes on his postoperative procedures, Sims concludes his case study with the following updates: "Two months afterward her husband, visiting Montgomery, informed me that she was in fine health, and no longer followed the injunction of living absque marito [without a husband]. Three years after this I heard she was a mother—the cure remaining permanent."[68] As "wife" and "mother," McRee is framed in ways that foreshadow Sims's later meditation on the implications of VVF's cure in his posthumously published autobiography, in which he describes his proprietary tools and procedures as "one of the most important discoveries of the age for the relief of suffering humanity."[69] Though Sims discusses McRee's postoperative life in terms of feminine normalcy and heteronormativity, Amy was, like Anarcha, Betsey, Lucy, and the unnamed others, returned to her enslaver. That her child, like the mother, was owned by the enslaver reveals how such concepts are ill suited to describe the realities of McRee's life.

The second case, that of "Mrs. A. F., aged 40 years, very large, weighing nearly 200 pounds"—and her distinction from McRee, who receives no honorific in her description—functions as another indication of the duplicity in the text's use of terms, as it illustrates how discourses of privacy and protection demarcated racial and gender differences (and perhaps racial *as* gender differences) for which flesh remained a key apparatus for perceiving the political and ethical dimensions of VVF's condition and cure.[70] Relatedly, "Two Cases" indicates again how medicoscientific language produces deviations from norms (recall Anarcha's smell), which is to say that illness and disability are as much a social as a physical concern.

A little more than a year after "Two Cases" was published, Sims founded the Woman's Hospital, financially backed by some of the wealthiest white women of New York and administered by a "board of lady managers."[71] According to Sims, at its opening, in May 1855, the hospital of thirty beds was full to capacity, and within six months it was forced to expand its staff. As he wrote in his autobiography, "It was a charity; there were no 'pay-patients' admitted."[72] The patients were typically indigent immigrant women. Their class status and position as non- or not-yet-white provided Sims ample opportunities to perform operations in a surgical theater before his peers and possible donors. By 1857, the Woman's Hospital received its charter, and along with this recognition came a restructuring of governance (being now placed in the hands of "the leading men of the city") and plans to erect a new building, modeled after Saint Luke's.[73] It took ten years to complete the hospital's relocation, eclipsing the span of the U.S. Civil War, its construction prolonged by the removal of forty-seven thousand coffins of cholera victims from an outbreak in 1832.[74]

According to his biography, Sims traveled in the summer of 1861 "to take a little rest and vacation, to learn something at first hand of the Old-World medical centers . . . and to investigate trends in hospital construction in Great Britain and France."[75] The trip, according to Harris, was the idea of his wife, Theresa, who observed "with loving concern her husband's growing chagrin at the war's disruption of all his plans."[76] Sims wrote in a letter to Theresa from Paris of "the unfortunate state of political affairs" that placed him "in a very precarious position."[77] Believing that the Confederate Army would win the war, Sims told his wife that pledging allegiance to the "Northern States" would make him "worse off pecuniarily but better off professionally."[78] Though Sims was trepidatious about his prospects abroad, he found warm welcome in Dublin, his first port of call. He quickly left Dublin for London, spent time in Edinburgh, and eventually, upon arrival in France, found the perfect conditions for prospering professionally and financially as a physician to European nobility. As Harris notes, "Paris at [that] moment was in a mood to feel very favorably disposed toward all Southerners, for the prevailing French attitude toward the war in America was one of strong sympathy for the South." Some prominent Frenchmen, including Emperor Louis Napoleon III, thought that France and England "ought to ensure the Confederacy's permanent separation from the North by joining openly in its fight instead of merely building ships to help it break the Northern maritime blockade."[79] During this, Sims's first visit to Paris, he treated the Countess de F.'s vesicovaginal fistula alongside and at the request of her primary physician, Auguste Nélaton, who acted as surgeon to Giuseppe Garibaldi and Louis Napoleon III. The surgeries came with myriad complications, precipitated by the countess's reaction to the anesthesia and, one might reason, Sims's lack of experience with its application and effects, given that his experiments on the chattel "patients" never included it. Sims, however, established connections and cultivated a reputation that would allow him to return to France—this time with family in tow—and begin a lucrative medical practice.

Upon return from his first trip, Sims received news that he would be awarded the Knight of the Order of Leopold I by the government of Belgium, though the honor would be rescinded before it was bestowed. Harris conveys that this incident demonstrated "that as long as [Sims] remained in the United States during the war in the despised role of neutral he might expect one after another of his old friends to turn against him."[80] Yet as Sims's 1861 letter from Paris had confirmed, Sims's position was far from neutral: "My sentiments I can not help, for I lived forty years of my life at the South. The companions of my youth are the leaders of the great Southern rebellion. My father, now seventy-three years of age, is one of its soldiers; our whole family . . . [is] in arms."[81] Along with financial incentives for relocation, Sims cited this "slight" by the Belgian government as one of the precipitates for his nine-year stint in France beginning in 1862. While in Paris, Sims counted among his patients the Duchess of Hamilton and Empress Eugénie de Montijo, wife of Napoleon III; he also wrote and published *Uterine Surgery*. Regarding its publication, Sims wrote in *The Story of My Life*: "Before that time there was not a professorship of gynaecology, worthy of the name, connected with any of our medical schools, and now we have professorships of this department in every school . . . throughout the civilized world."[82]

Although his editorial flourish here signals the various ways Sims viewed his medical career as part of a civilizing project—his instruments, procedures, and writings in gynecology producing knowledge for "the civilized world"—it also opens lines of inquiry about "power-knowledge" as a correlative of flesh. That is, Sims's research, international practice, and reputation carried a critical object lesson on the ways gender and race were articulated, illustrated in part in the unresolved matter of blackness in science (and nature) in the contemporaneous wave of European colonial-imperialist expansion in Africa and Asia, which was also expressed under the banner of civilization.

In his lectures at the Collège de France in 1974–1975, Michel Foucault described the "complex and floating domain of the flesh" as a "correlate of . . . [a] new technique of power . . . what can be called a new procedure of examination." For Foucault, the disparagement of the body as flesh engendered "an analytic discourse and investigation of the body" that rendered it culpable and available for objectification.[83] Foucault's presumption of a temporal sequence of corporeal ontological primacy, in which the discourse of flesh emerges after the (discourse of the) body, is not simply incompatible with the rise of gynecology in terms of the field's narration but also indexes Foucault's failure to connect racialization to power's procedural efficacies, here as elsewhere. In his move to describe power as capillary and productive, as more generative than repressive, Foucault overlooks how race functions as a necessary prefix to the particulates of his compound term ("power-knowledge"), altering knowledge and power. Characterizing the negative or repressive view of power as "a sort of daguerreotype of power in a slave society, a caste society, a feudal society, and in a society like the administrative monarchy," Foucault critiques this conceptualization for its inability "to grasp what is specific and new in what took place during the eighteenth century and the Classical Age."[84] As the zenith of transatlantic slave-trading activity occurred in the eighteenth century, and as the classical age was also a slaving age characterized by a succession of administrative monarchies (particularly in the case of ancient Rome), Foucault's insistence on the "new" and "specific" presents a historical and methodological problem for his articulation of a cleft between negative and positive modes of power, as it also identifies another concern with his thinking on coloniality and race. As Greg Thomas argues in his trenchant analysis of the coloniality of gender and sexuality, Foucault's history of sex refuses to understand "sex categories as explicit categories of empire" wherein "the colonial vocabulary of sex is part and parcel of the modern production of heterosexuality as a defining feature of Occidentalism."[85]

Tarrying with the daguerreotype, which for Foucault was a metaphor for an outdated conception of power, offers a visual grammar for reading the imbrications of "race" and "gender" under captivity. After being exposed in a camera, daguerreotype images were produced by treating highly polished sheets of silver-plated copper with mercury vapors. Fragile and malleable, the images were immediately placed under glass. To view a daguerreotype is to look at an image that does not sit on a surface but appears to be floating in space. Rather than an antiquated form of modern photography, as Foucault's characterization implies, the daguerreotype provides a series of lessons about power, and racial power in particular, as a form in which an image takes on myriad perspectives because of the interplay of light and dark, both in the composition of the shot and in the play of light on the display. That the image does not reside on the surface but floats in an unmappable elsewhere offers an allegory for race as a procedure that exceeds the logics of a bodily surface, occurring by way of flesh, a racial mattering that appears through puncture in the form of a wound or covered by skin and screened from view.

Flesh is, above all else, a thing that produces relations—real and imagined, metaphysical and material. As Nicole Ivy argues, "[N]ot only were black women made to be the ciphers through which medical knowledge about an imagined constituency of suffering white womanhood could be telegraphed, they also remained rendered knowable and fungible across time and geographic space."[86] The founding of American gynecology and the distinct contrast between chattel experimentees and an "imagined constituency of suffering white womanhood" highlights how flesh acted as a condition of possibility for the hospital as laboratory, creating a structure in which bodies were made flesh by way of medicoscientific discourses, techniques of examination, and objectification born from a possessive scopophilic dynamic that characterized the enslaver's relation to the captive. The medical plantation thus served as a key site for the refinement of biopolitical and necropolitical techniques in the production of medical knowledge that critically disavowed chattel slavery as a constitutive grammar to express sex and gender as effects of racial science.

Although Sims essentially relocated to Europe to sustain his financial standing during the U.S. Civil War, while in Paris he participated in the Franco-Prussian War, organizing the American-Anglo Ambulance Corps, of which he was made surgeon in chief.[87] Upon his return to the United States, in 1871—a decision precipitated by the possibility of facing charges for assaulting an American dentist in Paris—Sims continued to maintain a thriving practice, returning to the Woman's Hospital and turning his attention to cancer and syphilis, among other illnesses.[88] In a spectacular scene at the hospital's anniversary party in November 1874, Sims resigned from the Woman's Hospital over new protocols limiting the number of spectators at surgeries and a ban on surgeries related to cancer. However, Sims remained generally well regarded by his colleagues in the twilight of his career, continuing to receive honors and awards from European and American institutions and becoming the president of the American Medical Association in 1876 and the president of the American Gynecological Association in 1880. Upon Sims's death, in 1883, the Medical Society of the District of Columbia issued a series of resolutions that included commentary on his later years in the profession, writing, "[T]he light of his genius had not grown dim with years, but . . . to him . . . [the society looked] for future discoveries of hidden truth in the yet unexplored regions of medical science, which can only be *penetrated and made manifest* by a genius like that of Sims."[89]

A little more than a decade after Sims expired from a heart attack at the age of seventy, on November 13, 1883, the City of New York dedicated a bronze statue of Sims, marking the first occasion that a physician received a publicly erected memorial in the United States. Rendered by Ferdinand Freiherr von Miller, the monument was first installed in Bryant Park in 1894. In 1934, it was moved across from the Academy of Medicine and remains at the intersection of Fifth Avenue and 103rd Street in Central Park in Manhattan. Other memorials were installed on the grounds of his alma mater, Jefferson Medical College in Philadelphia, Pennsylvania, as well as at the South Carolina and Alabama capitol buildings in Columbia and Montgomery, respectively. The marker of Sims's birthplace in Lancaster County, South Carolina, most clearly expresses the romantic plot that organizes these various memorialization efforts to venerate, in its words, "his service to suffering women, empress and slave alike."[90]

Anarcha is sometimes referred to as the mother of gynecology, standing in for the named and unnamed captives whose penetrated flesh produced gynecology as a particular form of medicoscientific knowledge. Rebecca Wanzo notes how "Anarcha's name, rather than Lucy's or Betsey's, seems to resonate most strongly . . . perhaps because Sims wrote that Anarcha was the first case he saw."[91] Her designation as the mother of gynecology raises a number of questions about the politics of memorialization, about how it is possible to venerate flesh, and about the potential violence that underwrites this form of emplacement. Although offered as a recuperative gesture, the logics of substitution that impanel Anarcha as the mother of gynecology replicate the legal, economic, and cultural dynamics of chattel mothering, in which the mother and the offspring are subject to the owner. From this view, positioning her as the mother of the field, which also implies a set of perturbing relations to Sims, reiterates what Jennifer Morgan explains are the "implicit expectations that [enslavers'] wealth and, indeed, that of entire colonial empires, derived from the reproductive potential of African women."[92]

The theopolitical justification that Sims gave in his 1857 lecture on silver sutures to the New York Academy of Medicine reappears in the familial language that constructs the founding of American gynecology. As G. J. Barker-Benfield argues, "Sims's fathering of himself in the conventional terms of self-making was integral to his fathering of modern gynecology."[93] Creating oneself and the environment of one's emergence through the language of fatherhood echoes Christianity's language of invention. Achille Mbembe explains:

> Breaking with Judaism, Christianity brought the divinity back within the framework of family relations and situated it in a family universe including a son and a mother. . . . In its abstract determinations, however, the god escapes a purely familial logic. He is both father and son; since the son is realized within a woman while at the same time being innate to the father, one can conclude that the mother is innate to the son, and thus the feminine becomes an integral principle of the phantasm of the One.[94]

To the extent that gynecology's language of invention casts Sims and his "offspring"—his instruments, positions, and procedures—as one and the same, the "mother," in this instance being "innate to the son," is traceable as the flesh in the objects. The objects are, in turn, another instantiation of the flesh.

Given that the appearance of flesh is often an index of injury, "the narratives of Anarcha, Betsey, and Lucy," as Wanzo observes, "add another nuance to the iconographic history of black suffering."[95] Brutality under captivity is frequently captured through images of proud flesh—of the black back overlaid with intricate patterns of keloid scars, of an attenuation of the multiple orders of flesh on display in the narrative of VVF's surgical cure. Kuppers argues against the impetus to memorialize the experimentees exclusively as "medical victims," as this approach obscures more complex understandings of the named and unnamed chattel women as "whole beings."[96] Kuppers offers "disability culture" as a space to remember them more fully, and her critique also invokes Evelynn Hammonds's earlier meditation on black holes and the possibility of wholeness for black female sexualities in matters of theory and practice. Hammonds raises two questions, which bear directly upon the matter of flesh, its metaphysical properties, effectivities, and relations: "How do you deduce the presence of a black hole? And "what is it like inside of a black hole?"[97] Hammonds addresses the first question by calling for an analysis attuned to the effects of an undetectably present thing.[98] This is the ground on which many scholars have critiqued American gynecology's foundation and the political terrain on which activists have sought to memorialize the named and unnamed experimentees in contesting the presumed authorship of the instruments and procedures that produced vesicovaginal fistula's cure.[99]

Hammonds's second question, however, brings to the fore the problem of representability, a concern which is distinct from issues of visibility and the dominant calculus that privileges more over less. Accessing and assessing the quality inside the black hole—or of flesh itself—requires a different analytic, what Hammonds describes as a "different geometry," to explore and generate the conditions of possibility for such a description to take place. Put differently, addressing the question of what it is like to be flesh necessitates a mode of thinking capable of discerning the conditions of possibility for the conditions of possibility. As the narratives of the named and unnamed experimentees articulate how the development of "women's medicine" was grafted from ungendered flesh, their stories, as circumscribed by Sims's archive, also invoke a series of consternating questions about the relations between sex and flesh: In what ways is sex an effect of flesh? Does sex require flesh as its condition of possibility? Or, to reiterate the question posed in this chapter's introduction, what is sex without flesh? To pursue this line of inquiry, I turn to two images that were produced long after the deaths of Sims and his experimentees, which depict the relations between the anarranging of flesh and the transorienting of sex and gender. In what follows, I take up two key examples of gynecological visual culture in the United States for what they reveal about the metaphysics of sex and gender, which cohere by way of the instrumentality of flesh.

Anarranging Flesh, Transorienting Sex and Gender

In 1911, Johns Hopkins University instituted the Department of Art as Applied to Medicine, which was the first of its kind to train students in medical illustration in the United States. Max Brödel, who is sometimes referred to as the "father of modern medical illustration," became its first director and presided over the program until his retirement at the age of 70, in 1940.[100] Prior to his appointment, Brödel worked as an illustrator for Johns Hopkins's gynecology and obstetrics department, contributing drawings and diagrams for Howard A. Kelly's *Operative Gynecology* (1898) and Thomas S. Cullen's *Cancer of the Uterus* (1900), among others. He and his colleagues August Horn and Hermann Becker have been described as revolutionaries in the field of medical illustration, heralded for creating the defining works of their time, which, according to Cullen, happened "just as medicine and surgery were making greater strides than they had done in centuries and when many new illustrations were necessary."[101] Although Brödel's vast catalog depicted myriad medical phenomena, his initial placement and training in gynecology indelibly shaped his view of the role of illustration in medical literature. In an address to the AMA in June 1907, which was later published as an article in its flagship journal, Brödel articulated his concern for the state of the profession: "The trouble is that the medical illustrator is not familiar with the objects he is to draw or paint. To him, they are obscure in meaning, indefinite in form, and sometimes repulsive in character; as a consequence he shuns original study, the only means of preparing for the work."[102]

For Brödel, in order for a medical illustration to analyze, interpret, and teach, the artist was required to have prior and direct access to medical knowledge. In an essay published a few months before his death, he pronounced, "[N]o drawing was made by me without original study by injection, dissection, frozen section or reconstruction."[103] Such a process was necessary, he suggested, for the artist to fully comprehend "the subject-matter from every standpoint: anatomical, topographical, histological, pathological, medical, and surgical. From this accumulated knowledge grows a mental picture, from which again crystal-lizes the plan of the future drawing."[104] As a gynecological illustrator, however, depicting the nude female form required improvisation, given the paucity of models for such endeavors. In a tribute written for Brödel after his death, Cullen addressed the matter directly: "On a few occasions, when he was a relatively young man, and when he was illustrating Dr. Kelly's new method of examining the bladder and ureters, he required a model from which to sketch the knee–chest posture. Every time I see the drawings he made on those occasions I cannot help smiling broadly. I was Max's model, and you may rest assured that it was easier for me to assume the knee–chest posture at that time than it is now."[105] According to Ranice Crosby and John Cody, "The jokes and laughter of the two young men as Max labored to transform Tom's muscular rump into something gracefully feminine echoed undiminished down the years."[106] Brödel's artistic translations from male to female form also crossed racial classifications, as in his "Method of Introducing Long Rectal Speculum to Examine Entire Length of Lower Bowel," published in the second edition of Kelly's *Medical Gynecology* (1912).[107]

Placed in the first chapter, "Consulting Room and Gynecological Examination," and depicting a doctor bearing an uncanny resemblance to Kelly in the process of examining a patient posed in "knee–breast position," the illustration—through the placement of white sheets—obscures all but the rectum and top of the head of the blackened form. (Incidentally—but not coincidentally—"Method" appears within one page of a pair of images depicting Sims's position for vaginal examination.) Including 165 drawings of blackened and white forms, of men,

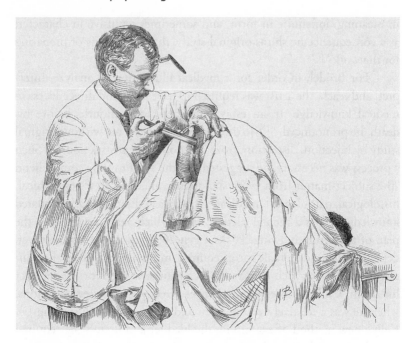

From the 1912 edition of Howard Kelly's *Medical Gynecology*, Max Brödel's illustration "Method of Introducing Long Rectal Speculum to Examine Entire Length of Lower Bowel" was drawn from a scene of Kelly, founding doctor of Johns Hopkins's gynecology department, and fellow white professor Dr. Thomas Cullen. Courtesy of Johns Hopkins Medical Archive.

women, and children, fully clothed and completely nude, *Medical Gynecology* does not, at first glance, seem to conform to any necessary formula regarding race and nudity. Many of the illustrations depict "white genitalia," determined by the figure's shading and the rendering of hair, such that it would not seem that black figures were featured, in order to secure white women's bodily integrity. Among the images, no blackened figure is depicted fully clothed. In some instances, white bandages obscure the faces of blackened forms as their breasts and buttocks are meticulously rendered, underscoring a pornotropic gaze that informs, subtends, and frequently subsumes the medicoscientific one, which is to say that flesh also expresses how the examination room is also a libidinous site.

The reappearance of the white sheets, which in "Method" reads as a perverse and parodic take on Harris's earlier description, reveals itself

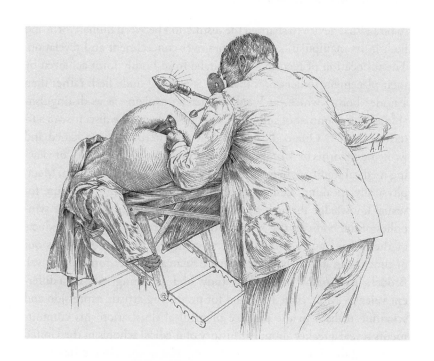

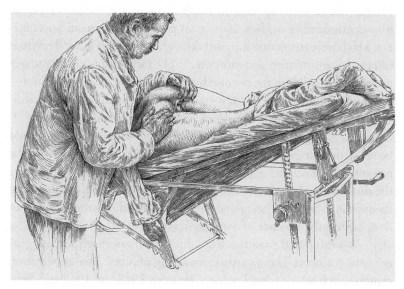

Illustrations of Sims's position for vaginal examination in Kelly's *Medical Gynecology* (1912). Courtesy of Johns Hopkins Medical Archive.

to be a visual device to sharpen the distinction between human form and flesh in its manipulation of anxieties over concealment and revelation. The dislocation of rectum and genitalia from bodily form achieved by their placement underscores that one is viewing nude flesh rather than a nude "body," which, as Frank Wilderson explains, is as distinguishable as "the grammar of suffering's discourse" from "the discourse of suffering itself."[108] One could reason that the interplay of blackened and white nude forms in *Medical Gynecology* produces an apparatus for viewing medical nudity as being structured by and distinct from flesh. Metaphysically speaking, flesh then becomes the capacitating structure for sexual knowledge through its constitutive position outside of the symbolics of the body. In this sense, Brödel's illustrations are not "products of their time" but a perpetuation of codifying blackened flesh as out of time, as an untimely referent that demarcates other forms of arrival. Brödel's investments in "original study" and "planning" take on a different valence. More than a method for producing artistic expression and scientific realism in the practice of medical illustration, his commitments reveal a reality about the history of medical schools in the United States and medical instruction's ongoing reliance on black cadavers. As Harriet Washington explains, the emphasis on anatomical instruction in nineteenth-century medical classrooms produced a demand for cadavers, which were frequently supplied through the theft of black flesh from cemeteries, mortuaries, and morgues.[109] The racial disparities in cadaver use persisted well into the twentieth century, and, as Washington notes, in a study conducted in 1933, it was found that "many southern medical schools . . . still used only black cadavers for teaching anatomy."[110] From this vantage point, one might ask a number of questions that should be taken up alongside the chapter's previously stated concern about the metaphysics of sex and gender, including these: How does flesh express the distinction between the living and the dead, between ontology and its opposite? between being and nonbeing? In other words, how does flesh express the violence of metaphysics itself?[111]

As a thing that produces relations, flesh transorients sex and gender, which Robert Thom's artistic rendering of Sims's first examination expresses in terms of time. Produced between 1948 and 1965 and commissioned by the Parke-Davis pharmaceutical group, Robert Thom's eighty-five oil paintings depicted a range of medical phenomena, loosely organized as forty centuries of medical advancement and pharmaceutical invention.[112] Beginning in 1951, Parke-Davis distributed reproductions of the paintings throughout Canada and the United States as boxed sets. The images were eventually collected into two volumes—*Great Moments in Medicine* (1961) and *Great Moments in Pharmacy* (1966)—with additional description provided by Parke-Davis pharmacist and self-trained historian George Bender. Prior to their collection in book form, as a mode of soft advertisement for the pharmaceutical company, each image also circulated as a subsidized monthly insert in the magazine *Modern Pharmacy: A Practical Journal for the Retail Druggist.*[113] Jonathan Metzl and Joel Howell note the immense popularity of the series, which "soon adorned the walls of countless waiting rooms, pharmacies, and private homes . . . was widely reproduced in calendars, popular magazines, and educational brochures, [and] became the subject of a full-length promotional movie."[114] Thom's *J. Marion Sims: Gynecologic*

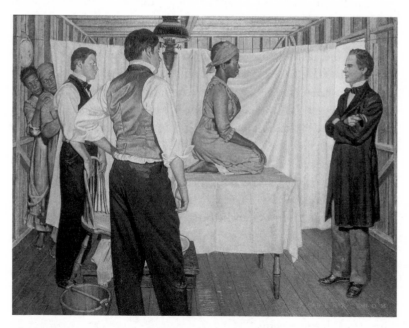

Robert Thom's *J. Marion Sims: Gynecologic Surgeon* is one of eighty-five oil paintings included in the *Great Moments in Medicine* series, by George A. Bender and Robert A. Thom (Detroit: Parke-Davis, 1961). Courtesy of the Collection of the University of Michigan Health System, Gift of Pfizer Inc.

Surgeon was, according to Metzl and Howell, the "most controversial image in the *Great Moments* series"; the aesthetic rendering of plantation medicine was unable to allay concerns about the unethical grammar of suffering that structures this scene of "medical advancement."[115]

On the far right of the painting, Sims is pictured in an overcoat with arms crossed and, according to Harriet Washington, holding in one hand "a metroscope (the forerunner of the speculum)."[116] Sims's likeness was made from the various portraits taken during his life. His formality of dress and posture distinguishes him from the other white men in the scene, who, in shirtsleeves, waistcoats, and bow ties, are meant to represent his assistants (whether students or fellow physicians); their rolled-up sleeves and posture mark the scene as anticipatory of a later moment, in which they will be enlisted to restrain the figure seated in a kneeling position. All eyes are directed at Sims, including those of two black women peering from behind a large white sheet. In contrast to the individuated figures imaged in front of the sheet, the two are posed in close proximity to each other, with one figure's hand placed upon the other's shoulder. Some critics have read their expressions as "childlike," but one could also perceive their expressions as a consequence of their partial embrace, an action that mirrors the gesture of the figure on the table, whose hand is placed across her chest, perhaps in an attempt to soothe herself.[117] Although the painting's caption describes her as "the slave girl Lucy," Washington identifies the kneeling figure as Betsey, noting how she is depicted "as a fully clothed, calm slave who kneels complacently on a small table" in an "innocuous tableau [that] could hardly differ more from the gruesome reality."[118] Though Washington does not explain why she calls the kneeling figure "Betsey" rather than "Lucy," her analysis calls attention to the interchangeability of Lucy and Betsey in Sims's autobiography and the logics of fungibility that situate Sims's experimentees within his archive. As another dimension of how fungibility animates the scene of gynecology's founding, Thom cast his housekeeper Barbara White to represent Lucy/Betsey, an artistic decision that re/produced black women as fungible flesh more than a century after Sims's initial experiments.[119]

As Deborah Kuhn McGregor suggests, "[T]he background of a draped white curtain and a table covered by a white sheet" presents a sanitized scene for the ensuing examination.[120] Other objects, including the smaller table, additional cloth, and bowl, reinforce the decorum of medical professionalism and scientific exploration. The large ceiling lamp is nearest the center of the image, a visual metaphor for the enlightenment that would ensue. The abundance of white sheets in Thom's painting recalls again Harris's description of the nineteenth-century woodcut of the white female patient, fully clothed and covered in an additional sheet, which, for Harris, represented a paucity of information among physicians about women's bodies and health. As a visual trope of unrepresentability, the sheets in Thom's painting mark a shift from masking the patient (and the unrepresentability of the white female form as flesh) to obscuring the environment, yet the "examination room" cannot quite conceal the more than a dozen chattel persons—some of whom Sims personally enslaved. Put succinctly, the sheets distinguish the medical setting from its double, a site of slavery. The ornate dress worn by one of the figures partially obscured by the sheet as well as what McGregor notes as the lack of "wear and tear" on the subject's bare feet buttress the scene's romantic depiction of Sims as an emblem of scientific neutrality.

Whereas all eyes are presumably on Sims, he seems to be looking at the clock across the room, a gesture that indicates the significance of temporality to the image and the *Great Moments* series. As the caption explains, the scene depicts Sims in a moment of preparation, the figures therein pictured in expectant repose. In a sense, one could read the image as a portrayal of anticipatory time, cohering within the grammatical tense of the future perfect to express Sims's wish fulfilled. Freud's final sentence of *The Interpretation of Dreams* is instructive here: "By representing to us a wish as fulfilled the dream certainly leads us into the future; but this future, taken by the dreamer as present, has been formed into the likeness of that past by the indestructible wish."[121] Thom's depiction of Sims's wish is also an expression of the dream of American gynecology, its founding in the commingling of past and future that confirms its existence in the present. As Hans-Dieter Gondek explains, the dream-cum-wish is "indestructible because, as a simulacrum of the past, as its double, its repetition, it projects itself into the future and brings the future image into the staging of the dream by presenting it and making it present. . . . The wish is indestructible because it is repetition; but the fact that it is repetition is brought to the fore only in deferment."[122] Just as repetition marks the temporality of the wish fulfilled, the image visually rejoins (or perhaps anticipates) Judith Butler's theory of gender in *Gender Trouble: Feminism and the Subversion of Identity*. As Butler relates,

> In a sense, all signification takes place within the orbit of the compulsion to repeat. . . . The injunction *to be* a given gender produces necessary failures, a variety of incoherent configurations that in their multiplicity exceed and defy the injunction by which they are generated. . . . The coexistence or convergence of such discursive injunctions produces the possibility of a complex reconfiguration and redeployment; it is not a transcendental subject who enables action in the midst of such a convergence. There is no self that is prior to the convergence or who maintains "integrity" prior to its entrance into this conflicted cultural field. There is only a taking up of the tools where they lie, where the very "taking up" is enabled by the tools lying there.[123]

Butler's explanation of gender as a discursive convergence precipitated by and constitutive of "the tools lying there" rejoins and reanimates the biblical distinction between word and flesh. As described in the book of John, "In the beginning was the Word, and the Word was with God, and the Word was God" (1:1 [Berean Study Bible]); and "[t]he Word became flesh and made His dwelling among us" (1:14), such that "He who comes after me has surpassed me, because He was before me" (1:15).[124] Matters of flesh and word—of signification and ontology—are tied in scripture and theory through a complex temporality that presents origin by way of existence, which is another way of describing repetition by way of its deferment. In Butler's critique of the dominant interpretation of gender, as an "act of cultural *inscription*" that moves alongside and away from sex as the "material or corporeal ground upon which gender operates," she writes more explicitly about flesh, arguing, "[G]ender is not written on the body as the torturing instrument of writing in Kafka's 'In the Penal Colony' inscribes itself unintelligibly on the flesh of the accused. The question is not: what meaning does that inscription carry within it, but what cultural apparatus arranges this meeting between instrument and body."[125] The narratives of American gynecology's founding clarify how chattel slavery functioned as one cultural apparatus that brought sex and gender into arrangement; the instrument in such an encounter occurred in and as flesh. Thom's mid-twentieth-century painting of Sims renders the dynamics of flesh through a collapsed temporality of anticipatory time, highlighting that the history of American gynecology, which is also the transitive history of chattel slavery and medicine, was not firmly locatable in the past or, more properly, in linear time.

In excess of linear time, the existence (and persistence) of flesh gives rise to how sex and gender have been expressed and arranged according to the logics that sustained racial slavery. As Alexander Weheliye has written, in a riff on Spillers and Sylvia Wynter, flesh "operates as a vestibular gash in the armor of Man, simultaneously a tool of dehumanization and a relational vestibule to alternate ways of being that do not possess the luxury of eliding phenomenology with biology."[126] As a shared node in the collateral genealogies of blackness and transness, Sims's archive presents one side of flesh's vestibularizing paradigm, wherein Anarcha, Betsey, Lucy, and the unnamed other captives were rendered as raw materials for making the field of "women's medicine," from which they were excluded as women according to the attenuating frame of plantation medicine's sexual economies. In the chapter that follows, I pursue flesh as a capacitating structure for alternative modes of being by tracing the various ways black figures made use of fungibility for fugitive movement, such that flesh became their instrument to engender interstitial spaces of reprieve, as in what Harriet Jacobs called her "loophole of retreat."

2

TRANS CAPABLE
FUNGIBILITY, FUGITIVITY, AND THE MATTER OF BEING

[The] New World . . . marked a *theft* of the body—a *willful* and violent . . . severing of the captive body from its motive will, its active
desire. Under these conditions, we lose at least *gender* difference *in
the outcome*, and the female body and the male body become a territory of cultural and political maneuver, not at all gender-related,
gender-specific.

—HORTENSE SPILLERS, "Mama's Baby, Papa's Maybe:
An American Grammar Book"

"FUNGIBLE," ACCORDING TO ITS ETYMOLOGY, first appeared in the
English language in Henry Colebrooke's *Treatise on Obligations and Contracts, Part 1,* in 1818. Colebrooke, having spent a considerable period
of his life as a colonial bureaucrat and judge in India, returned to England to write about the particularities of British contract law; he also
wrote about Hinduism and Hindu philosophy before his death, in 1871.
Fungible articles, which he delineated according to their characteristic
quantifiability—"alike liquidate and exigible"—required legal definition
in relation to matters of compensation.[1] Yet, Colebrooke maintains,
"even things, which are not fungible, may be subjects of *compensation;*
being due under general obligation respectively as cattle, slaves, horses."[2]
The legal treatment of slaves and animals as both "subjects of compensation" and "not fungible" indicates, at least in part, the anxiogenic
time in which the *Treatise* was produced. By the time of publication,

Denmark–Norway (1803), Haiti (1804), the United Kingdom (1807), the United States (1808), Mexico (1810), Chile (1811), the Netherlands (1814), Uruguay (1814), Venezuela (1816), Spain (1818), France (1818), and Portugal (1818) had all passed legislation criminalizing transatlantic slave-trading activity. In some of these instances, slavery was also legally disestablished.

Although the United States formally abolished the importation of people for the purposes of enslavement in 1808, the internal slave trade remained legally intact until 1865. Some states, either by federal ordinance or through state legislation, passed laws that annulled or gradually phased out the legal practice of slavery within their territories. Alternately expressed in terms of "compromises," "provisos," and "clauses," the demarcation and annexation of territories and states evinced how slavery and settler colonialism structured official discourses of nation building and foreign policy, articulating a grammar rife with euphemism to disavow the violent processes by which land and persons would find primary legal expression as property. The variegated landscape of enslavement—its applications, abrogations, and diffuse rationales—staged the grounds for fungibility to emerge as a legal intercession intra- and internationally. How, then, would the "slave," as "not fungible" and as a "subject of compensation," come to emblematize a series of crises in imperial sovereignty, value, and ontology in the twilight of formal slavery? Relatedly, how did the legal categorization of the slave, in Saidiya Hartman's terms, link "the figurative capacities of blackness [with] the fungibility of the commodity"?[3] If, as Hortense Spillers explains in the epigraph, the capacity for gender differentiation was lost in the outcome of the New World, ordered by the violent theft of body and land, it would stand to reason that gender indefiniteness would become a critical modality of political and cultural maneuvering within figurations of blackness, illustrated, for example, by the frequency with which narratives of fugitivity included cross-gendered modes of escape.[4] Spillers named this process "ungendering," the not accidental coincident of "fungible" in the twilight of formal slavery—also described as the transition from slavery to freedom or from slaving economies to the free market—which prompts an understanding of the phenomena she identifies in terms of the transitive expressivity of gender within blackness.[5]

In this regard, captive flesh figures a critical genealogy for modern transness, as chattel persons gave rise to an understanding of gender as mutable and as an amendable form of being. Given that the ungendering of blackness is also the context for imagining gender as subject to rearrangement, this chapter examines how fungibility became a critical practice-cum-performance for blacks in the antebellum period. To suppose that one can identify fugitive moments in the hollow of fungibility's embrace is to focus on modes of escape, of wander, of flight that exist within violent conditions of exchange. Transitive—as in fungible passing into fugitive—and transversal—as in fugitivity intersecting fungibility, this chapter explores the fugitive (and at once fungible) narratives of black people—born free or into captivity—in the era of slavery's formal transition. Here, the transitivity and transversality of fungibility and fugitivity find expression in a line of a poem by Fred Moten, wherein the figures under principal review in this chapter "ran from it and [were] *still* in it."[6] Fugitive narratives featuring "cross-dressed" and cross-gender modes of wander and escape, most often described in terms of "passing," function as a kind of map for a neglected dimension of what Spillers defined as the semiotic terrain of black bodies under captivity, wherein gender refers not to a binary system of classification but to a "territory of cultural and political maneuver, not at all gender-related, gender-specific."[7]

William Still notes in his preface to *The Underground Rail Road* (1872) the different ways fugitives "disguised in female attire" or "dressed in the garb of men" made use of gender fungibility as a contrivance for freedom.[8] Providing numerous examples of this occurrence, Still's monograph included accounts of the escapes of Clarissa Davis of Virginia, alias Mary D. Armstead, in 1854; Maria Ann Weems of the District of Columbia, alias Jo Wright, in 1855; and Ellen Craft of Georgia, alias William Johnson, in 1848. Barbara McCaskill also describes how Harriet Tubman once "disguised a Black man as a bonneted woman in order to obstruct his arrest and re-enslavement by Northern deputies,"[9] and Harriet Jacobs narrated her cross-gender fugitive practice, as told from the perspective of the pseudonymous protagonist Linda Brent, in *Incidents in the Life of a Slave Girl, Written by Herself,* published in the United States in 1861.[10] Prior to these examples, northern white readers would have encountered the story of Mary Jones, alias Peter Sewally, also referred to as the Man-Monster or as Beefsteak Pete. Jones, although born free in New York City, was imprisoned in 1836 on charges of grand larceny in conjunction with pickpocketing.[11] This polyonymous figure, along with a later namesake, Mary Ann Waters, who appeared in a pickup notice—a genre of slaving media meant to notify enslavers of the location of their escaped property—in 1851, illustrated how the transitive and transversal relations between blackness and transness were narrated reiteratively in this period in terms of "cross-dressing and theft," not only as they both gave expression to the particularities of their criminalized acts but also as they pertained to the fungible, fugitive deeds carried out by actors figured as property-cum-persons.[12]

The first part of this chapter focuses on the two Marys and their emergence in the antebellum white press; the subsequent sections turn to Brent/Jacobs's *Incidents* and William Craft's *Running a Thousand Miles for Freedom; or, The Escape of William and Ellen Craft from Slavery* to explore how the fungibility of gender mapped the terrain of these fugitive passages. Even as the cross-gender aspects of the escapes titillated abolitionist audiences, they also required resignification in order to present these incidents as examples of the extreme measures fugitives took to escape the problems of slavery rather than as a contingency of a contemporaneous pseudoscientific project that linked blackness with gender and sexual polymorphous perversity. Most often this was achieved by framing such cross-gendered modes of escape in terms of cunning wit on the part of the fugitive actor, who manages to successfully assume and maintain an unnatural performance of artifice. In this narration, passing expresses a form of agency as well as a promise of restoration, which is to say that passing—as a limited durational performance—signals a "return" to a natural-cum-biological mode of being. This narratological strategy shaped how passing would be deployed as an interpretive frame for all manners of trans-identificatory practices—both contemporaneously and reiteratively into the twentieth and twenty-first centuries.

No less performative but lacking a clear biologized semiotic referent, fungibility in this chapter expresses how ungendered blackness provided the grounds for (trans) performances for freedom. By describing their acts as performances *for* rather than *of* freedom, I am suggesting that the figures under review here illustrate how the inhabitation of the un-gender-specific and fungible also mapped the affective grounds for imagining other qualities of life and being for those marked by and for captivity. Brent/Jacobs referred to this vexed affective geography as "something akin to freedom" that, perhaps paradoxically, required a "deliberate calculation" of one's fungible status.[13] Rather than regarding Jones, Waters, Jacobs, and the Crafts as recoverable trans figures in the archive, this chapter examines how the ungendering of blackness became a site of fugitive maneuvers wherein the dichotomized and collapsed designations of male-man-masculine and female-woman-feminine remained open—that is fungible—and the black's figurative capacity to change form as a commoditized being engendered flow. As the title "Trans Capable" suggests, disability figures prominently in this archive, and disability theory is indispensable for analyzing, for example, the visual and textual maneuvers by which Ellen and William Craft would become William Johnson and his servant, just as it was with rendering the lives of Anarcha, Lucy, Betsey, and the unnamed others as they were circumscribed and written out of James Marion Sims's archives in the preceding chapter. Together, this chapter and its companion, "Anatomically Speaking" (chapter 1), explore how transness became capable, that is, differently conceivable as a kind of being in the world where gender—though biologized—was not fixed but fungible, which is to say, revisable within blackness, as a condition of possibility.

The Two Marys: Fungible Fugitivity as "Cross-Dressing and Theft"

According to the *New York Herald*, Mary Jones took a "tour of pleasure" with Robert Haslem, a white master mason, one summer night in 1836, probably somewhere near the Greene Street bordello where Jones was a greeter and performed cooking and assorted domestic tasks for other sex workers associated with the popular brothel.[14] After their transaction, Jones and Haslem parted ways, with Jones carrying Haslem's wallet in tow. It was a perilous exchange, which required skill and with which Jones apparently had much practice. According to news coverage and the arresting officer's account, Jones was found with several wallets on her person at the time of capture. When Haslem eventually realized that his wallet and $99 were taken and replaced with another wallet containing a bank order for the then sizable sum of $200, rather than accepting his good fortune, he tracked down the second wallet's initial owner, convincing the other man to accompany him in reporting the crime.[15] They, along with the arresting officer and the officer's brother, devised and executed a plan to apprehend Jones that night. Jones was tried for grand larceny on June 16, 1836, in the Court of General Sessions. Induced to appear before the court in the same clothes worn on the night of her arrest, Jones was, as Tavia Nyong'o has described, "roundly mocked and prodded by a gawking and contemptuous crowd," in a surreal, spectacular scene.[16]

Asked at trial to account for her dress before the court, Jones responded: "I have been in the practice of waiting upon Girls of ill fame . . . and they induced me to dress in Women's Clothes, saying I looked so much better in them and I have always attended parties among the people of my own Colour dressed in this way—and in New Orleans I always dressed in this way."[17] Though the context of her confession undoubtedly shaped this response, Jones's description of three distinct geographies—the Greene Street brothel, the parties among people of her own race, and New Orleans, where she "always dressed in this way"—named variously scaled sites in which Jones's gender expression, as an intracultural maneuver, was met with a reception at odds with the ridicule she faced that day in the Court of General Sessions.[18] Though Jones pleaded not guilty, the *Herald* reported that the jury, "after consulting a few moments," returned with a verdict that found her culpable of the crimes of which she was charged. She was sentenced two days later to five years of hard labor at Sing Sing.[19]

Approximately one week after the trial, the lithographic portrait *The Man-Monster* began to appear in print shops across New York City. Without the inclusion of a sequence of names—engraved below the figure, as "Peter Sewally alias Mary Jones&c&c"—or the description of Jones's sentencing, the image would seem to have portrayed, as Jonathan Ned Katz has argued, "a rather ordinary-looking and unthreatening black woman in a clean white dress with small blue flowers."[20] The *New York World*'s description of her courtroom appearance was perhaps a referent for the subsequent caricature, referring to Jones as, "attired *a la mode de New York,* elegantly, and in perfect style. Her or his dingy ears were decked with a pair of snow white ear rings, his head was ornamented with a wig of beautiful curly locks, and on it was a gilded comb, which

THE MAN-MONSTER,

Peter Sewally, alias Mary Jones &c&c

Sentenced 18th June 1836, to 5 years imprisonment at hard labor at
Sing Sing for Grand Larceny

Published by H.R.Robinson, 48 Courtland St N.Y

The Man-Monster, Peter Sewally, alias Mary Jones. Published by H. R. Robinson, 1836. Collection of the New-York Historical Society.

was half hid amid the luxuriant crop of wool."[21] The cultural significance of the lithographic form explains, in part, *The Man-Monster*'s imagistic content. According to Erika Piola, lithographs became readily available in the 1830s, as "thousands of copies of a cartoon could be printed, issued, and sold in a short period, especially during political scandals."[22] The image's profitable reproducibility created a different, albeit familiar, articulation of racial-cum-sexual exchange, in which white value accrued in relation to black unfreedom, as the story of Jones's carceral life produced revenue for printmakers throughout the city.

The rise in lithographic production altered the imagistic landscape of slavery. As Jasmine Cobb notes, "[L]ithography advanced the circulation of caricatures as well as newspapers and advertisements for runaways," contributing to a "visual culture that readily enlisted Whites to search for Black people."[23] As a result, abolitionists hesitated to depict free black people in image form, choosing instead to pursue the question of and quest for black emancipation in and through text. Because lithography was instrumentalized in slaving culture, the image of *The Man-Monster* elicited a reading that worked on multiple registers, as caricature gave expression to the particularity of Jones's media spectacle and the visual antagonism toward imagining black freedom. In this sense, and in its depiction of a "rather ordinary-looking" black woman, the interplay of the lithograph's title and image worked to confirm a contemporaneous common sense about the fungibility of blackness, in which the interchangeability of gender figured one aspect of blackness's capacity, as it transversed captivity. A productive relation emerges between *The Man-Monster* and the fourteen colored lithographs that constituted Edward Williams Clay's cartoon serial *Life in Philadelphia* (1828), as coterminous representations of black freedom. Clay's caricatures of free black women, which, according to Cobb, depicted them as "unwomanly and outside of middle-class definitions of womanhood," also illustrated the gender fungibility of blackness in the antebellum United States, where visual culture elided and ambiguated the descriptive distinctions between captive and free, northern and southern forms of black life.

As Jones's commoditized caricature gave rise to a meditation on the gender fungibility of black flesh during slavery, her salacious coverage in the penny press illustrated that the matter of black freedom was equally vexed in print. Newspapers focused on the details of her "disguise" and on the question of whether Haslem recognized the gender of his sexual partner at the moment of their transaction. The *Sun* told its readership, *in Latin*, how Jones engaged in sex acts with her clients by wearing a "piece of cow [leather?] pierced and opened like a woman's womb . . . held up by a girdle."[24] This detail—apparently appropriate only for the eyes of the educated upper class—gave rise to the epithet "Beefsteak Pete," which appeared recurrently in subsequent media coverage. Though Jones initially served time for grand larceny, in the mid-1840s, she would re-emerge in the press in relation to charges of vagrancy, another iteration of "theft," which pivoted on her public perambulations and the appearance of freedom. On December 21, 1844, the *New York Herald* informed its readership that "the notorious Beefsteak Pete" had been "sent up to the Island for six months as a vagrant, and since that time . . . has been repeatedly sent back."[25] Katz also notes, that "on August 9, 1845 . . . the *Commercial Advertiser* reported that 'a notorious character, known as *Beefsteak Pete,* was arrested on Thursday night, perambulating the streets in woman's attire.'"[26] The frequency with which the moniker "Beefsteak Pete" was additionally modified by "notorious character" may suggest how the macho epithet was meant to invoke for the readers of the penny press an image of the "ordinary-looking" black woman who was labeled a man-monster.

The same *New York World* article, which seems to have served as a referent for Jones's lithographic caricature, also described her as a "great he negro" who conducted "a fair business [of] both . . . moneymaking, and practical amalgamation." As Nyong'o has argued, "the modifier 'practical' redoubles the satire insofar as it indexes the standard abolitionist charge that equality *in theory* meant amalgamation *in practice.*"[27] In addition and in practical terms, Jones's sex work and gender presentation also illustrated how fungible fugitivity conjoined matters of imagination and theft. Although it is not possible to declare definitively, and with all the force of the historical record, whether Jones's attire of women's clothes was a matter of personal definition—a kind of trans self-fashioning—it is clear that the practice of "cross-dressing," a process without a stable gender referent, created an imaginative context for Jones and her johns, as the ungendering of blackness created a space for emergence within dynamics of political, economic, and cultural modes of exchange. The praxis of emergence was most frequently criminalized such that (as Jones's narrative bears out) theft described the manner with which free blacks were seen as being in illicit possession of themselves and their perambulations, according to the logic of antebellum law, the press, and popular culture, requiring carceral containment as a response.

Nowhere were these dynamics more evident than in the pickup notice issued for Mary Ann Waters by the warden of the city and county jail in Baltimore, Maryland, in 1851. Like Jones, Waters was a black "cross-dressing" sex worker who emerged in discourse in relation to her capture. The pickup notice, in keeping with the conventions of the genre, provided the usual details regarding the age and appearance of the captive, in addition to information about the process and place for recovery of property. In this visualizing document—imaged through the eyes of the Fugitive Slave Act and the warden—Waters's "speech" is narrated in terms of a disavowal, as both an acknowledgment and a denial of how fungibility and fugitivity expressed Waters's condition, exemplified in the phrase "a Negro Man, who calls himself Mary Ann Waters" and later in the document: "Says he is free." As further illustration, the description of Waters's dress and the duration of time she had "been hiring out in the city of Baltimore as a woman" transverse the pickup notice's slaving discourse of visuality, simultaneously acknowledging her life "as a woman" in Baltimore while denying Waters's name, to articulate how fungibility—although it may have created different epiphenomenal relations in the ephemerality of sexual transactions embedded within larger economies of racial-cum-sexual exchange—did not exceed or provide refuge from slavery's hegemony over the material and semiotic arrangement of black flesh. Relatedly, the pickup notice, as a document for recapture, also conveyed the transitive relation between fungibility and fugitivity, wherein Waters's trans performance holds open the possibility of eventual discharge. (The question emerges, discharge into what?) The final address to the owner, "to come forward, prove property, pay charges, and take said negro away; otherwise he will be discharged according to the law," expresses both a set of instructions and a threat, as it also clarifies how the Fugitive Slave Act provided an enforceable narration for how to apprehend race and gender in terms of visuality and literacy. Just as Waters's gender fungibility articulated the terms in which fugitivity could be subsumed and reincorporated into captivity, it also produced a way of seeing how black flesh would animate the semiotics of gender, wherein sex and gender became inexhaustibly revisable according to the racial logic of consumption as they passed in and out of carceral states.

In this sense, the matter of whether Waters was *actually* a fugitive slave or a free black is not really the point, because the status of the slave as "not fungible" yet "subject to compensation" under racial slavery attenuated the supposed distinction.

Whereas Waters was captured and interred in the archive through the pickup notice, Jones reemerged in the press reiteratively into the twentieth century, even after the formal end of slavery and the period of Reconstruction. In an article entitled "Many Gastronomic Records Established," published on October 2, 1908, in the *Virginia Enterprise*, "'Beefsteak Pete,' a Bowery character" was reported to have "consumed 17 pounds of meat from which he takes his cognomen at one setting, and five days later he raised this figure to 24 pounds, thus making a total of 41 pounds of meat consumed in two days."[28] Here, Jones, in the twilight of her life, attempted to resignify that epithet constituted by the flesh of what Nyong'o described as a "surrogate vagina" into a "gastronomic record" based on a no less spectacular form of consumption.[29] As an anecdote and an archival trace, Jones's carnivorous feat illustrates what Vincent Woodard has argued is the question that emerged "long before the poignant questions of the color line and the Negro problem," as that "more pressing problematic" of "How does it feel to be an edible, consumed object?"[30] The temporal collapse of Du Bois's paradigmatic analyses and Jones's archival installation signals how the logics of consumption and exchange would continue to delineate black flesh.

WAS COMMITTED to the jail of Baltimore city and county, on the 23d day of September, 1851, by D. C. H. Bordley, Esq., a justice of the peace of the State of Maryland, in and for the city of Baltimore, as a runaway, a Negro Man, who calls himself Mary Ann Waters, about twenty-eight years of age, 5 feet 2½ inches high, stout built, very black complexion, and has a scar on his left ear. Said negro had on when committed a dark figured mousseline de laine dress, blue velvet mantilla, white satin bonnet, and figured scarf. Says he is free, was born in Elkridge, and has been hiring out in the city of Baltimore as a woman for the last three years.

The owner of the above described negro is requested to come forward, prove property, pay charges, and take said negro away; otherwise he will be discharged according to law.

WM. H. COUNSELMAN,

sep 29—9t   Warden of Baltimore city and county jail.

Pickup notice for Mary Ann Waters, 1851. Collection of the Maryland State Archives.

As this resignification occurred by way of eating, which, as Kyla Wazana Tompkins has described, functioned in nineteenth-century print culture to attach "extreme commodity pleasure to nonwhite bodies," Jones's "gastronomic record" conjoins and highlights the tacit link between certain gustatory practices and aspects of masturbatory gratification.[31] Consuming her surrogate flesh to make a new meaning for her name, Jones exemplifies what Spillers explains in her noted essay on psychoanalysis and race—that "there is an aspect of human agency that cannot be bestowed or restored by others," such that eating, in this sense, becomes a tactic "for gaining agency" that "is not an arrival but a departure, not a goal but a process."[32] As an erotic act that emerges by way of a familiar, if not commonplace, practice of racial-cum-sexual exchange, eating precipitates the question "What is (the discourse of) sexuality to the fungible?" (a demonstration of, at least, a temporal disordering of psychoanalytic and sexological rubrics in which these particular acts may be regarded as a psychosexual regression from the genital to the oral phase). Jones's archival installation also evinces how amalgamation sometimes occurs by way of mastication, wherein the combining of flesh—both hers and not hers—exists as a relay between self-fashioning and an ever-pressing "out there."[33] Here, Jones's mouth serves a double function of "processing food into digestible matter and in producing sense," wherein the eating, in this regard, becomes a way, as Tompkins has argued, "to reembody oneself, both as food and as its container."[34] Perhaps this reading figures Jones as ever the pragmatist, whose calculation to eat as much as she could of that stigmatized surrogate flesh produced a record in the archive of self-revision by way of accumulation and consumption. This is a consequence of reading the archive for gender as an always racial and racializing construction—as a strategy for living and dying—that in this instance provides a way for thinking about what forms of redress are possible in/as flesh.

On the Color of Gender: The "Loophole of Retreat" in the Morass of Racial Slavery

Although the publication of Harriet Jacobs's narrative followed *Running a Thousand Miles for Freedom* by one year, *Incidents,* in its discussions of the racialization of gender and the gendering of race, functions like a legend for reading the Crafts' fugitive narrative, as well as a prism for reviewing the political and cultural maneuvers of the two Marys. Published in 1861 under the titles *Linda; or, Incidents in the Life of a Slave Girl* and *Incidents in the Life of a Slave Girl, Written by Herself,* the text at the titular level reflects the interanimating antagonisms between the subject, object, and voice of its author (Jacobs), its narrator-cum-protagonist (Linda Brent), and its editor (Lydia Maria Child). As scholars have noted, Jacobs began to conceptualize her story in book form as early as 1851 or 1852.[35] After an unfruitful attempt to secure Harriet Beecher Stowe— author of the best-selling novel *Uncle Tom's Cabin*—as her amanuensis, Jacobs began writing her book on her own. Having completed the manuscript in 1858, after at least two publishers expressed interest only to go bankrupt before releasing the text in print, Jacobs ultimately paid to have the book privately printed in early 1861.[36] Initially conceived to address an audience of northern white women, the narrative takes a cross-genre form, having been described as a fugitive narrative that includes elements of sentimental, gothic, and antislavery novel forms, that carried particular racial and gender significance for its various audiences, including critics, given that it was the first text of its kind to be published by a black woman in the United States.[37] Valerie Smith notes how *Incidents* contravened the plot of the standard fugitive narrative, which, according to convention up until that point, traced "not only the journey from slavery to freedom but also the journey from slavehood to manhood."[38] Partially through its manipulation of form, Jacobs's narrative, according to Hazel Carby, also "revealed the concept of true womanhood to be an ideology, not a lived set of social relations."[39] *Incidents* is rife with intertextual signs, offering numerous metaphors, allegories, and "incidents" that speak both to the conditions of Brent's fugitive passage and to the context of Jacobs's narrative production.

Brent's dramatic escape maps a terrain of ungendered blackness that simultaneously marks the intersection and mutual envelopment of fugitivity and fungibility. Narrative portrayals of the protagonist's sexual negotiations clarify aspects of Brent/Jacobs's ungendering. Saidiya Hartman has described how *Incidents* underlines the "unwieldiness of sexuality—the entanglements of instrumentality and pleasure" expressed by a chattel person, constituted by an "indifference to injury, the extended use and dispossession of the captive body, the negation of motherhood, and the failures and omissions of the law"; "these elements or 'incidents' determine the condition of enslavement and engenderment."[40] As Spillers also suggests, "Though this is barely hinted on the surface of the text, we might say that Brent, between the lines of the narrative, demarcates a sexuality that is neuter-bound, inasmuch as it represents an open vulnerability to a gigantic sexualized repertoire that may be alternately expressed as male/female."[41] In the delineation of the various ways captivity coercively decouples bodily comportment from the dominant symbolics of gender and sexuality in *Incidents*, Brent/Jacobs's maneuvers forcefully raise the question once more: What is sexuality to and for the fungible? As a partial response, Brent's "deliberate calculation" to bear children for Mr. Sands is an instance of the kinds of actions available under captivity; the narrator-cum-protagonist relates, "It seems less degrading to give one's self, than to submit to compulsion. There is something akin to freedom in having a lover who has no control over you, except that which he gains by kindness and attachment."[42] The numerous circumscriptions and qualifications in Brent's description shed light on Jacobs's critique-cum-exposition of the impossibility of normative gender and sexual reciprocity under captivity. Rather, gender and sexuality appear by way of their constitutive injury, such that, as Aliyyah Abdur-Rahman argues, Jacobs's narrative highlights how "incidents of abuse serve as both metonym and metaphor for the lived experience of American slavery."[43]

Though Brent determines a sexual relationship with Sands to be "less degrading" than compulsory concubinage to her enslaver, Dr. Flint, that calculation, as some critics have argued, came with little measure for protection.[44] Sands's decision to make their black daughter the personal slave of his wife and Brent's concern over her daughter's imminent life in captivity catalyze Brent/Jacobs's conscripted movement, inaugurating the narrative action of the fugitive drama of *Incidents*. The choreography of Brent/Jacobs's escape begins as it ends, with the protagonist finding harbor in the home of a "sympathetic" white woman. The circumstances of her earliest hiding place foreshadow the garret that she later labels a "loophole of retreat," which Hartman defines as a "space of freedom that is at the same time a space of captivity."[45] Brent's dependence on the unnamed white woman also prefigures the vexed form of "freedom" the protagonist experiences as a servant in the North. The recurring theme of finding spaces for maneuvering within confinement aptly describes, as Christina Sharpe has suggested, Brent/Jacobs's condition—as fugitive, abolitionist, and author—in terms of being "still protected and unprotected in her relationships with whites."[46]

Before her temporary concealment within the white mistress's storeroom, Brent/Jacobs describes having been bitten by "a reptile of some kind"—a detail in the narrative that not only explains some of the perils of fugitivity but also foreshadows the protagonist's various encounters with the Snaky Swamp. The recurrence of the swamp, as yet another site of temporary refuge for the protagonist, amplifies her narrative's elucidation of freedom in terms of the vexed spaces of ongoing fugitivity that emerge, however briefly, from within more general conditions of unfreedom and constraint. Just as the "loophole" refers to both the small space in Brent/Jacobs's grandmother's attic that contains the protagonist for seven years and the hole that Brent makes in that space in order to see outside, the swamp stages the transversal relationship between fugitive life and death, as it also allegorizes how fungibility emerges as a tactic of maneuvering from within the morass of slavery's identity politics. To and from the Snaky Swamp Brent moves in "disguise," and in these "crossdressed" perambulations enacts a fugitive plot that stages through Brent's ungendered body the various ways fungibility and fugitivity pass into one another. That crossing in form, narrative, and flesh condenses the text's narration of the conditions of captive life, as it provides a way to interpret Brent/Jacobs's numerous calculations in *Incidents* in terms of fungible fugitivity.

In the chapter "New Perils," readers learn how Betty, the enslaved cook and servant of the "sympathetic" white woman, brings Brent "a suit of sailor's clothes,—jacket, trousers, and tarpaulin hat."[47] Donning her "disguise," Brent passes through town twice, describing her return trip in this way: "I wore my sailor's clothes, and had blackened my face with charcoal. I passed several people whom I knew. The father of my children came so near that I brushed against his arm; but he had no idea who *it* was."[48] Jacobs's use of the transitive verb "pass" to describe moving through space also portends the intransitive sense of the term, as the scene renders the mechanisms by which gender and racial subversion are assumed. This intransitive passing, as the performance of false identity, reached its peak of usage in print in the mid- to late 1800s, coinciding with the initial publications of both Jacobs's and the Crafts' fugitive narratives, though its particular meaning had emerged in the mid-fifteenth century during the first wave of European colonization.[49] Many of the accounts of cross-gendered escape explicitly articulated themselves as "passing narratives," particularly in the case of the Crafts, who, from the first printed iteration of their story, in 1849, are referred to as a pair of passing figures: one passing as a disabled white gentleman; the other, as his servant.

As Jacobs's scene relates, for fugitive movement Brent completes her attire of sailor's clothes by blackening her face. Cobb suggests that this blackening may have been an anticipatory gesture; when James Norcom (Jacobs's enslaver) published a description of her in the 1835 issue of the *American Beacon,* he presumed that she would be "seeking whiteness and dressing as a free woman, not accentuating her Blackness" and finding a "cross-dressing" and ungendered mode for escape.[50] Although the description of sartorial arrangements seems to conform to passing's logic of movement for protection or privilege, Jacobs's use of charcoal to darken her complexion tropes—by inverse logic—on more commonly held beliefs (and fears) about racial passing. As "passing" became a term to describe performing something one is not, it trafficked a way of thinking about identity not only in terms of real versus artificial but also, and perhaps always, as proximal and performative. Like a vertical line with arrows on either end, passing is figuratively represented by moving up or down hierarchized identificatory formations. This articulation of vertical identity also coordinates with forms of binary thinking, typified, for example, by the language of "the opposite" sex.

As passing is most commonly understood, one ascends into privilege, being, and distinction, or, as Jacobs's blackening suggests, into the converse of those things, which is to say, into fungibility, thingness, and the interchangeable. In this vertical model, blackness functions as the possibility of distinction in which fungibility acts as the requisite grounds from which distinction is forged. Here, blackness, as it was for the two Marys and in the numerous narrations of the Crafts—particularly in William's fugitive performance as slave—points to a place where being undone is simultaneously a space for new forms of becoming. Brent/Jacobs's blackened blackness gives expression to her condition as fungible within the logic of U.S. slavery, in which the system of colorism, as Nicole

Fleetwood has argued, "produces a performing subject whose function is to enact difference . . . an act that is fundamentally about assigning value."[51] As it relates to the scene of Jacobs's brushing past Sands, her status as "it" also indicates how blackness-as-fungible engenders forms of nonrecognition, as Jacobs's performance elucidates how blackness and going blacker become an embrace of the conditions that might allow one to pass one's friends and lovers undetected. In this encounter, fungibility sets the stage for gendered maneuvers on a terrain constituted by modes of viewing blackness, in which Jacobs's blackness and going blacker color her gender as well as her face.

The ecological characteristics of the Snaky Swamp serve an allegorical function in illustrating how fungibility produced what Brent/Jacobs describes as a "hiding-place" for those "in no situation to choose."[52] While preparing herself to enter that fugitive space that articulated a simultaneous promise of life and death, Brent/Jacobs tells the reader of how her previous snakebite and fear of snakes filled her with an especial dread. Narrating the encounter with the swamp in detail, Brent describes how the lush natural environment that concealed her and her companion also teemed with predatory and poisonous wildlife:

> Peter landed first, and with a large knife cut a path through bamboos and briers of all descriptions. He came back, took me in his arms, and carried me to a seat made among the bamboos. Before we reached it, we were covered with hundreds of mosquitos. In an hour's time they had so poisoned my flesh that I was a pitiful sight to behold. As the light increased, I saw snake after snake crawling round us. I had been accustomed to the sight of snakes all my life, but these were larger than any I had ever seen. To this day I shudder when I remember that morning. As evening approached, the number of snakes increased so much that we were continually obliged to thrash them with sticks to keep them from crawling over us. The bamboos were so high and so thick that it was impossible to see beyond a very short distance. Just before it became dark we procured a seat nearer to the entrance of the swamp, being fearful of losing our way back to the boat. . . . I passed a wretched night; for the heat of the swamp, the mosquitos, and the constant terror of snakes, had brought on a burning fever. I had just dropped asleep, when they came and told me it was time to go back to that horrid swamp. I could scarcely summon courage to

rise. But even those large, venomous snakes were less dreadful to my imagination than the white men in that community called civilized.[53]

Incidents portrays the swamp as a death-space for human life, or, more precisely, a space of near death into which some other quality of living is assumed out of necessity. Its perception as uninhabitable is what also constitutes the swamp as a "loophole of retreat." Yet the protagonist also notes at the conclusion of her description how she prefers the terror of the swamp and its inhabitants over the forms of racial and gender terror exercised by white men in so-called civilization. Though Brent/Jacobs has direct experience of both, the passage elects the use of "imagination" to describe the differences between the two sites. This word choice elicits a reading of the passage in terms of its referentiality to an abolitionist literary and public imaginary. As Anne Bradford Warner describes, the Snaky Swamp is, on one level, an "intertextual parody" of Stowe's recurrent depiction of black fugitive life set within a romanticized backdrop of the swamps and particularly pronounced in Stowe's characterization of the Dismal Swamp in the 1857 novel *Dred*.[54] John J. Kucich has additionally argued that the African spiritualist symbolism in Jacobs's representation of the Snaky Swamp functions as a mode of literary or textual concealment, rendering the swamp in ways that remain "irreducible to European-American norms."[55]

Yet here, as with flesh, the swamp is both material and metaphysical. In addition to being a polyvalent literary device, the Snaky Swamp is a real place. Located west of Edenton, North Carolina, it bears a geographical proximity to the Great Dismal Swamp, a site for the longer-durational inhabitation of marooned Africans and native people, that conveys how its ecological features produced an adversarial terrain for human life, rife with the imminent and ever-present difficulties of co-habitation with its nonhuman animal inhabitants for the displaced and dispossessed. *Incidents* returns to the (idea of the) Snaky Swamp in a brief exchange between Brent and the sea captain who eventually transported her to Philadelphia: "As we passed Snaky Swamp, he pointed to it, and said, 'There is a slave territory that defies all the laws.' I thought of the terrible days I had spent there, and though it was not called Dismal Swamp, it made me feel very dismal as I looked at it."[56] The captain's characterization of the Snaky Swamp as defiant of all laws bespeaks what Sylvia Wynter describes as the development of a "new world view," a system of ordering logics that accompanied the "discovery" of the Americas and that were expressed according to a series of binary oppositions including master and "natural" slave, rational and irrational, and habitable and uninhabitable territories.[57] As Katherine McKittrick relates, "Post 1492, what the uninhabitable tells us . . . is that populations who occupy the 'nonexistent' are *living* in what has been previously conceptualized as unlivable and unimaginable. If identity and place are mutually constructed, the uninhabitable spatializes a human Other category of the unimaginable/native/black."[58] The captain's pronouncement also invokes the swampland's transversal histories of maroonage with a more dogmatic and theological sense of slavery. Whether for two days, as in *Incidents,* or ten generations, as Daniel Sayers contends in his research on the archaeological remains in the Great Dismal Swamp, the region's inhabitation by marooned beings is figured and transversed according to a colonial-settler "subjective understanding" of the swamps as sites of terror and lawlessness beyond the parameters of god's grace.[59]

Though the wetland region the Great Dismal Swamp was named by Col. William Byrd of Virginia in 1728, Brent/Jacobs offers here an alternative explanation for why it bears the name Snaky Swamp from the lived experience of a fugitive inhabitant.[60] It is a landscape that slavery produces and reiteratively capacitates as a viable option, or, more precisely, as the choice/nonchoice for those "in no situation to choose" between one form of mortality over another. In this sense, one returns to the seemingly paradoxical construction of fungible fugitivity and its relation to the swamp's material and metaphysical region of mortality. Gesturing toward a similar epistemic structure, the swamp expresses the conditions for the fugitive's experience of "something akin to freedom," enabled by modes of apprehension, domination, and control introduced and refined within the morass of plantation identitarian logics. In this sense, Brent's cross-gender foray to and from the Snaky Swamp is a redoubled articulation of the fugitive possibilities within and structured by the geographical and metaphysical architecture of slavery: a dissent into the mud, a blackening of blackness, the mutability of a body defined as inexhaustibly interchangeable, an inhabitation of the virtually uninhabitable, being within the zone of nonbeing.

The oft-quoted conclusion of *Incidents*, in which Brent tells her reader that "my story ends with freedom; not in the usual way, with marriage" includes a qualifying confession: "The dream of my life is not yet realized. I do not sit with my children in a home of my own."[61] This description of freedom—or "something akin" to it—punctuates the fungible fugitivity that *Incidents* stages, wherein blackness is that vestibularizing paradigm that is both within and outside the nation-as-home, and in which black people find no home but a loophole of retreat—in life and within the symbolics of gender.

Whereas the earlier discussion of the two Marys offers a way to understand gender fungibility in terms of cross-dressing and theft, this section's focus on Brent/Jacobs's fugitive theater explores how blackness functioned as a site for an elaboration of gender in which the fungible interchangeability of sex for chattel persons revealed gender within blackness to be a polymorphous proposition. The ungendering of blackness, then, opens onto a way of thinking about black gender as an infinite set of proliferative, constantly revisable reiterations figured "outside" of gender's established and establishing symbolic order. Its symbolic order, which is simply one articulation of the ordering of things, relies upon gendered others to maintain an epistemological coherence. Using *Incidents* as a legend to read the Crafts' fugitive narrations, the balance of this chapter explores how fungibility articulated the Crafts' thousand-mile run for freedom. Reading the Crafts' escape as an example of fungible fugitivity wherein the gender and race of Ellen and William were reiteratively rearranged in their quest for freedom highlights how matters of self-determination and personal sovereignty were regarded as existential *and* ontological concerns. This chapter, in complement to the preceding one, examines fungibility as another expression of the multiple deployments of black flesh, in its capacity to make and remediate personhood through ontological rearrangement.

Crafting Fugitivity with Fungibility

In 1848, a little more than three years after Sims began his series of experiments on his named and unnamed "patients," William and Ellen Craft executed a plan to flee the conditions of enslavement on their respective plantations in Macon, Georgia. Different versions of their escape would be reported periodically over time, first in a letter from William Wells Brown to William Lloyd Garrison, published in *The Liberator* on January 12, 1849; with greater elaboration in Josephine Brown's biography of her father, Wells Brown, in 1856; and later in the 1860 publication of William Craft's *Running a Thousand Miles for Freedom*, among many others. Their escape received ongoing international news coverage and became fodder for fictional representations in the forms of novels and plays, and as orators, the Crafts were prized speakers on the antislavery circuit in the United States and the United Kingdom.

The particular details of their escape varied across the numerous iterations. The earliest circulations of their narrative conveyed the Crafts' relationship with the prominent abolitionist, operative of the Underground Railroad, and their eventual manager William Wells Brown, who escaped from slavery more than ten years before the Crafts, in 1834. In his abbreviated first telling, a paragraph-length letter published in the *Liberator*, Wells Brown employed the intransitive use of "pass" three times to describe the Crafts' four-day fugitive journey, referring to Ellen as "so near white, that she can pass without suspicion for a white woman."[62] In his brief account of their escape, Wells Brown told Garrison and the readers of *The Liberator* of how "Ellen dressed in man's clothing . . . passed as the *master*, while her husband passed as the *servant*."[63] Passing would become a recurring refrain in subsequent narrations of the Crafts' escape. Wells Brown further explained in the brief letter that the Crafts' illiteracy, which reflected the law for chattel persons, precipitated further sartorial adjustments: "Ellen, knowing that she would be called upon to write her name at the hotels, &c., tied her right hand up as though it was lame, which proved of some service to her, as she was called upon several times at hotels to 'register' her name."[64] For Wells Brown, the disability Ellen assumed to become her husband's master, Mr. William Johnson, acted as further evidence against the popular proslavery adage that framed slaves as unable to "take care of themselves." In the conclusion to his letter, Wells Brown simply wrote, "Ellen is truly a heroine." In this first iteration of their fugitive tale, Ellen Craft receives considerable and, according to Daphne Brooks, unprecedented attention as "an equally heroic counterpart to that of her husband."[65] Although his version of the Crafts' narrative would receive greater elaboration in subsequent retellings, the tone set in the letter to Garrison remains consequential to how contemporaneous and contemporary audiences interpret what Wells Brown described as "one of the most interesting cases of the escape of fugitives from American slavery."[66]

Ellen's complexion as "near white" has been a focal point for abolitionists, journalists, and scholars. As many have noted, Ellen's color aired the taboo of miscegenation, even as it also underscored the frequent occurrence of sexual violence for those held in captivity.[67] In addition, especially as it played out in the United Kingdom, Ellen's white aesthetic visually amplified the horrors of slavery. For British audiences, it was further proof of the provincial brutality of their former colony. The difference in color between William and Ellen also produced a rationale for her cross-gendered escape. Although she may have been expected to be read as a white woman, her coupling with William would have brought greater scrutiny and surveillance during their fugitive passage, necessitating Ellen's gender transformation so that the Crafts could travel together homosocially, as was mandated by a legal and social invective against interracial heterosociality—particularly for white mistresses—within slavery's sexual-cum-racial logics. This is not to imply that the appearance of homosocial interracial couplings should be perceived as absent of sexual activity, for, as Aliyyah Abdur-Rahman argues, slavery's "economies of desire and sexuality . . . provided a cover under which aberrant sexuality flourished." According to Abdur-Rahman, "The institution granted to *all* whites—slaveholders and non-slaveholders—the full-fledged legal right and unchecked personal authority to exploit, consume, and destroy the slave's psyche and body in whatever ways they chose."[68]

Before her escape, Ellen was held captive by her half-sister, Eliza Collins, for whom Ellen acted as a "ladies' maid."[69] According to William Craft's account, "Notwithstanding my wife being of African extraction on her mother's side, she is almost white—in fact, she is so nearly so that the tyrannical old lady to whom she first belonged became so annoyed, at finding her frequently mistaken for a child of the family . . . [that she] gave her when eleven years of age to a daughter, as a wedding present."[70] Ellen's father and first enslaver, Maj. James P. Smith, possessed Ellen's mother, Maria—who was half-white—as his slave. Less is known about William Craft. He was skilled as a cabinetmaker in Macon, Georgia, and, like Ellen, as a child he and his family were separated and sold. Described in Wells Brown's letter in *The Liberator* as "much darker" than his wife, William remained relatively circumspect about his mixed-race heritage throughout his abolitionist career.[71] William's description in the first *Liberator* article is also curiously circumspect, as Wells Brown notes only three things about the hero: his complexion, his "pass[ing] as the servant," and his illiteracy at the time of their escape. William, however, in speech and in print, proved a pivotal figure in the transmission of details surrounding their fugitive moves.

Several years before the publication of William Craft's *Running a Thousand Miles for Freedom,* Josephine Brown published a biography of her father under the title *Biography of an American Bondman.* In her monograph, she depicts the dialogue between Ellen and William that launched their escape. According to Brown's retelling, Ellen conceived of the entire plan, formulating each aspect of their fugitive plot in response to William's skeptical questions. Ellen proposed to cut her hair and wear men's clothes—high-heeled boots, a top hat, a covering about her mouth, a sling for her right arm, and binding around her right hand—in order to present herself as Mr. William Johnson, a "most respectable-looking gentleman."[72] Even still, according to *Biography of an American Bondman,* William voiced suspicion about Ellen's capacity to carry out the plot. Brown wrote:

> "I fear you could not carry out the deception for so long a time, for it must be several hundred miles to the free States," said William. . . . "Come, William," entreated his wife, "don't be a coward! Get me the clothes, and I promise you we shall both be free in a few days. You have money enough to fit me out and to pay our passage to the North, and then we shall be free and happy." This appeal was too much for William to withstand, and he resolved to make the attempt, whatever might be the consequences.[73]

Brown provides nearly every detail of Ellen Craft's sartorial plan to become Johnson except for the pair of green spectacles that would later be imaged in the engraved portrait and frontispiece of *Running a Thousand Miles for Freedom.* Brown's depiction contrasts most sharply with William's later description around the ascription of the plot's authorship. In his biography, William credits himself with conceiving their elaborate plan for escape and then describes how he had to convince his wife to join him in his detailed plot. In reference to the discrepancy between Brown's and Craft's accounts, Barbara McCaskill compellingly argues that William's revision of the narrative "stands as an example of how black abolitionists often wrote formerly enslaved Africans into conventional gender roles."[74] Yet consider that McCaskill's explanation on this particular matter might be extended to rethink the various contrivances that constitute the Crafts' narrative, chief among them the frequency with which the Crafts are taken up as passing performers par excellence.

In the form of a question, one might ask, How does the story of the Crafts pass as a passing narrative? The political effect of framing their story as such produces and naturalizes the Crafts within a dominant heteropatriarchal conscription, and it also gestures toward the popularity and long public memory for their tale as a fugitive narrative told in the form of a transatlantic romantic adventure. Passing, particularly as it is invoked to describe the Crafts' performance of false identity, suppresses the violence that maps the relationship between fungibility and blackness under captivity. Returning to Wells Brown's first formulation—"Ellen dressed in man's clothing . . . passed as the *master*, while her husband passed as the *servant*"—one notes how these concerns become more pronounced around William's figuration. What does it mean for a (fugitive) slave to "pass" as a slave? In their autobiography, William Craft describes an exchange between Mr. Johnson, a white mistress, and a "very respectable-looking young gentleman," as it occurred on a train ride between Virginia and Baltimore during the Crafts' fugitive passage. I quote Craft here at length, as the scene throws the aforementioned questions into stark relief:

> At Richmond, a stout elderly lady . . . took a seat near my master. Seeing me passing quickly along the platform, she sprang up as if taken by a fit, and exclaimed, "Bless my soul! there goes my nigger, Ned!"
>
> My master said, "No; that is my boy."
>
> The lady paid no attention to this; she poked her head out of the window, and bawled to me, "You Ned, come to me, sir, you runaway rascal!"
>
> On my looking round she drew her head in, and said to my master, "I beg your pardon, sir, I was sure it was my nigger; I never

in my life saw two black pigs more alike than your boy and my
Ned."

After the disappointed lady had resumed her seat . . . she closed
her eyes, slightly raising her hands, and in a sanctified tone said
to my master, "Oh! I hope, sir, your boy will not turn out to be so
worthless as my Ned. . . . Oh! I was as kind to him as if he had
been my own son. Oh! sir, it grieves me very much to think that
after all I did for him he should go off without having any cause
whatever."

"When did he leave you?" asked Mr. Johnson.

"About eighteen months ago, and I have never seen hair or hide
of him since."

"Did he have a wife?" enquired a very respectable-looking young
gentleman, who was sitting near my master and opposite to the
lady.

"No, sir; not when he left, though he did have one a little
before that. She was very unlike him; she was as good and as faithful a nigger as any one need wish to have. But . . . she became so
ill, that she was unable to do much work; so I thought it would be
best to sell her, to go to New Orleans, where the climate is nice
and warm."

"I suppose she was very glad to go South for the restoration
of her health?" said the gentleman. "No; she was not," replied the
lady, "for niggers never know what is best for them. She took on a
great deal about leaving Ned and the little nigger; but, as she was
so weakly, I let her go."

"Was she good-looking?" asked the young passenger, who was
evidently not of the same opinion as the talkative lady. . . .

"Yes; she was very handsome, and much whiter than I am; and
therefore will have no trouble in getting another husband. I am
sure I wish her well. I asked the speculator who bought her to sell
her to a good master. . . . [S]he has my prayers, and I know she
prays for me."[75]

The scene functions as a *mise en abyme,* as a smaller copy within the
larger portrayal of the context and logics that shaped the Crafts' escape.
Among the numerous mirrored images, the description of the young
passenger as a "very respectable-looking young gentleman" is nearly iden-
tical to Craft's description of his wife-cum-master, inviting a reading of

the unnamed abolitionist and William Johnson as somehow related by the Droste effect, a recursive imaging, in which a picture appears within itself. In addition to the separated chattel couple, which trope William and Ellen, particularly in the inclusion of details about their complexion, Craft also stages a conversation between a cruel and clueless white mistress, who might stand in for Ellen's first enslaver's wife or for her half-sister or for any number of white women who benefited from and were complicit with slavery, as well as an abolitionist who by the scene's conclusion exclaims to Mr. Johnson, "What a . . . shame it is for that old whining hypocritical humbug to cheat the poor negroes out of their liberty!"[76]

The passage's opening flourish makes use of "passing" to describe William Craft's movement through the train car, a display of mobility that immediately arouses the white mistress's suspicion. William Johnson is compelled to account for William Craft, hailed as Ned and curiously called "sir" in the dialogue, and his movement in the scene. Johnson's declaration of ownership of Craft in the scene—"No, that is my boy"—is, however, ignored until the nameless white mistress has visually confirmed for herself that William Craft is not Ned. This detail amplifies how William Johnson, cast as a "clever disguise," cannot fully come into view in the retrospective retellings of their fugitive passage. In one sense, Johnson must fail in the narrative so that Ellen Craft, the near white woman, can emerge as a more compelling version of her "true self." In another sense, William Craft writes a scene that resounds with his role on the antislavery speakers' circuit and as the author of *Running a Thousand Miles for Freedom,* casting himself as an authorizing and interpretive figure for William Johnson.

Johnson quickly falls from view after uttering his ineffectual claim to Craft as his property, and the scene turns to the dialogue between the "stout elderly lady" and the "young passenger." In the description of the separated chattel couple, which the white mistress provides, readers are brought into a tragic romance between Ned and his very handsome, very white, and disabled wife. The resemblance here is striking, as the scene belies that though Ned and William Craft are not the same, they are at least mirrors of each other (a variation of Colebrooke's description of the fungible/not-fungible condition of slaves under contract law). The resonances in descriptions between Ned's nameless wife and Ellen Craft figure William Johnson as Ellen's negative image, a textual formulation

ELLEN CRAFT,

The fugitive Slave.

In the frontispiece of *Running a Thousand Miles for Freedom*, Ellen Craft is posed as William Johnson, bearing several key discrepancies from the narrative description.

that imagistically opens the monograph in the frontispiece, where Ellen is presented as William Johnson sans the signifiers of disability. Moreover, the turn to dialogue between the white mistress and the young passenger illustrates how the figure of the abolitionist is heralded as William Craft's most effective interpreter, over and against the figure of William Johnson, his mirrored double.

At every narrative turn, the specter of violence is suppressed within the scene: first in the use of "sir" in a dialogue that conveys how the train ride between Virginia and Baltimore could quickly become a scene of William Craft's recapture; and second, in the extended dialogic depiction of the tragic romance of Ned and his wife, who run along a gauntlet track both parallel to and interlaced with William and Ellen Craft. The impetus to mitigate the violence in this scene, on one level, highlights how *Running a Thousand Miles for Freedom* was developed to satisfy particular audiences, as represented by the abolitionist figure written into the dialogue. Yet, perhaps more importantly, this impetus also subtends how passing became a way to suppress the violence that constructed the Crafts as fungible under the conditions of slavery. As Daphne Brooks wrote in her introductory comments to *Running a Thousand Miles for Freedom*, the logic of the Craft narrative "calls attention again and again to the serious 'joke' that the couple plays out in order to reach freedom."[77] The biography operates, then, by offering its readers the promise of being let in on a "joke," and in so doing offers up a preferred way to read their escape narrative in a manner that confirms who they had become—or were becoming—in a contemporaneous international imaginary. In this sense, not only *Running* but also Wells Brown's initial letter and William Still's 1872 account in *The Underground Railroad* function as textual maneuvers to secure the Crafts' status as husband and wife, against all the ways—legal, social, and ontological, to name a few—in which their marriage could be imminently and immanently revoked as a consequence of their status as (fugitive) slaves.

Their status, as it animates the phrasing of the title of Craft's monograph, in which the couple would "run" a thousand miles *for* (rather than *to*) freedom, also frames how black freedom, and the degree to which blackness could come to modify freedom as a concept, would be approached as matters of ethnology and ontology. Frank Wilderson argues, "For the Black, freedom is an ontological, rather than experiential question," and in this formulation he distinguishes ontology from experience in order to convey how black freedom is thinkable only in terms of categories of being.[78] A consideration of the temporality of the Crafts' escape illustrates how the matter of black ontology (and the question that rests upon it: black freedom) was far from settled in science, with its frequent interchange of "race" and "species"; or in law, as illustrated in the form of further remunerative policies (such as the Fugitive Slave Law of 1850) to guard against slavery's formal abrogation in a period marked by the disestablishment of transatlantic slave trading. One might read Wilderson's assertion here as, at the very least, an important warning against the taken-for-granted ascription of (fugitive) slaves as categorically free and concomitantly vested with the symbolic trappings of personhood, of which gender would be included. But Wilderson also suggests that the violence, "which turns a body into flesh . . . destroys the possibility of ontology because it positions the Black in an infinite and indeterminately horrifying and open vulnerability, an object made available (which is to say, fungible) for any subject."[79] Yet, as Spillers has pointed out, gender (and the categorical exclusion from its symbolics) becomes its material staging ground.[80] Wilderson's assertion of the impossibility of black ontology is buttressed by a theory of gender that draws on Judith Butler and on which he writes that there is "no philosophically credible way to attach an experiential, a contingent, rider onto the notion of freedom when one considers the Black—such as freedom from gender or economic oppression."[81] In posing gender as contingent to blackness, Wilderson's argument becomes incapable of perceiving un/gendering as a mode of violence that makes black fungibility palpable, which is to say that his assertion rests on a refusal of the ways gender is itself a racial arrangement that expresses the transubstantiation of things.

The logic of passing would apprehend Ellen's cross-gendered fugitivity as the primary case of gender fungibility here, but it is true for both Crafts, as a disability analytic brings into sharper focus. As Ellen Samuels has argued in her essay "'A Complication of Complaints,'" the Craft narrative not only highlights how matters of narration are inextricably linked to questions of authority, but also indexes how the Crafts' story is shaped by the Derridean concept of supplementarity "as that which is added to an apparently complete text but is actually necessary to its meaning, 'the not-seen that opens and limits visibility.'"[82] For

Samuels, illiteracy might be understood as a kind of disability, and thus for Ellen to become a white master, she must become differently disabled, to inhabit simultaneously a "complication of complaints" that mask her structurally imposed impairment.[83] In addition, as Samuels explains, "If we understand the invalid as 'one who is served,' it is clear that William's presence as the servant of 'Mr. Johnson' is as fundamental to Ellen's successful performance of invalidism as are the sling, poultice, and green spectacles she wears."[84] Here, Samuels's formulation opens a way for thinking about how William Craft's (fugitive) slave status engendered him as another disability "prop" in a polysemous supplementarity in which Craft's narration would reveal how Mr. Johnson's gender was formed from that fungible "it," which fashioned Ellen into Johnson and William into any thing. Captivity became the terrain for the Crafts' exclusion from the dominant semiotics of gender, providing the conditions that would allow fungibility to become fertile ground for flight. Indeed, in one key sense, as the Crafts' narrative illustrates, fungibility and fugitivity figured two sides of a Janus-faced coin, in which the same logic that figured blackness as immanently interchangeable would also engender its flow.

Transnationalism and the Transubstantiation of Things

William and Ellen Craft were legally married in Boston in the same year the U. S. government passed the Fugitive Slave Law. The confluence of these two events framed the couple's transatlantic crossing and inaugurated their nineteen years in exile in the United Kingdom. After spending two weeks in Halifax, Nova Scotia, the Crafts boarded the SS *Cambria* on December 11, 1850, and disembarked approximately eight days later in Liverpool, England.[85] Throughout the mid- to late eighteenth century, Liverpool's docks had been enmeshed in a long and bloody history of transatlantic trading activity; after the legal disestablishment of transatlantic slave trading, in 1807, and the abolishment of slavery throughout the British Empire, in 1833,[86] port cities across the United Kingdom acted as sites of convergence for blacks colonized by the British Empire and moved by its ongoing imperialist projects. As McCaskill notes, upon their arrival, the Crafts would "have heard British, African, and Caribbean accents rising and falling around them."[87]

William Craft described their arrival in Liverpool as the first time the couple were "free from every slavish fear."[88] His pronouncement might be interpreted as another indication of the geographical and financial conditions that gave rise to the publication of his autobiography, which William most clearly articulated in the narrative's final bit of prose: "In short, it is well known in England, if not all over the world, that the Americans, as a people, are notoriously mean and cruel towards all coloured persons, whether they are bond or free."[89] Speaking to a transnational audience of abolitionists and others, whom he hoped to persuade to an antislavery position, Craft frames the "cruelty" of American slavery as an ethnological issue, which is to say that he casts American whiteness in terms of its particular species' characteristics. His use of ethnological language in his closing prose is instructive for reading how the Crafts' transnational circulation contributed to their symbolic slip in a secularizing chain of being, as ethnological rationales intervened to make sense of the movement of different bodies across the Atlantic in the decline of imperialist reliance on chattel slavery. The purity of geo-racialized groups came under particular scrutiny. As Ellen's form symbolized, and as the numerous cases of white enslavement in *Running* further illustrate, anxieties over the racial purity and locational boundedness of ethnological forms required complementary discursive strategies to explain the order of things. Within shifting contexts of national sovereignty and modes of capitalist accumulation, such strategies would also engender a kind of transubstantiation for the Crafts, from fugitive slaves to diasporic actors.

Not unexpectedly, the Crafts—first William, and later Ellen—participated in the U.K.'s antislavery lecture circuit as a way to support themselves financially upon arrival. As R. J. M. Blackett notes, "Although British audiences had heard and read of the daring escapes of slavery of men like [Frederick] Douglass, [Moses] Roper, and [Josiah] Henson, never before had they heard a tale which involved such boldness and romance."[90] Their narrative played on audiences' romanticized affective attachment to the idea of the American frontier, and in their presentations William and Ellen choreographed their story to have a maximum impact on the attendees: "William told of their escape, and at the end of his narrative, in a tear-jerking scene, Ellen was invited up on the stage."[91] As Blackett explains, Ellen's appearance—and the visual-cognitive dissonance her white aesthetic produced—was frequently greeted with audible shock from the crowd, and she became a "symbol of Southern slavery's barbarity (particularly the defilement of women) for British abolitionist[s]."[92]

In June 1851, the Crafts, along with William Wells Brown and several members of the British antislavery movement, staged a demonstration at the Great Exhibition of All Nations in London's Crystal Palace. In a letter from William Farmer to William Lloyd Garrison, published in *The Liberator,* Farmer narrated that once the party arrived at the U.S. artist Hiram Powers's sculpture *Greek Slave* (1844), they produced an image of *Punch*'s "The Virginian Slave: Intended as a Comparison to Power's [*sic*] 'Greek Slave,'" to illicit a response from visitors from the United States regarding the meaning of juxtaposing the two figures. The U.S. government selected the *Greek Slave* to represent American art in the Great Exhibition in part because of its popularity with audiences in the United States. In conjunction with its 1847–48 tour, Powers's friend and tour manager composed a pamphlet to explain the statue's significance, as "an emblem of the trial to which all humanity is subject."[93] Antislavery newspapers, such as Frederick Douglass's *North Star* and the *National Era,* discussed that tour in terms that foreshadowed the Crafts' later demonstration, signifying on the degree to which the *Greek Slave* could be made to reflect on the conditions of U.S. slavery. Farmer wrote that, after producing the *Punch* image at the Great Exhibit, "the comparison of the two soon drew a small crowd, including several Americans, around and near us. Although they refrained from any audible expression of feeling, the object of comparison was evidently understood and keenly felt."[94]

While the controversy over the nudity of Powers's sculpture galvanized an estimated hundred thousand patrons to view the *Greek Slave* on its 1847–48 tour, the Great Exhibit demonstrators made use of the taboo of interracial sexuality to draw on their audiences' emotions. In their political performance, the juxtaposition between the sculpture and the drawing worked in tandem with the arrangement of the groups to convey the meaning of their protest. As Farmer noted in his letter, "Mr. McDonnell escorted Mrs. Craft, and Mrs. Thompson; Miss Thompson, at her own request, took the arm of Wm. Wells Brown, whose companion she elected to be for the day; Wm. Craft walked with Miss Amelia

On display at the 1851 Great Exhibition of All Nations in London's Crystal Palace, Hiram Powers's *Greek Slave* (1844) provided a context for a group, which included the Crafts and William Wells Brown, to provoke audiences to contend with the ongoing realities of U.S. slavery.

THE VIRGINIAN SLAVE.

INTENDED AS A COMPANION TO POWER'S "GREEK SLAVE."

Published in 1851 in the satirical weekly *Punch,* Joseph Tenniel's "The Virginian Slave: Intended as a Companion to Power's [*sic*] 'Greek Slave'" was presented by the demonstrators in an effort to illicit an affective (and preferably verbal) response to the juxtaposition of U.S. slavery and slavery within antiquity.

Thompson and myself. This arrangement was purposely made in order that there might be no appearance of patronizing the fugitives, but that it might be shown that we regarded them as our equals, and honored them for their heroic escape from Slavery."[95] Although Farmer explains how the groupings were representative of their egalitarian aims, the presence of differently raced, differently gendered bodies walking arm in arm made use of the spectacle and specter of miscegenation to frame and amplify the juxtaposition of black and white slaves for potential onlookers at the Great Exhibit. Ellen's white aesthetic, as it had been instrumentalized on the antislavery speakers' circuit, again played a key role in making sense of the scene. As Uri McMillan notes, the promenade of couples throughout the Exhibit would function by the logic of "readymades," prompting their viewers to reconsider the quotidian existent landscape through "highly aestheticized and experimental self performances" that made their bodies into sites for art.[96] Ellen's proximal presence to the staging of black and white enslaved female forms highlighted how such a juxtaposition required the erasure of miscegenated figures; her appearance made a triptych of agitprops against contemporaneous visualities of race. Yet, as the only fugitive woman among the group of demonstrators, Ellen in her participation also produced a reading of her gender through a similar logic of proximity, placing her form in relation to the sculpture as well as to the other women in her party. Fully clothed and presumably dressed in her fineries for the occasion, Ellen sharply contrasted in her presentation with the nudity of the enslaved female representations and the visual access that subtended the logics of slavery, placing her in nearest proximity to the other white women participants. Her act of looking was yet another dimension of her performance for freedom.

In 1852, during the Crafts' time at the Ockham School in Surrey, rumors began to circulate about Ellen's supposed unhappiness in England. False reports proffered by proslavery activists suggested that Ellen wished to return to enslavement in Georgia. McCaskill explains, "In the false reports circulated in the press, Ellen is described as a passive, possessed, and commodified item of negotiation, property, and exchange," "as accruing no more or no less value than the fluctuating currency of [the slaveholding South's] mercantile economy."[97] Such propagandistic speculations conferred and confirmed Ellen's status as "fungible," as they also ventriloquized William Craft's desire for that category of being. On December 23, 1852, Ellen responded with an open letter published simultaneously in the *Pennsylvania Freeman* and the *National Anti-slavery Standard*. Laying the rumors to rest, Craft wrote, "I had much rather starve in England, a free woman, than be a slave for the best man that ever breathed upon the American continent."[98] Here, the syntax belies gender's forms, as Ellen explicates the corollary between freedom and womanhood, which is to suggest not that women did not face gendered oppression but that the ontology of gender required freedom as its prerequisite. The sentence conveys this point by making use of "free woman" to describe her "starved" position in England as preferable to a structural re/inhabitation of an ungendered, fungible "slave."

Her published letter, one of the few occasions in which audiences would engage her prose, confirmed what was previously staged at the Great Exhibit—that even amid their hardships in England, the Crafts' changed legal and geographical context gave rise to a different experience of life and being. As Cobb notes, "Fugitivity, as a state of being and a matter of fleeing justice, was also about the way in which the runaway had no clear place to go, no clear place of belonging in the context of slavery."[99] Thus, fugitivity could not mitigate the logic of slavery and the attendant ordering of the category of the "slave" to the nation, nor could it provide escape from slavery's legal, scientistic, and optic modes of capture and reinstatement. No longer fugitives but diasporic actors, Ellen and William tried on different legal language to articulate a complex form of not quite belonging, a life in exile in England. The Crafts were not among the first black Americans to live as refugees there; in the late eighteenth century, the Black Loyalists found temporary residence in London before relocating more permanently to the then British colony of Sierra Leone.[100]

After three years at Ockham, the Crafts relocated to West London, where they continued to grow their family, which would eventually include five children: Charles Estlin Phillips, William, Brougham, Alfred, and Ellen. The elder Ellen regularly entertained prominent abolitionists on tour in England and served as the primary caretaker for their five young children. William resumed his activity as an antislavery speaker, and they both, according to some accounts, developed the 1860 text that chronicled their escape from slavery. The publication of *Running a*

Thousand Miles for Freedom went into reprinting twice in its first two years, and the revenue from sales of the frontispiece caused William to speculate about whether he could use the income to secure his sister's release from enslavement.[101]

In the year following *Running*'s release, William Craft would join the African Aid Society, whose aim was "to make the Niger the Mississippi of West Africa and through commerce and Christianity bring 'civilization' to [that] part of the world."[102] The founding of the society just preceded the Lancashire Cotton Famine, a four-year depression in the textile industry in northwest England produced by the dramatic decrease of availability of cotton from the U.S. South during the American Civil War. As Blackett explains, "The emergence of emigrationism among black Americans after 1855 and the growing interest in African colonization gave a new fillip to the search for an alternative source"; the society thus consisted primarily of a "growing group of abolitionists and Lancashire cotton men eager to promote the cultivation of cotton by free labor in the British dominions," principally through the establishment of official trade agreements with the Kingdom of Dahomey (now Benin), located on the western coast of Africa.[103]

Throughout the winter and spring of 1862, Craft raised funds to visit Dahomey. His aims were manifold: to convert the peoples of Dahomey to Christianity, to persuade the king to cultivate and trade cotton with Great Britain, and to abolish the Dahomean customs of human sacrifice and enslavement. The Aborigines Protection Society commented on his mission in its twenty-sixth annual report: "There is something truly noble in the idea of a coloured man, himself rescued by his own exertions and those of his devoted wife from the barbarism of American slavery, so disinterestedly giving his services to the cause of degraded Africa."[104] His expressed dedication to the project of "civilizing" Dahomey was far from disinterested. According to Dorothy Sterling, Craft's trips to Dahomey functioned as an alternative to his possible enlistment in the Civil War, which he had considered briefly.[105]

After receiving approval from the British Foreign Office, Craft set sail for Dahomey in November 1862; after spending five months in Lagos, he eventually met the king in May 1863. In a report prepared for the Dahomean Committee, Craft wrote his appraisal of his first mission:

The Dahomians who now make palm-oil, and grow cotton on a small scale, seem fully to appreciate my arguments, and expressed their willingness to act promptly upon my suggestions, provided I would return to Whydah and assist them in carrying them out. And as the King gave me a large place of business at Whydah and as much land and as many people as I may wish to have to teach cotton growing, I shall return there as soon as possible to assist in civilizing the people, and endeavoring, by the blessing of God, to prepare their minds for the better reception of his truth.[106]

Craft's procolonial prose underscored what he would write in less official documents about his first trip, which included "baffled descriptions of the polygamous relationships that he observed" and critical assessments of the existent missionary presence in the region.[107] His report to the society was the first of many that William made about Dahomey for British audiences. On the heels of his return, he also made a speech, under the title "On a Visit to Dahomey," for the British Association for the Advancement of Science.[108]

The *London Times* covered the association meeting in detail, focusing on several interactions between Craft and two ethnologists at the annual conference: "On this occasion Section E, devoted to geography and ethnology, was most densely crowded, partly to hear Mr. Crawfund's paper on Sir Charles Lyell's *Antiquity of Man,* and partly Dr. Hunt's paper on the *Physical and Mental Character of the Negro,* to which latter it was known that Mr. Craft, a gentleman of color, recently from Dahomey, and formerly, it was stated, a slave in the Southern States, would reply."[109] The threefold description of William Craft in the *Times*—a "gentleman of color," a recent traveler to Dahomey, and a former slave—is instructive for determining how Craft's transatlantic perambulations would recast him within a symbolic chain of being. His encounters with the ethnologists staged his transubstantiation to supreme effect.

Both Crawfund and Hunt imparted theories of humankind that were premised on African inferiority and European superiority. Leaving the question of monogenetic versus polygenetic structures of being unsettled, Crawfund's presentation, as quoted in the *Times,* concluded that "no one is more strongly convinced than I am of the vastness of the gulf between civilized man and the brutes; or is more certain that, whether *from* them or not, he is assuredly not *of* them."[110] Crawfund also extended

Lyell's and others' earlier work on the distinction between human and animal to affirm U.S. (southern) law, as an articulation of the proper ordering of humankind and the logical expression of a natural antipathy between races and species, citing that "neither the freedman in the Caribbean nor the slaves in areas where they were a majority in the United States had assumed dominant positions over whites."[111] According to Blackett, Craft responded to Crawfund's paper "by pointing out that rather than any natural antipathy a considerable portion of the black population of America was in fact mixed, and that in spite of the laws which banned inter-racial marriages. The generally degraded state of the black population was due, he observed, not to any inherent racial characteristics but to social oppression."[112]

Hunt's paper, as it was reported in the *Times* and recorded in the *Report of the British Association for the Advancement of Science, 33rd Meeting* (1863), made three points, which affirmed Crawfund's earlier presentation. Hunt argued that "many cases of civilized blacks are not pure negroes" but individuals who were able to advance due to their inheritance of admixture with other races, which he deemed higher in an order of being.[113] The black race, he claimed, was without history, and as such, "there is as good reason for classifying the negro as a distinct species from the European as there is for making the ass a distinct species from the zebra."[114] The *Times* reported Craft's response to Hunt's presentation at length:

> Mr. Craft (an escaped "contraband" who has resided for some years in this country) said that,—"Though he was not of pure African descent, he was black enough to attempt to say a few words in reference to the paper which had just been read." His grandmother and grandfather were both of pure negro blood. His grandfather was a chief of the West Coast; but through the treachery of some white men, who doubtless thought themselves greatly his superiors, he was kidnapped and taken to America, where he was born. He had recently been to Africa on a visit to the King of Dahomey. He found there considerable diversities even among the African[s] themselves. Those of Sierra Leone had prominent, almost Jewish features. Their heels were quite as short, on the whole, as those of any other race, and upon the whole they were well formed. . . . When Julius Caesar came to this country, he said of the natives that

they were such stupid people that they were not fit to make slaves
of in Rome. (Laughter.) It had taken a long time to make English-
men what they now were, and, therefore, it was not wonderful if
the negroes made slow progress in intellectual development. . . .
He pointed to Hayti as furnishing an instance of independence of
character and intellectual power on the part of the negro, and con-
tended that in America the degraded position which he was forced
to occupy gave him no chance of proving what he was capable of
doing.[115]

In this fourth description of Craft, the *Times* depicts William (again) as
formerly enslaved and, with the use of "contraband," signifies on the
distinction between his refugee status in England and his fugitive position in the former colony. The direct quote from William, which claims
a mixed racial heritage even as it also confers and confirms that he is
"black enough" to respond to Hunt's claims, posits a double articulation of authority, a kind of deployment of double consciousness in
which his former enslavement stands as a testament to his acculturation
to whiteness—and, by metonymic extension, to "civilization"—and his
blackness positions him as a translator between two worlds. Though
Craft did not discuss his family in any depth in *Running a Thousand
Miles for Freedom,* he offers a genealogy here that would include West
African nobility and that subtly frames his interactions with the Dahomean king for his British audiences.

As in *Running,* William makes use of the language and logic of
ethnology to point out racial and intraracial difference. Mia Bay has
described black ethnology as a form of "self-defense" that blended science, history, and scripture to highlight "the mutability of human
affairs."[116] Black ethnology is also another expression of the transubstantiation of things, in the sense that its spiritual, historical, and scientific underpinnings created (alternative) modes of exchange that revalued
and redefined objects and essences, persons and populations, according
to its internal logic. In describing the physical characteristics of various
African nationalities, Craft alludes to the ways Hunt's (and Crawfund's)
paper cannot account for variation within racial categories. Turning to
Julius Caesar, William conveys, in one sense, that the English were once
characterized in similar terms, a declaration met with laughter from the
audience of scientists. Yet in another sense, Craft is also speaking here

to the contemporaneous ethnological distinction between British and American forms of whiteness, a difference that pivoted on their legal dispositions toward slavery. It is perhaps no surprise, then, that William Craft would conclude with the matter of Haiti, the former French colony, which, in addition to demonstrating how the "independence of character and intellectual power" spurned the disestablishment of transatlantic trading, also acted as a counterpoint and a possible (ethnological) future for blacks in the United States.

The *Times* reported that William was "loudly applauded"[117] for his response, and, as Blackett notes, "The debate at the Association's meeting reverberated through British intellectual and philanthropic circles for some time, adding fuel to the debate over race" and the "place of the Negro in Nature" during Great Britain's new wave of expansion in Africa in the 1860s.[118] The Crafts would participate in this new wave of British colonial expansion; William returned to Dahomey for three years beginning in January 1864, and Ellen established a "ladies' auxiliary" of the British and Foreign Freedman's Aid Society, which, among their activities, solicited money for the establishment of a girls' school in Sierra Leone, "where the young women of this British colony would receive their first Christian and industrial education."[119] The Crafts' activities corresponded with Britain's approach to blackness as a global "problem." As Sterling notes, "After the [American] Civil War, the British antislavery movement shifted its emphasis to encompass black people everywhere. In addition to sending clothing, books, and farming implements to the newly freed people of the American South, the former abolitionists . . . turned their attention to the British colonies in Africa and the Caribbean, where, they believed, the most pressing need was to bring Christian civilization to 'the heathen.'"[120]

As the formal abrogation of slavery in Europe and its colonies coincided with an uptick in European colonial-imperialist expansion, the Crafts' personae and activities found interpretation through a different—though no less antiblack—lens. In this shifting terrain of human precarity, marked by an ongoing, unfinished project of subjectifying and subjugating blackness through the mechanisms of law and science, the Crafts gained a kind of distinction through their efforts to articulate themselves in relation to fluctuating modes of sovereignty by taking up the British colonial-imperialist project. As *Running* reveals, U.S.

forms of whiteness proved so cruel—and so totalizing—as to make fungibility the Crafts' mode *for* freedom. Yet within a differing geography of black life, one indexical of the simultaneous expansion and contraction of forms of exploitation, violation, and violence that constructed racial difference on a global scale, the question of freedom, and the attendant question of ontology, forcefully reemerged. Though one might conceive of this particular conjuncture of time (post–American Civil War) and space (England) as a rupture or break that yielded the capacity to upend the order of things, this would not be completely accurate. It was not a break in thought or being but a shift or slip (subtle yet violent) in an ordering of things that would, to riff on Sylvia Wynter, continue to reflect the proverbial colonial knot of being/power/truth/freedom that overrepresented the ethnological form of European Man as human.[121]

It is in this sense that one returns to the image that constituted the frontispiece of *Running a Thousand Miles for Freedom*. The engraving of Ellen Craft had a distinct, mass-produced life before *Running*'s publication, appearing in various British and American periodicals throughout the 1850s, often deployed to announce an upcoming lecture or sometimes purchased for a shilling for personal use. As Michael Chaney notes, "[T]he earliest publications of the engraving cannot be classified technically as illustrations since they do not visualize referents outside of their immediate context."[122] In other words, they were produced as fungible artifacts, which is to say that they were made to conform to any given context by the very logic of accumulation that underwrote the project of chattel slavery. In another sense, the portrait illustrated, by way of preface and through its preceding circulation, how fungibility contextualized the Crafts' narrative. Whereas *Running* showcased William's illicit literacy, the engraving represented the crime of self-possession, not in a metonymic sense, for, as other scholars have also noted, the image fails to represent accurately either Ellen Craft or William Johnson.[123] As McCaskill writes, "Her top hat, jacket, heraldic tassel, tartan, and tidily tacked tie—all status symbols of white male authority and privilege—and her closed-mouthed, reflective smile jointly tell a story of dignity, patience, and reason."[124] In this sense, the portrait tropes on the genre of portraiture, which is to say that the imaged figure portrays the subject for whom the genre was developed: man. Yet the frontispiece and the various narratives discussed in this chapter also illustrate how "gender," "race," and "sex" found reiterative arrangement in an imbricated field wherein the designations between human and person, black and white, and sex and gender were not easily mappable as distinctly biological or social terrains.

PART II
TRANSIT

Identity and subjectivity are acts of creation whose aesthetic is logic. Being and becoming, however, require an act of creating the self shaped by transaesthetics.

—L. H. STALLINGS, *Funk the Erotic: Transaesthetics and Black Sexual Cultures*

3

READING THE "TRANS-" IN TRANSATLANTIC LITERATURE
ON THE "FEMALE" WITHIN *THREE NEGRO CLASSICS*

[T]he black American male embodies the *only* American community of males handed the specific occasion to learn *who* the female is within itself, the infant child who bears life against the could-be fateful gamble, against the odds of pulverization and murder, including her own. It is the heritage of the *mother* that the African-American male must regain as an aspect of his own personhood—the power of "yes" to the "female" within.

—HORTENSE SPILLERS, "Mama's Baby, Papa's Maybe: An American Grammar Book"

THE COLLECTION'S TITLE was apparently a consequence of editorial concern over space on the cover. In a letter of correspondence between then editor at Avon Books Peter Mayer and volume editor John Hope Franklin, Mayer explained: "I want to call the book 3 NEGRO CLASSICS but I wonder if this is not an awkward title. They are obviously more, but I have a terrific space problem since I must have a book title on the cover, plus 3 book titles and 3 authors—and the titles are long—and your name as well."[1] Perhaps it is surprising that such a banal rationale would come to frame how these texts would be read together; the inclusion of "they are obviously more" invites speculation about what other titles might have materialized within a different economy of words. Communication between Franklin and Mayer also conveyed that this was not the first time a publisher wanted to link *Up from Slavery* (1901), *The Souls of Black Folk* (1903), and *The Autobiography of an Ex-Colored Man* (1912). Poet, novelist, and Fisk University librarian Arna Bontemps was commissioned several years earlier by a different press to introduce and curate the three texts.[2] In his introduction, Franklin described the 1965 publication of *Three Negro Classics* as an "auspicious event."[3] As he suggested, although the texts "are as different from each other as the three authors who wrote them . . . each reveals the deep apprehensions and the troubling dilemmas that virtually every sensitive Negro American has experienced."[4]

The juxtaposition of these three texts has often signaled a spectrum of political views on the "Negro question." Indeed, much has been made of the relationships between and among Booker T. Washington, W. E. B. Du Bois, and James Weldon Johnson; and concomitantly, their personal antagonisms and affinities are frequently extrapolated as evidence of the times in which these texts were initially penned. The repackaging and recirculation of the texts in 1965 as linked cultural artifacts ushered a return to these works for insights into how to approach a racial environment profoundly marked by what Du Bois succinctly described as the ever-unasked question between him and the "other world": "[H]ow does it feel to be a problem?"[5]

That *Three Negro Classics* went into reprint four times within the first five years of its initial publication also indicates, in some way, the commercial imperatives that underpinned meditations on race in the early twentieth century for the time at hand. Readers would witness in the year of the collection's publication Malcolm X's assassination (February 21), Selma, Montgomery's, "Bloody Sunday" (March 7), the passage of the Voting Rights Act (August 6), and the Watts Rebellion (August 11–17). It was undoubtedly auspicious that Avon Books would publish a collection of works that, in the words of Franklin, might instruct its reader on how "he can at least maintain his equanimity and his dignity and his self-respect."[6]

Franklin's reiterative use of masculine pronouns indexes how these texts were also concerned with what Du Bois referred to as the issue of "manhood rights."[7] For Du Bois, the issue of manhood rights, or the securing of legal rights for black men, worked in tandem with women's suffrage; both were critical to his vision for building and bettering democracy. Although these ideas contravened the prevailing logic, which figured white masculinity as a prerequisite for liberal personhood and full citizenship at the turn of the century, they remained shaped by modernist conceptions of identity, which regarded race and gender as distinct but comparable constructs.[8] Yet the status of the black man, as both a cultural and a legal being, was inextricably bound to the status of his mother. Hortense Spillers, Jennifer L. Morgan, Saidiya Hartman, and other black feminist critics have described how slavery, in its practices and codifications, structured certain matrilineal arrangements that at their root were concerned with black women's capacity to produce black children as property.[9]

Spillers notes, "[U]nder the condition of captivity, the offspring of the female does not 'belong' to the mother, nor is s/he 'related' to the 'owner,' though the owner 'possesses' it, and in the African-American instance, often fathered it, *and, as often,* without whatever benefit of patrimony."[10] For Spillers, the enslaved black child was essentially "orphaned," yet became, "under the press of patronymic, patrifocal, patrilineal, and patriarchal order, the man/woman on the boundary, whose human and familial status, by the very nature of the case, had yet to be defined."[11] The production and codification of the "slave" thus created a crisis in definition for blacks in the antebellum New World at the familial and anthropomorphic levels. Jennifer Morgan explains how the reproductive capacity of enslaved Africans, native peoples, and indentured servants was managed according to a "mathematics of 'mastery.'"[12] As Du Bois wrote several years before the publication of *Souls,* in "The Study of the Negro Problems" (1898), "The inability of the Negro to escape from a servile caste into political freedom turned the problems of the group into problems of family life."[13] Such problems were created, according to Du Bois, by colonists' responses to the issues inherent to creating a systemic code according to race (as caste) rather than condition (as laborer). Yet, as he suggests, "Even as this slave code was developing . . . there was also created by emancipation and the birth of black sons of white women a new class of free Negroes."[14] By birthright, black sons of white mothers inherited a sui generis classification, as "free Negroes." Their collective status, as Du Bois describes it, gestured toward the many ways gender and sexuality organized racial classification during the antebellum period of U.S. history. As Frank Wilderson explains, black and white women figured two sides of a laceration produced by "civil society's phallic wound," in which reproductivity for the black was "a vector of spatial and temporal capacity: space cohered as place: the womb, time cohered as event: childbirth."[15] In contradistinction to black women's figurations as wombs, as producers of property, as always consenting and unable to (not) consent, white women's sexualities were constructed as "inaccessible, forbidden (until marriage)" and, by metonymic extension, were made to stand in for the white family, private property, and the state.[16]

The association between being black and having a black mother was critical to maintaining the biopolitical ordering of slavery and continued as a question for consideration and redefinition through and in the wake of Reconstruction. As Laura Doyle explains, "In the race-bounded economy the mother is a maker and marker of boundaries. . . . She is forced across a border, or she is prohibited from crossing a border; in either case her function is to reproduce, through offspring, the life of the border."[17] In light of this interrelation, one could rearticulate the problem of the color line in terms of reproduction, such that one substitutes the question of what it feels to be a problem with what it means to have a black mother. This metonymic move—a linguistic ordering that mimics the transubstantiation of things—which is also a play on how the logics of synecdoche and substitution structure the racial real in Afromodernist literature, organizes this chapter along a series of routes into the "'female' within" the *Three Negro Classics*.

As a symbol and metonym for black life, the black mother is, as David Marriott describes in a riff on the depiction of mothers and mothering in Richard Wright's Afromodernist novel *Native Son*, "degraded, even abject. . . . [B]ecause she carries the riven consciousness, the dereliction that [is associated] with black culture in America, she is herself a figure of that dereliction."[18] The question emerges, How might one constitute a self from such abjection? Or, put differently, What is the function of the black mother, as an embodied category and figuration, to a sociogenic process? Addressing this matter requires at least what Sylvia Wynter described as the goal of Frantz Fanon's *Black Skin,*

White Masks: "to effect the black man's extrication from his very sense of self, from his identity."[19] As Fanon wrote in the introduction to *Black Skin, White Masks:*

> Supply a single answer and the color problem would be stripped of all its importance.
>
> What does a man want?
>
> What does the black man want?
>
> At the risk of arousing the resentment of my colored brothers, I will say the black is not a man.
>
> There is a zone of nonbeing, an extraordinarily sterile and arid region, an utterly naked declivity where an authentic upheaval can be born. In most cases, the black man lacks the advantage of being able to accomplish this descent into a real hell.
>
> Man is not merely a possibility of recapture or of negation. If it is true that consciousness is a process of transcendence, we have to see too that this transcendence is haunted by the problem of love and understanding. Man is a *yes* that vibrates to cosmic harmonies. . . .
>
> The black is a black man; that is, as the result of a series of aberrations of affect, he is rooted at the core of a universe from which he must be extricated.[20]

Here, Fanon describes blackness as an exclusion from the dominant symbolics of gender, which is to say that within an antiblack patriarchal formulation, the black man cannot be a man.[21] The black is not a man insomuch as his "*yes*" does not vibrate to "cosmic harmonies"; he does not register as Enlightenment man but indicates a result of antinomic projections that center him in a universe that requires his destruction.

The bridge between Fanon's paradoxical declarations of the black as (not) a man—or perhaps as antinomic man—is his discussion of the "zone of nonbeing," that "extraordinarily sterile" place which serves as a site for the reproduction of an "authentic upheaval." This zone, a scene of abjection, is fertile grounds—perhaps the demonic grounds—for Sylvia Wynter to propose the sociogenic principle as a praxis to address the metaphysical and scientific conundrum of human consciousness.[22] In addition, there are connections to be drawn here between Fanon, Wynter, and Julia Kristeva in her 1982 treatise on the potential utilities of abjection for self-construction. Kristeva seemingly unwittingly rejoins the conversation held between Fanon and Wynter by emphasizing how the project of constructing a self from abjection is analogous to the subjective experience of desire, or the phenomenology of "want." "But if one imagines," Kristeva explains, "the experience of *want* itself as logically preliminary to being and object—to the being of the object—then one understands that abjection, and even more so abjection of self, is its only signified. Its signifier, then, is not but literature."[23] What Kristeva seems to take for granted as a self that antecedes abjection is troubled by Fanon's articulation of the self—or selves—produced by racial abasement. At the same time, one could read *Black Skin, White Masks,* and particularly the chapter on the lived experience of the black, as a signifier of the black's want for liberation from himself.

Just as the experience of wanting locates a domain of subjectifying abjection, black masculinist/modernist literature demonstrates the degree to which the experience of wanting has corporeal effects, such as in the description of Fanon's splayed body in *Black Skin, White Masks,* or in the second-sightedness that engenders double consciousness in Du Bois's *Souls of Black Folk.* Literary depictions of corporeal splintering could be read as a symptom of an encounter with the zone of nonbeing, a space figured outside of Enlightenment legibility that is concurrently a site for a different sociogenic possibility in saying/being a different "yes," or what Spillers argues is "the heritage of the *mother* that the African-American male must regain as an aspect of his own personhood—the power of 'yes' to the 'female' within."[24] Reading Fanon's and Spiller's "yes" concurrently informs the analytical framework for this chapter, as it illustrates the ways in which the black mother has been rendered as the zone of nonbeing, in which her figuration becomes a portal to an articulation of a black (modernist) self. What follows then is an examination of *Up from Slavery, The Souls of Black Folk,* and *The Autobiography of an Ex-Colored Man* as they demonstrate the interface between the zone of nonbeing and Afromodernist modes of subjectification, an encounter profoundly marked by the complex figuration of the black mother, who maps blackness as an impossibly public experience, even as she also delimits the possibility of a black interiority. In this sense, the black mother is a metonym for black sociality, an emblem of race as a problem and product of the social that bears upon a project of self-narration in Afromodernist literature. She—herself a corporeally splintered body—

is a pivotal figure in revealing and reworking antinomic blackness, which is to say, her representation reproduces the borders between a black self, endowed with an interiority, and racial blackness, as it is always and only given by the social.

This chapter posits that what makes each text a potent example of Afromodernism is identifiable by way of the figuration of the mother, as she is deployed to render a racial "subject" in the absence of the symbols of the father. Though notably different in approach and circumscribed by the politics of production and reception, each text confronts the conundrum of how to represent black personhood. Lindon Barrett described this ontorepresentational practice as carrying the potential to rupture the continuity of Western modernism, where the evidence of black literacy threatened the logic of post-Enlightenment subjectification.[25] This quality of disruption has been identified with blues and jazz aesthetics, signaling an idealization of improvisation in Afromodernism's forms. This nod to improvisation also underscores the kinds of circumnavigation on display in *Three Negro Classics*, which is to say that the "trans-" in "transatlantic" is not only about movements across space but also about movements across time and being, and concomitantly about movements across blackness. This perhaps explains what makes the purported perspective of an "ex-colored" man a "Negro classic."

In pursuing a question about the degree to which the "trans-" in transatlantic literature bears a resemblance to the "trans-" that modifies conceptions of gender, I turn to the various paradoxes revealed in reading for the black maternal figure in *Up from Slavery, The Souls of Black Folk,* and *The Autobiography of an Ex-Colored Man,* for what her figuration illuminates in these texts is the palpable experience of the phenomenon known as black sociality, which occurs even under the conditions of social death. She, as the progenitor of race, is the emblem of this complex, even paradoxical form of sociality. The black mother's gender is vestibular, a translocation marked by a capacity to reproduce beings and objects. But one should not mistake her figuration for the real. As Du Bois relates in his damning of Reconstruction and its inevitable demise, the inhabitation of the structural position of blackness produces black gender as "mother-like," a concept he invokes to describe how inhabiting blackness produces not a gender in a dominant symbolic sense but a figuration of gender that is inextricably linked to a metaphysics of time.

Du Bois's formulation precipitates a need to distinguish Fanon's and Spillers's deployments of "yes" as they emerge in relationship to how power is conceptualized in each instance. Whereas power remains a tacit—and normative (read: patriarchal)—context for Fanon's expression, Spillers's construction—the "power of 'yes' to the 'female' within"—articulates how the political praxis of accessing the black mother requires a reading of her as the onto-epistemological framework for black personhood.[26]

In the section that directly follows, I attend to the relationships between modes of production, circulation, and reception as they have constructed how the texts, authors, and a black body politic have been perceived contemporaneously and recursively over time. However, this chapter is principally interested in the apertures into "the specific occasion [for African American males] to learn *who* the female is within itself," which in Spillers's emphatic expression pivots on the question of "who" but which I pursue in an anagrammatical rearrangement as the problem of "how."[27] Given that the color line was produced and policed by black women's reproductive capacity, the project of defining black manhood within a modernist idiom would necessitate an encounter with the figure of the black maternal as a character and as the ground of nonbeing that engenders black manhood.

On the Human Document: Metonymy and Making the Racial Real

Though the three texts at issue are represented as generically distinct from each other, their ability to signify on the conditions of blacks in America was secured by the production of their authors as "native informants" on contemporaneous race relations. This figuring of texts and authors bears a direct relation to the contexts of production and circulation of antebellum slave narratives, in which abolitionist sentimentality and primitivism framed the texts as indexes of embodied authorial transparency. As Philip Gould notes about the development of the slave narrative, abolitionist meetings prefigured the style and content of the genre, as they also placed "limits on black expression in public and literally staged [black] bodies for public consumption. Ex-slaves were asked only to state the basic 'facts' of their lives; they sometimes bared their backs as texts that 'proved' their stories."[28] The term "anatamopoiesis" conjoins "anatamo-politics," or what Foucault described as the disciplining of the body constitutive to biopower, with "poiesis," which refers to all manners of creative and cultural production. I offer the term here to describe the relations between race and author to highlight the ways black literature has been multiply corporealized as the author's black body and, by metonymic extension, a black body politic.

In her examination of *Up from Slavery, The Souls of Black Folk,* and *The Autobiography of an Ex-Colored Man,* Deborah McDowell highlights how the generic conventions of antebellum slave narratives influenced black literature well into the 1920s, as she also gestures toward the ways Washington, Du Bois, and Johnson contravened the genre: in their abstention of a description of black suffering under slavery, in a refusal of the "slavery to freedom" plot, and in the questioning of racial identity's certitude, respectively.[29] Yet even as their works revised the generic conventions of the slave narrative, the marketing and contemporaneous reception of Washington's, Du Bois's, and Johnson's texts restaged their authorial bodies in ways that harked back to the preceding and precedent-setting genre, in producing at least two couplets: of the texts with the bodies of their authors, and of black literary works with black populations.

Of the three, Washington's autobiography is figured as most exemplary of its author. Rebecca Carroll, in her introduction to a book commemorating the one hundredth anniversary of the text's publication, describes *Up from Slavery* as "the very embodiment of legacy, something that has been handed down from the past from an ancestor."[30] She notes, "[T]he style and tone of Washington's writing . . . succeed in mirroring its message in near precise measure. Humility, consistent hard work, attentive behavior, and great faith in humanity can well set the foundation for a strong sense of self and the achievement of individual sovereignty."[31] Washington prepares his readers to understand his book as such when he writes in the preface, "I have tried to tell a simple, straightforward story, with no attempt at embellishment."[32] Washington also explains in the prefatory comments that this version of his autobiography was born from a series of articles prepared for *Outlook,* a Christian weekly magazine published in New York City. The serialization contributed to developing a larger audience for this, Washington's second autobiographical work, as subsequent installations of his story were attentive to the questions and concerns of a particular demographic of would-be consumers, assuring them that *Up from Slavery* would not replicate the mistakes of *The Story of My Life and Work*, which had been published in the previous year and was described by *The Nation* as "a subscription book of the cheapest character."[33] Alongside the episodic treatments of Washington's life, *Outlook* frequently

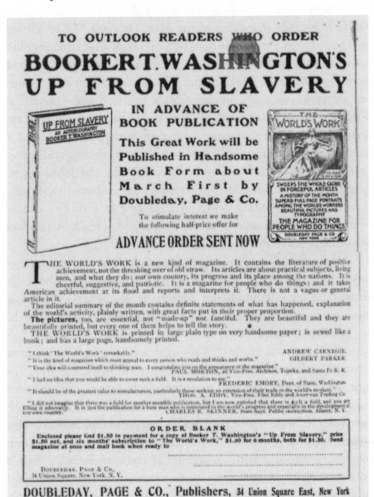

An advertisement for Booker T. Washington's *Up from Slavery*, featured in *Outlook* magazine in 1900.

printed advertisements that provided discounts for its readers who ordered the book in advance of the autobiography's publication.[34]

In a correspondence with *Outlook* editor Lyman Abbott, Washington described his plan for the new project: "to give the *first place* to facts and incidents—taking for granted that the average reader is more interested in an interesting fact than in a generalization based on the fact." Presenting his facts in chronological order, Washington wrote that he "sought not to use too many generalizations and when they [were] used to have them well sugar-coated with some interesting incident," for "only his generalizations went 'beyond the natural order.'" Washington's insistence on giving pride of place to facts and incidents harks back to white abolitionist framings of antebellum black life, and the rare "generalizations" served as anachronistic ruptures to a story "conceived and influenced by some of the leading editors and publishers [of the time] . . . and carefully designed to enhance Washington's image among the general public and to promote his school, his social philosophy, and his career."[35] Moreover, according to Louis R. Harlan, *Up from Slavery* was "to some degree ghostwritten" by Max Bennett Thrasher.[36]

The point here is not to disparage Washington's role in producing *Up from Slavery* but to convey how anatamopoiesis characterized the production and reception of the work. Take, for example, a comment made by Hamilton W. Mabie, then associate editor of *Outlook,* that describes the book as "one of the most important human documents which has come to light in this part of [the] world for many years."[37] Not only does Mabie's praise reveal the highly collaborative process by which the text came into being, but in his use of "human documents" he underscores the dual practice of anthropomorphizing texts and thingifying persons, an animating politic of consuming black literature. Such reading strategies relied on the transubstantiation of the text for a (particular figuration of the) body and called attention to the racial-cum-sexual logics of consumption that contributed to the text's commercial success; until the publication of the *Autobiography of Malcolm X,* in 1965, *Up from Slavery* was regarded as the most popular African American autobiography.[38] That *Three Negro Classics, Autobiography of Malcolm X,* and the first English translation of Frantz Fanon's *A Dying Colonialism* share the same year of publication is fodder for speculation about the publishing industry and the thanatopolitics of the texts' receptions. One might raise the question, albeit tentatively, of whether and how it matters that these works found even wider reception after the deaths of their authors. How do the authors' deaths engender different lives for these manuscripts? Relatedly, in what ways do their meditations on race become more assimilable into teleologies of progress after their demise? The interrelation of texts and authors—both in life and in afterlife—indexes an appetite for a racial real whetted by the collapse of black literature with black bodies.

In the case of Du Bois, the constitution of text as author bore a great deal on the reception of *The Souls of Black Folk* as a kind of literary representation that could rupture the Progressive Era's political real. Robert Gooding-Williams, for example, describes Du Bois's work as "both a call to arms and an aesthetic event. . . . [It is] a book that demands to be read equally as political argument and literary art.[39] Although Du Bois and Johnson—at least after Johnson became publicly known as an author—are viewed as less subjected to the expectation to directly embody their texts than Washington, the frequency with which the authors' commentaries about each other serve to contextualize their respective works indicates a common understanding of the literature as brokering a kind of access to their authors, producing readings of the fictive elements of *The Souls of Black Folk* and *The Autobiography of an Ex-Colored Man* as figurations of their authors' political ideals and personal beliefs.[40] Like the publication history of *Up from Slavery,* earlier iterations of parts of *The Souls of Black Folk* were initially published, albeit more sporadically, in the *Atlantic Monthly,* which described itself as a journal of literature, politics, science, and the arts. When *The Souls of Black Folk: Essays and Sketches* was published by A. C. McClurg, in 1903, it would evidence more significant transformation than did the translation from Washington's episodic writings in *Outlook* magazine to *Up from Slavery.* As a text, *Souls* is a palimpsest of forms, including poetry, fiction, musical scores, speeches, essays, and more. As Cheryl Wall argues, part of its literary distinctiveness is due to "the text's self-consciousness of its participation in an ongoing tradition of African American expressivity."[41] In her reading of *Souls* as self-conscious, Wall invokes Du Bois's later essay on the topic of African American art and letters. More than twenty years later, Du Bois would publish "Criteria for Negro Art," often regarded as a reflection on *Souls,* to discuss the relationships between and among black aesthetics, art, and politics.

Du Bois's essay, however, is as much about the issues that emerge in locating a racial real in black representation as it is concerned with delimiting criteria for black cultural production. "Criteria for Negro Art" cast his earlier writings as propaganda, which he articulated was a professional hazard for black artists: "[I]t is the bounden duty of black America to begin the great work of the creation of beauty, of the preservation of beauty, of the realization of beauty, and we must use in this work all the methods that men have used before . . . [such as] truth—not for the sake of truth, not as a scientist seeking truth, but as one upon whom truth eternally thrusts itself as the highest handmaiden of imagination, as the one great vehicle of universal understanding."[42] According to Du Bois, truth is both imbricated with and subordinated to figurations of imagination, and therefore "[t]he apostle of beauty [the black artist] . . . becomes the apostle of truth and right not by choice but by inner and outer compulsion."[43] Originating in the seventeenth century and referring to practices deployed in Catholic missionary work, the term "propaganda" clarifies how Du Bois's conception of black art reflects the word's earliest usage, as a *congregatio de propaganda fide*, translated as a "congregation for propagating the faith."[44] The plurality evoked in the original sense of the term also informs a formal reading of *Souls,* a text marked by a multiplicity of forms and voices.

Black art and black personhood are at least doubled in this formulation; black art is beautiful (aestheticized) and truthful (sociological, ethnographic), as black artists-cum-intellectuals imagine different (plausible) political outcomes through formal innovation and invention. As Marlon Ross explains, both Washington and Du Bois utilized ekphrasis to render race visually through the use of descriptive language and allegory. Ross suggests that the interplay of visual and discursive forms allowed "the author[s] to stage the race in two senses: (1) to mark and document the particular stage that the race has reached in the race toward modernity; and, simultaneously, (2) to place a visual embodiment of the race on a metaphorical stage."[45] As a matter of staging, the aesthetics of black literature (and art) shaped the way blackness—marked and marketed as male—was apprehended.

As a dialectical formulation that is shaped by "inner and outer compulsion," black art is less about distinguishing the real from the unreal than it is about the precariousness of *representing* the *real* in and through representation.[46] In a less frequently cited portion of "Criteria for Negro Art," Du Bois warns against the impulse to read notable black artists as indicative of racial progress. "They are whispering," he writes sardonically, "'Here is the way out. Here is the real solution of the color problem. The recognition accorded Cullen, Hughes, Fauset, White and others shows there is no real color line.'"[47] Then, citing numerous examples that illustrate how racism produces myriad institutional impediments for black artists while also undermining a myth of meritocracy, which would suggest that those black people who have been successful have done so because their work is so exceptional as to transcend race or racial prejudice, Du Bois explains that the popularity of black artists does not indicate more positive conditions for black people.

In its critique of celebrity, which highlights how racial capital shapes the production and reception of black art, "Criteria for Negro Art" provides additional insight on Wall's reading of *Souls* as self-conscious. The chapter titled "Of Mr. Booker T. Washington and Others," for example, often cited as proof of the disagreement between the two men, also indicates Du Bois's concerns with the troubling confluence of black celebrity, art, and politics:

> [T]his very singleness of vision and thorough oneness with his age is a mark of the successful man. It is as though Nature must needs make men narrow in order to give them force. So Mr. Washington's cult has gained unquestioning followers, his work has wonderfully prospered, his friends are legion, and his enemies are confounded. To-day he stands as the one recognized spokesman of his ten million fellows, and one of the most notable figures in a nation of seventy millions.[48]

Washington's singularity, exceptionalism, and ability to stand in for millions of black people are as equally odorous as his program, which Du Bois characterized as a "silent submission to civic inferiority" that would inevitably "sap the manhood of any race in the long run."[49] The deleterious effects of *Up from Slavery* on the (black) public sphere, Du Bois notes, are not the "direct results of Mr. Washington's teachings; but his propaganda [that] has, without a shadow of a doubt, helped their speedier accomplishment."[50] Here, the use of "propaganda" to refer to Washington and his program is in keeping with the more commonplace pejorative use of the term, and it derides the representational value of

Washington's symbolic form as a spectacular text/body that suggests all black people might attain wealth and influence in their path up from slavery. Yet, as Erica Edwards explains, "Du Bois [also] scripts a cast of exemplary black leaders into his classic meditation on black American life in the 1903 *Souls of Black Folk,* writing of a 'peculiar dynasty' of black leaders and listing the 'new' leaders of the century as foils to Booker T. Washington."[51] Edwards's reading of a "charismatic scenario" in *Souls* partially explains how the text quickly positioned Du Bois as emblem of the black masses, even as the text, in its investment in producing multiplicity, seemed to work against producing the author's narrative/body as exceptional. As the advertisement in *The Colored American* illustrates, in the inclusion and position of Du Bois's image and the selection of editorial praise for the text, which describes *Souls* as "the most interesting publication by a colored man up until this time," the marketing and reception reinscribed the collapse of text and author to figure the writing as another installation of a literary racial real.

The Autobiography of an Ex-Colored Man, particularly in the shifting dynamics of reception before and after authorial attribution, provides a Janus-faced example of the cultural logics that animate an interrelation of body and text. Its production history could be regarded as an explication of contemporaneous modes of racial capital that contributed to a desire to read the realities of U.S. race relations through the metonymic figuring of ex-/black texts as ex-/black authors. Published by a small Boston press, *Autobiography* was designed to cultivate its status as a classic. As Jacqueline Goldsby explains, "From the seductions of its fake first-person narration to the rich and discreet appearance of the text itself (cloth-bound in maroon leather with gold lettering on the front cover and spine), Johnson deliberately styled his novel to parody publishing's modern protocols."[52] Johnson enlisted family members as press agents, hired a press-clipping service, and, after receiving indications that the novel would be a success, "changed his given name—James Williams—for a more marketable one, James Weldon."[53]

Attentive to the material form and circulation of the novel, Johnson, through his involvement in marketing *Autobiography,* exploited the metonymic structuring of black author-as-text by conscientiously promoting the text-as-author. As Johnson relates in his genuine autobiography, *Along This Way* (1933), most of the reviewers "accepted it as a

The Souls of
Black Folk

By W. E. B. DuBois

Detroit Informer :

"Should be read by every intelligent negro in the land."

The Freeman (Indianapolis):

"Without doubt the most interesting publication by a colored man up until this time."

The Guardian (Boston):

"A great book by a great scholar, touching the spiritual life of colored people."

The New York Age:

"A work of peculiar power and penetration."

The Ohio Enterprise:

"From every point of view can well be termed a masterpiece."

3d Edition $1.20 *net*   Published by
A. C. McClurg & Co., Chicago

An advertisement for W. E. B. Du Bois's *The Souls of Black Folk*, published in the Washington, D.C., magazine *The Colored American* on July 4, 1903.

human document," as was his wish.[54] In one of the earliest reviews of the text in the *Cleveland Gazette,* in 1912, the reviewer framed the novel as "a book with a peculiar interest and value [that] shows the relations clearly of the two races" and that would give white people the opportunity to understand "the black race [figured as] somewhat of a sphinx."[55] In the same review, the *Gazette* attributes the work to Mr. Alexander, whom it described as "destined to take his place as one of the foremost writers of the day."[56] "Mr. Alexander" most likely referred to Dr. Charles Alexander, a reviewer of the manuscript for *The Freeman* and other outlets.

The anonymous publication of *Autobiography* coincided with Johnson's move back to New York from Nicaragua. In New York, as Shana Redmond explains, Johnson became a "contributing editor to the oldest of New York's Black newspapers, the *New York Age.*" From this position, Johnson would, according to Sondra Kathryn Wilson, "'become visible as a national race leader' through columns that offered his social and political philosophy."[57] Johnson explains in *Along This Way* that he initially

The Autobiography *of* an Ex-Colored Man

ANONYMOUS

A book unique in the annals of the Negro race. As a document it reads more strangely than fiction.

Professor Charles Alexander, the well-known lecturer, says of the book:

"It should have a wide reading among the Negroes of this country because it tells the story of a soul-life of the race in an inimitable manner, by a member of the race who has lived two lives, or in two worlds, the black and the white."

Although just off the press, the book has already created much interest and the attention of the press, secular and religious, Negro and white, has at once centered upon it. We quote briefly three well-known papers:

"A unique publication of surpassing interest to our people."—Cleveland *Gazette.*

"An intensely interesting and exceedingly able portrayal of the experiences of a man in an exceptional situation, and with very unusual opportunities to observe the condition of the colored race in this country."—Zion's *Herald.*

"The most wonderful story of self-revelation, either in fact or fiction, that has been published in many years."—Springfield (Mass.) *Union.*

210 pages; handsomely bound in cloth; $1.30 postpaid

SHERMAN, FRENCH & COMPANY, Publishers

6 BEACON STREET, BOSTON

An advertisement for *The Autobiography of an Ex-Colored Man,* published in August 1912 in the National Association for the Advancement of Colored People's magazine, *The Crisis.*

received "a certain pleasure out of anonymity": "The publishers themselves never knew me personally; yet the fact gradually leaked out and
spread."[58] According to literary historian Dickson Bruce, it was *Crimson
and Gray*, the publication of Johnson's alma mater, Atlanta University,
that first mentioned Johnson's authorship.[59] By November 1914, the *Chicago Defender* opined that Johnson's decision to publish the book anonymously reflected "such humility" as to be "the best test of [his] genius."[60]
Certainly, black authors had been writing anonymously and pseudony-
mously, even for black audiences, since the early nineteenth century.
Generally, it was considered a way to politely address impolite topics,
and sometimes authors used pseudonyms even when readers were already
aware of the writer's identity.

As knowledge of Johnson's authorship increased, the linking of
text with author accomplished a few things. First, it secured Johnson's
place in a literary milieu of authors legible to white and black audiences. For example, beginning in November 1919 and throughout 1920,
Johnson republished *Autobiography* in serial form in *Half-Century Magazine*, billed as "A Colored Monthly for the Businessman and the Home-
maker."[61] *Autobiography* was also translated into German and Swedish
by 1929, which marked, as the *Negro Star* reported, "four countries
[including the United States and England] and three languages in which
the book ha[d] appeared to date."[62] Second, it mitigated the novel's critique of the publishing industry generally, and of the politics of black
authorship more specifically. Much as in Du Bois's case, the celebration
of Johnson as author influenced contemporaneous and future readings
of the text. Affixing his name to the novel produced two forms of speculation about the text and author. On the one hand, a rationale emerged
to explain away the political reasons for absenting his name originally.
On the other, an additional narrative took shape in some readers' minds
to situate *Autobiography* as Johnson's life story. Johnson would later
explain that such mis/readings—"I continue to receive letters from persons who have read the book inquiring about this phase of my life as
told in it"—were his raison d'être for writing *Along This Way*.[63]

In a letter to the initial publishers, Johnson explained that his hope
was to have the work read as nonfiction in order to demonstrate that
"the black race consisted of many kinds of people and groups, each of
which had distinctive ways of relating to the others and to whites."[64] In

his desire for *Autobiography* to be read as a "human document" and in his description of what he hoped the text would accomplish, one is reminded again of the collusion of literature with the disciplining discourses that give shape to the human form. Indeed, the relation between *Autobiography* and its initial author, "Anonymous," could be staged as a "autopbiography," a term which Grant Farred coined to describe "the critical act of taking apart—autopsying—the life of the author before that life is (physically) over."[65] As autopbiography, *Autobiography*'s initial publication attempted to mark, dissect, and classify contemporaneous inter- and intraracial political and sexual dynamics. The news of Johnson's authorship and the persistent marketing of black texts as provisioning routes into a particular kind of intimacy with their authors situated *Autobiography* (and Johnson) within the more familiar anatamopoietic terrain.

Just as *Up from Slavery, The Souls of Black Folk,* and *The Autobiography of an Ex-Colored Man* were made to stand in for a black body politic, they also demonstrated how masculinism sometimes functioned as a mask for gender fungibility. Put differently, in the production of blackness as monolithic and of black people as interchangeable, gender difference continued to be lost. The question emerges, What would be necessary, then, for these texts, as "manhood rights" projects, to articulate themselves within and in response to an order of knowledge predicated on understanding blackness as an instrumental mode of difference that necessarily (or perhaps consequentially) mitigated gender differentiation? At the very least, it would require that each author contend with the inheritances of his mother to address this symbolic exclusion from, in the words of Spillers, a "patronymic, patrifocal, patrilineal, and patriarchal order."[66] Relatedly, these narratives would need to write about the black maternal in relation to one of her most potent caricatures: the black mammy.

"The Black Mammy" and Other Flights of Fancy

Five years after the initial publication of *The Autobiography of an Ex-Colored Man,* Johnson published *Fifty Years and Other Poems* (1917), which included the short work of poetry "The Black Mammy." In the poem, the narrator describes a black woman with a kind face and "crude, but tender hand," a "simple soul" with a song "so plaintive and so wild."[67] Written as an ode to the black mammy, the poem details the domestic and affective labor she is compelled to perform for white children who, "swift like a stab, / . . . some day might crush [her] own black child."[68] Whether through her compensatory labor in service of a whiteness that would ensure a slow death for her offspring or by her own hand with which she might accelerate her child's death, the black mammy, in Johnson's verse, serves a filicidal function. According to its etymology, "mammy" precedes the words "mam" and "mama," which presumably derive from it.[69] Emerging in the sixteenth century, "mammy" came into circulation along the routes of the Atlantic slave trade. In parts of western Africa, "mammy" is used in conjunction with other terms to form compound words, like "mammy-boat" and "mammy-chair," which describe the wicker baskets slung over the sides of boats used for the transportation of persons.[70] The earliest use of the word to refer to enslaved black women tasked with caring for white children appears in a travelogue of the American South in 1810, and from that moment, as Kimberly Wallace-Sanders explains, the mammy's figuration became central in an "interracial debate over constructions of loyalty, maternal devotion, and southern memory."[71] As a matter of representation, the mammy was made to reproduce racial borders; her mythology was critical to developing an image that would perpetuate, in the words of Saidiya Hartman, a "racial and sexual fantasy in which domination is transposed into the bonds of mutual affection, subjection idealized . . . and perfect subordination declared the means of ensuring happiness and harmony."[72] As a matter of labor, the mammy figured a social relation of production that brought surplus value to white families, private property, and the nation. Conversely, the mammy came to epitomize the black mother as a "problem," figured as such for any number of reasons, including her purported acts of neglect or filicide, but also, and more importantly, as the symbolic progenitor of racial identity.

There is a related, or perhaps embedded, conversation to have about the type of relation figured between the black son and the "mammy" here. As Amber Musser describes in her explication of Deleuze's work on masochism and its applications for the conceptualization of queer subjectivity, the masochist cannot be "thought as a singular entity— s/he requires a symbolic dominator to be complicit in the illusion of powerlessness. Yet, this dominant, gendered female because of her part in the psychoanalytic return to the maternal and its affiliated heterosexual matrix of desire, loses the potential for autonomy and separate desire. As a result, the masochist and his/her dominant *only* exist in their interrelation[;] neither can be thought as individuals."[73] The black subject/son and black mother/mammy form an "intersubjective complex" in which racial and sexual subjection/subjectification occurs through repeated encounters with the abject, cast as the maternal.[74] As a feature in intramural black life, black being is interrelated with the figuring of the black maternal as nonbeing, just as she is also deployed in an intercultural milieu (think: the Moynihan report or the overrepresentation of controlling black mothers in film and television) to produce a grammar for thinking/expressing blackness in relation to a Western ethnocentric conception of personhood. As Darieck Scott contends, "[W]ithin human abjection as represented and lived in the experience of being-black, of blackness—we may find that the zone of self or personhood extends into realms where we would not ordinarily perceive its presence; and that suffering seems, at some level or at some far-flung contact point, to merge into something like ability, like power."[75] Reading Scott alongside Spillers's contention in the chapter's epigraph, the power of "yes" to the "female within" is thus expressible in masochistic terms.

One might anticipate a metonymic figuring of black mothers for black domestic life. In *The Souls of Black Folk*, for example, readers are privy to varied descriptions of black mothers as "strong, bustling, and energetic," "incorrigibly dirty," or "plump, yellow, and intelligent," which correspond to depictions of their homes and the status of other inhabitants.[76] *Up from Slavery* follows a similar pattern in the chapter "Early Days at Tuskegee," as it includes a mention of an awkward dinner Washington had with a black family. Though few specifics are given about the meal, he describes the mother's morning activities in some detail:

> The mother would sit down in a corner and eat her breakfast, perhaps from a plate and perhaps directly from the "skillet" or frying-pan, while the children would eat their portion of the bread and meat while running around the yard. . . . The breakfast over, and with practically no attention given to the house, the whole family would, as a general thing, proceed to the cotton-field. Every child . . . was put to work, and the baby—for usually there was at

> least one baby—would be laid down at the end of the cotton row,
> so that its mother could give it a certain amount of attention.[77]

Washington's focus on the mother's behaviors paints a picture of the impact of sharecropping on black family life. From her propensity to eat straight from the "skillet"—the scare quotes conveying a developing class-based distinction between the speech acts of the host family and Washington's authorial voice—and her giving "practically no attention" to household chores, to the "certain amount of attention" that she pays to her infant after picking a row of cotton, conceptions of womanhood and motherly duties are re/cast in light of her responsibilities in the cotton field. As Patricia Hill Collins has explained, black women's "mother-work" is indelibly shaped by "histories of family-based labor," and, as Washington's example further demonstrates, black mothers are affected by myriad expectations and demands for their attention.[78]

One might also suspect from these texts, which interface with the autobiographical genre, that when each work turns to the protagonist's mother, it is frequently in reference to acts of knowledge transmission toward the development of his character. Whereas *Up from Slavery* and *Autobiography* are rife with descriptions of mother–son interactions that highlight how the maternal function aided in their ability to become men, *Souls* includes only one mention of Du Bois's mother, in a parenthetical formulation—"(for my mother was mortally afraid of firearms)"—embedded in a discussion of Du Bois's search for employment after graduating from Fisk University.[79] Her phobia provides a rationale for why Du Bois has heard of the enjoyments of the hunt only "from hearsay," to which he rejoins, "I am sure that the man who has never hunted a country school has something to learn of the pleasures of the chase."[80] In the same chapter, Du Bois describes in great detail the families whose children would attend the country school where he eventually found a post. These familial descriptions place an emphasis on the appearance and mannerisms of the mother, and it is in this sense that the chapter titled "Of the Meaning of Progress" could be regarded as a meditation on the shifting dynamics of black motherhood after Reconstruction.

This is most evident toward the end of the chapter, when Du Bois describes how the schoolhouse where he once taught had been rebuilt and renamed Progress. Here, he realizes that the first pupil he met, a young woman named Josie, who, in his words, "seemed to be the centre of the family . . . nervous and inclined to scold, like her mother yet faithful, too, like her father," has died. Her "gray-haired mother" reports the news, adding, "We've had a heap of trouble since you've been away."[81] The inclusion of a detail regarding the mother's personal appearance is instructive, particularly when juxtaposed with a description of another student's mother, which comes in the final pages of the chapter: "The strong, hard face of the mother, with its wilderness of hair, rose before me. She had driven her husband away, and while I taught school a strange man lived there, big and jovial, and people talked. I felt sure that Ben and 'Tildy would come to naught from such a home. But this is an odd world."[82] The recourse to Ben and 'Tildy's mother is similarly marked by an impression of her hair, described in the third-person-singular "it." This aspect of depersonalization highlights the mother's abject status in the narrative, which, as Noliwe Rooks explains about the period, relied upon the description of physical characteristics, such as hair texture, hair length, and eye color, as indicative of a woman's character.[83] Counterposing the gray-haired mother, a feature that descriptively emphasizes the "trouble" the family has encountered in the ten-year lapse, with the memory of Ben and 'Tildy's mother's wild hair and corresponding "reckless" behaviors sets the stage for Du Bois's chapter-defining question regarding the meaning of progress. "How shall man measure Progress there where the dark-faced Josie lies?" Du Bois asks as he muses on the revelation of his favorite pupil's death, whose mother he earlier described as having "an ambition to live 'like folks.'"[84] How could it be that Josie had not made a way for herself, or at least survived, when Ben and 'Tildy had done both in spite of their mother's apparent shortcomings? At this, an indication of the "odd world" that Progress marked, he muses: "[I]s it the twilight of nightfall or the flush of some faint-dawning day?"

Du Bois's bemusement over the outcomes of his former students contextualizes his question about temporality. In the era of post-Reconstruction, the architecture of Progress, described as a "necessarily ugly" board house, figured the relation between "the Old and the New"—a kind of structure of feeling—that in its materiality evoked the shifting power relations of the time.[85] The concomitant meditation on mothers, which includes his brief aside about his own, punctuates his discussion on time and the meanings of Progress (and progress) to reveal an attendant and intrinsic question: What kind of mothering would be necessary to produce a generation able to navigate this particular orientation to time and space, both in the literal sense (the Progressive Era American South) and as a metaphysical supposition?

In direct discussions of the Reconstruction, which occur in both *Souls* and *Up from Slavery*, the black maternal figure is evoked metaphorically to index persisting and shifting power relations. In the latter book, Washington suggests, "During the whole of the Reconstruction period our people throughout the South looked to the Federal Government for everything, very much as a child looks to its mother. This was not unnatural. The central government gave them freedom, and the whole Nation had been enriched for more than two centuries by the labour of the Negro."[86] Confirming much of the contemporaneous discourse about recently emancipated black people, particularly in likening them to children, the passage casts the federal government as mother and as a replacement of the (father) figure of the master. The use of "our people" and "them" to describe "the Negro" is symptomatic of the various relations Washington is made to emblematize, as a champion of black people, as a mediator between black and white people, and as an interceder between southern and national interests. That the Reconstruction period coincides with Washington's adolescence provides additional insight into the kind of maternal relation that is being articulated here. Washington writes, "Even as a youth, and later in manhood, I had the feeling that it was cruelly wrong in the central government, at the beginning of our freedom, to fail to make some provision for the general education of our people in addition to what the states might do, so that the people would be the better prepared for the duties of citizenship."[87] In his critique of the actions of the Bureau for the Relief of Freedom and Refugees, popularly referred to as the Freedmen's Bureau, Washington constructs the federal government as a surrogate mother, ignorant and ill equipped to attend to black people's needs. In this sense, the central government, as a political entity, bears a deep resemblance to representations of plantation mistresses, as both were typically imaged as being unaccustomed to the day-to-day activities of mothering.[88]

Up from Slavery then highlights what Washington perceived as evidence of an increasing frivolity among black youth during and in the

wake of Reconstruction. Black young men, according to him, were spending more than half of their weekly wages on weekend carriage rides, and
black young women were turning away from their mothers' teachings on
"the industry of laundrying" to begin classes in the public schools. These
observations punctuated Washington's concern that programs initiated
by the Freedmen's Bureau were providing an education that increased
black people's wants, whereas "their ability to supply their wants had not
been increased in the same degree."[89] This moment in the text sounds
very much like the discourses that would later crystallize as "culture of
poverty" rhetoric, even as it indicts the federal government for producing the conditions for such behaviors to flourish.

In casting the federal government as a mistress, culturally figured
as responsible for instilling norms but legally unable to confer wealth,
name, or an inheritance, *Up from Slavery* continues a critique offered in
Du Bois's earlier analysis of Negro problems. In both instances, the family functions as a rhetorical device that organized race-as-caste during
slavery and in its afterlives. Although white mothers, according to Du
Bois, produced a different legal status for their offspring in antebellum
America, their capacity to generate positive effects/affects for their prog-
eny is circumscribed in Washington's characterization of Reconstruction.
Thus, Washington's criticism uses the relation of government-mistress
to the black child to signal how white (family/property/national) depen-
dency on the black was systematically subverted as a matter of institutional practice during Reconstruction. One might view his critique
of the government, taken to its logical conclusion, as Washington does
when he bemoans how black young women have turned away from their
mothers' profession, as a concern over the suppression of a black maternal function. What the black maternal function means to the project
of moving "up from slavery" is made clearer in his invocations of his
mother in the text, which I will attend to later in this chapter.

When Du Bois makes use of family metaphors to characterize
Reconstruction's failures, he renders two characters as spatiotemporal
figurations: "one, a gray-haired gentleman . . . and the other, a form hov-
ering dark and mother like."[90] With regard to the "mother like" form,
Du Bois writes, "[H]er awful face black with the mists of centuries, had
aforetime quailed at that white master's command, had bent in love over
the cradles of his sons and daughters, and closed in death the sunken

eyes of his wife,—aye, too, at his behest had laid herself low to his lust, and borne a tawny man-child to the world, only to see her dark boy's limbs scattered to the winds by midnight marauders riding after 'cursed Niggers.'"[91] Juxtaposed with Washington's reference to the "labour of the Negro," which might include the household work of laundering but primarily indexes the contributions black people made to wealth accumulation through the industries of cotton, sugar, and tobacco, *Souls* attunes its readers to a trans/gendering labor occasioned by a violent proximity to whiteness. Set in the domestic sphere of the plantation owner's home, gender stages the relation between whites and blacks, as blackness-as-womanhood (regardless of sex) is depicted as the result of a compulsory labor of care. In this formulation, black people are *all* mammies compelled to produce white value through their intimate labor and, by their reproductive capacity, surplus value in the form of the production of additional laboring bodies.[92] The "mother-like" who comes to stand in for all black people in this passage might be read as a gesture toward a feminization of black men based on their barred access to white patriarchal power. It would be more instructive, however, to read this instance of mammy-fication as the articulation of certain gendered dimensions of blackness in which the black "mother-like" is neither a black "woman" nor a black "man" but rather an emblem of a masochistic relation and a symbol of the processes by which black gender becomes fungible in slavery's political and visual economy of indifference to black gender difference.

The inclusion of the white mother's death could be read as the white father's capacity to reproduce himself insomuch as his sanctioned reproductive mate is disposable in the perpetuation of white patriarchal power. Yet, as Du Bois notes, these racial-gender configurations are representations of time, "two passing figures of the present-past" that structure the relation that "their children's children live to-day."[93] The "mother-like," then, signifies a temporal continuity as well as a disjuncture marked by the seemingly apocryphal nomenclature of pre- and post-Emancipation and indexed by the hyphenated term "present-past."

If Du Bois's depiction of the "mother-like" bears a close resemblance to the representational figure of the black mammy, it is expressed most acutely in the chapter "Of the Coming of John," which is most recognizable as fiction in *Souls*. Here, Du Bois crafts a narrative of perpendicular stories of black and white Johns, that is, of John Jones and John Henderson, respectively. As white John departs for Princeton, black John, spurred on by his mother, leaves home to attend preparatory school: "But [the whites] shook their heads when his mother wanted to send him off to school. 'It'll spoil him,—ruin him,' they said; and talked as though they knew."[94] Popular interpretations present the story of black John as staging the differences between "old" and "new" Negroes in one narrative arc. Before attending school, John was well liked by the whites in Altamaha, Georgia; he was industrious and handy, an "old" Negro who fit into the political economy and social order of the town. While away, John was marked and remarked upon in town through the circulation of the adage "when John comes," a spatiotemporal phrase that carried with it the import of temporality to sociogenesis—to the possibility of being beyond being in a temporality of emergence yet to be determined. John's mother is most frequently associated with the expression, and her presence, as the chapter bears out, signals his process of becoming in his absence.

As the story relates, black John did not acclimate well to the Institute in Johnstown at first. Having been dismissed by the dean for "tardiness . . . carelessness . . . poor lessons and neglected work," John responded with a promise and plea: "But you won't tell mammy and sister,—you won't write mammy, now will you? For if you won't I'll go out into the city and work and come back next term and show you something."[95] Following this encounter, John threw himself into work: "he grew in body and soul, and with him his clothes seemed to grow and arrange themselves; . . . a new dignity crept into his walk. . . . He had left his queer thought-world and come back to a world of motion and of men."[96] Thus, what John had become, which is curiously described as a return—a "comeback"—was, as a matter of narrative, linked to the figuration of the mammy as well as his sibling. The use of vernacular in the scene between John and the dean clarifies how gender inflects John's process of becoming. The juxtaposition of "mammy and sister" rather than "mother and sister" or "mammy and sissy (or sis)" provides an aperture into the animating presence of the mammy's figuration in forging a particular iteration of black modernist masculinity. Thus, for John to "come back to a world of motion and of men," he first has to negotiate his relationship to his mother by externalizing her in such a way that he too might benefit from her presence as a figuration of inexhaustible resource for the production of legible manhood. Put differently, through casting her as his mammy rather than his mother, black John moves within a symbolic order of masculinity by psychically disentangling himself from his mother's particular inheritance.

When John did come back, he was greeted warmly by those he left behind but found it difficult to acclimate to the ways of blacks in his hometown. Perhaps it was because it was not that "comeback" that "restored" black John's masculinity; rather, it was, by the narrative's logic, a regression, in the statistical sense, which is to say that it reflected a relation between black John and his corresponding environment. Black John's return to his mother's house coincided with a series of events, including suffering the indignities of white John's racist father when applying for work, being dismissed from his post as teacher at the school for black children, and witnessing his sister's sexual violation by white John. In response to this last event, which is figured as the ultimate affront to black John's manhood,

> He [black John] said not a word, but seizing a fallen limb, struck him [white John] with all the pent-up hatred of his great black arm; and the body lay white and still beneath the pines, all bathed in sunshine and in blood. John looked at it dreamily, then walked back to the house briskly, and said in a soft voice, "Mammy, I'm going away,—I'm going to be free."
>
> She gazed at him dimly and faltered, "No'th honey, is yo' gwine No'th again?"
>
> He looked out where the North Star glistened pale above the waters, and said, "Yes, mammy, I'm going—North."[97]

In this final tableau before John's march toward "the Sea" and the "coiling twisted rope," and in the wake of a reassertion of a manhood that was figured as being at odds with his environment and at risk in proximity with white John's, the narrative reinscribes the mammy's importance to the symbolism of black masculinity, as it gestures toward the distance that might be put between black sons and black mothers in pursuit of a particular conception of freedom.[98]

The details of John's march, including his humming softly Wagner's "Song of the Bride" in his procession toward the water, elucidates one aspect of what Spillers might mean by the "'female' within." As Charles Nero explains, the song functions as a nondiegetic accompaniment to the narrative action that "comments on John's female interiority as the bride."[99] For Nero, this feminine interiority resounds with Eve Kosofsky Sedgwick's analysis on homosocial desire in English literature, in which she argued that men risk permanent feminization when misunderstood as "the kind of property women are or the kind of transaction in which alone their value is realizable means."[100] Nero adds that the characterization of John Jones as messianic in nature also indexes the various ways gender-inversion theories circulated at the turn of the twentieth century.[101] John's feminine interiority also indicates a pervasive modernist generic convention, which, as Tamar Katz has argued, "is shaped to an idea of the 'feminine mind,'" in which femininity is important to "simultaneously establishing and complicating modernist cultural authority."[102]

Although Nero's reading of John as a meditation on the queerness produced by Du Bois's racial exclusion from public heterosexuality is very compelling, other potentialities of the narrative take shape when locating this moment of John's feminine interiority in relation to the figuration of his mother.[103] That is, if one reads the narrative as one in which black manhood is produced as a matter of interiority, as orchestrated through a series of centrifugal and centripetal movements in relation to his mother, "Of the Coming of John" may figure a crossroad—an intersection (and the dangers that accompany that kind of conjuncture) of "old" and "new" Negro along an axis of an old and new social order. John's mother becomes the border, a passage that simultaneously enables and condemns. In contradistinction to *Up from Slavery* and *The Autobiography of an Ex-Colored Man*, *The Souls of Black Folk* provides a narrative that situates the mother and the "mother-like" in relation to the project of black manhood such that John's demise acts as further evidence of the seeming impossibility of inhabiting the position of a "new" man in an "old" world. Like the logics of gender inversion, for which a mind's view of the self has yet to become legible on the body for others, John's interiority is shaped by the psychic collision of mammy into mother and mammy again. His death, then, becomes the only distance, narratively imagined, to disentangle black John from his mother's cruel inheritance. Yet, at the very beginning of the chapter, one notes that it is through his mother's "want" to send him to school that he embarks upon this journey. This detail, as it recalls abjection's underlying relation to sociogenesis, might prompt readers to consider the degree to which John's mother was ever distinguishable from the mammy's underside, for even with her good intentions, she sets his death in motion.

Conversely, in both *Up from Slavery* and *Autobiography*, the narration of the mother's death coincides with the availability of a different life for her son. Washington narrates his mother's death in a chapter entitled "Helping Others." Though home on vacation from Hampton University, Washington explains that he was unable to reach his mother before her death: "When I had gotten within a mile or so of my home I was so completely tired out that I could not walk any farther, and I went into an old, abandoned house to spend the remainder of the night. About three o'clock in morning my brother John found me asleep in this house, and broke to me, as gently as he could, the sad news that our dear mother had died during the night."[104] The chapter narrates the impact of his mother's death, described as the "saddest and blankest" as well as "the most dismal period of [Washington's] life," as a matter of domestic devolution: "[A]fter the death of my mother our little home was in confusion. . . . Our clothing went uncared for, and everything about our home was soon in a tumble-down condition."[105] After her death, Washington's mother functions as a superego within the text, invoked at various parts in the narration and serving a tethering function for the protagonist as he moves up from slavery to circulate among the wealthy and influential. Nowhere is this more apparent than in the penultimate chapter, "The Secret of Success in Public Speaking," which is also the final time his mother is mentioned:

> I rarely take part in one of these long dinners that I do not wish that I could put myself back in the little cabin where I was a slave boy, and again go through the experience there—one that I shall never forget—of getting molasses to eat once a week from the "big house." Our usual diet on the plantation was corn bread and pork, but on Sunday morning my mother was permitted to bring down a little molasses from the "big house" for her three children, and when it was received how I did wish that every day was Sunday! I would get my tin plate and hold it up for the sweet morsel, but I would always shut my eyes while the molasses was being poured out into the plate, with the hope that when I opened them I would

be surprised to see how much I had got. When I opened my eyes I would tip the plate in one direction and another, so as to make the molasses spread all over it, in the full belief that there would be more of it and that it would last longer if spread out in this way. So strong are my childish impressions of those Sunday morning feasts that it would be pretty hard for any one to convince me that there is not more molasses on a plate when it is spread all over the plate than when it occupies a little corner—if there is a corner in a plate. At any rate, I have never believed in "cornering" syrup. My share of the syrup was usually about two tablespoonfuls, and those two spoonfuls of molasses were much more enjoyable to me than is a fourteen-course dinner after which I am to speak.[106]

This sentimental rendering of a childhood memory of black life in captivity sits alongside tips on public speechmaking, accounts of worldly travel, and, as the excerpt elucidates by way of a critique, the opulence that characterized Washington's ascended status. On one level, the tableau depicts a moment of care under the conditions of slavery. Yet slavery is also everywhere in the scene: in Washington's description of himself as a "slave boy," in the method by which the molasses is procured from the "big house," and in the larger process by which the molasses was sourced—in the circuits of trade between Caribbean and U.S. plantation economies. Narratively, there is a metonymic link between Washington's mother and the molasses, as the passage figures the mother's relation to her son through syrup. As a matter of fabulation, the death of the mother gives way to a haunting (spread all over the plate), as it also mediates the boundary between slavery and freedom in Washington's life. Here, what might appear to reaffirm Washington's commitment to humility and frugality is also about the degree to which Washington's mother, in this final accounting, is made palatable, ingestible, as a diffuse presence that reminds her son from whence he came. In this edible arrangement, Washington incorporates his black mother by rendering her a delectable resource in making sense of his self-propulsion.

Autobiography, on the other hand, stages a different kind of maternal incorporation, as the unnamed narrator's varying gender expressions emblematize and emphasize his racial ambiguities. As Siobhan Somerville has argued, "[A]s a 'hybrid' racialized subject, symbolically both black and white, the narrator is also gendered 'between' male and female, like the bodies of the inverts who were subjected to the taxonomizing gaze of sexologists. In the case of the ex-coloured man, his own gaze importantly constructs and internalizes an eroticized version of the mulatto as invert."[107] These aspects of the novel are in part shaped by Johnson's interest in portraying typologies of blackness, as he discussed in correspondence with his publishers. Yet the protagonist's construction of mulatto as invert also means that scenes of racial awakening are frequently coupled with cross-gender identification.[108]

Early in the narrative, the protagonist is positioned as displaying a rivalrous attitude toward his mother. Take, for example, the interaction with his mother that occurred after the protagonist's encounter with the fact of his blackness at school:

> I looked up into her face and repeated: "Tell me, mother, am I a nigger?" There were tears in her eyes and I could see that she was suffering for me. And then it was that I looked at her critically for the first time. I had thought of her in a childish way only as the most beautiful woman in the world; now I looked at her searching for defects. I could see that her skin was almost brown, that her hair was not so soft as mine, and that she did differ in some way from the other ladies who came to the house; yet, even so, I could see that she was very beautiful, more beautiful than any of them.[109]

In this description, which directly follows the noted mirror scene, the narrator details the ways his greater proximity to whiteness marks him as closer to a white feminine ideal than his mother is. Though the mother is still "very beautiful, more beautiful than any" of the other black women he has encountered in his mother's home business, she is ultimately lacking in the protagonist's description because of the ways white supremacy structures gender's expressivities. This scene's sequencing after the mirror scene amplifies the transgender dynamics of the protagonist's description. Although this scene is typically read according to what it reveals about processes of racialization, as Jay Prosser notes, mirror scenes frequently recur in transsexual autobiographies as well. Prosser contends, "[M]irror scenes in transsexual autobiographies do not merely initiate the plot of transsexuality. Highly staged and self-conscious affairs . . . mirror scenes also draw attention to the narrative form [of] the plot, to the surrounding autobiography and its import for transsexuality."[110]

By the time the narrator finishes secondary school, his mother is "mortally ill." Following her passing soon thereafter, he eventually liquidates his mother's assets to the total of $200 and proceeds south in pursuit of further education. The narrator explains in regard to his mother's death, "I will not rake over this, one of the two sacred sorrows of my life; nor could I describe the feeling of unutterable loneliness that fell upon me."[111] Although the protagonist does not elaborate on the affective impact of his loss, as a matter of narration her death signals a shift in genre from a coming-of-age narrative to a travel memoir. His mother is invoked twice after her death: in the dissolution of his relationship with his white benefactor, and in his summation of the decision to be "ex-colored" at the end of the narrative. When the protagonist breaks with his millionaire companion to return to the United States to "live among the people" and "begin to do something," his benefactor guffaws at the decision.[112] This is a recurring dynamic between the duo, which critics have compellingly read to reflect on economic exploitation, racial hierarchy, and the role of erotic subjugation in the production of black masculinity.[113] As the narrator notes, their relationship existed as an exchange that made the protagonist "a polished man of the world" and that gave his patron the opportunity to evade "the thing which seemed to sum up all in life that he dreaded—time."[114]

Upon the relationship's dissolution, the protagonist heads to the U.S. South with a parting check of $500, in addition to the several hundreds of dollars he saved from money previously given by the millionaire. The narrator writes, "And so I separated from the man who was, all in all, the best friend, I ever had, except my mother, the man who exerted the greatest influence ever brought into my life, except that exerted by my mother. My affection for him was so strong, my recollections of him so distinct, he was such a peculiar and striking character that I could easily fill several chapters with reminiscences of him; but for fear of tiring the reader I shall go on with my narration."[115] Though Somerville argues that in this description, "Johnson suggests that the narrator's feelings toward the patron exceed the limits of what is representable," the repetitious comparison to the protagonist's mother underscores the quality of relationship fomented between the two figures.[116] The inclusion of details about the sums of money that accompanied the two breaks ($200 from the liquidation of his mother's assets and an uncalculated total of well over $500 from the millionaire) foreshadows the narrator's decision to become "ex-colored," influenced, at least in part, by his adjudication of a lesser valuation placed on blackness. His underestimation of blackness, materialized in an undervaluing of his black mother's assets, frames the narrator's regret over his "cheaply sold birthright" and estrangement from his "mother's people."[117] As Darieck Scott notes, and as it relates the protagonist's ex-colored status to his mother, the narrator's "mistake," then, lies in his refusal to embrace blackness-as-abject (personified as the black mother/mammy), which calls "into question 'race,' 'gender' and the like: by pushing those categories to the edge of their defining capabilities, where they nearly tip over into the death which they are meant to defend against, and which simultaneously, as 'black' or 'woman,' they are meant to represent."[118]

In terms of narration, whereas the mother's death catalyzes the protagonist's expulsion from a black social world in the form of his mother's home and business and in his relationships with childhood friends, the dissolution of his affiliation with the millionaire signals (an affective longing for) a departure from his multicultural cosmopolitan existence in Europe for a return to black sociality. Notably, the narrative portrays a spectacular disruption of the enactment of this longing, as the protagonist's course irrevocably changes again after he witnesses a lynching. But the return of his mother in the description of his break with the millionaire highlights the construction of the interior world of an "ex-colored man," dramatizing what Matt Richardson described in his reading of Jackie Kay's *Trumpet* as the transformative potential of positionality in which "black queerness provides the site from which this burden of decision can be more clearly rendered, given its positionality outside the nation and even outside of blackness."[119]

Near the end of the narrative, the protagonist proclaims that sometimes he feels as if he has been a "privileged spectator" of black "inner life," even as he has "never really been a Negro." "At other times," he rejoins, "I feel that I have been a coward, a deserter, and I am possessed by a strange longing for my mother's people."[120] On the one hand, the distinction between having a privileged perspective on black interiority without being black seems to cast the protagonist within Richardson's reading of black queerness as a position outside of blackness. Yet, on the other hand, the ascription of the black race as his "mother's people," particularly when coupled with his feelings of regret, opens up a different, though not incompatible, interpretation that stages how black interiority and black sociality are both produced through a black maternal figuration. In both the opening and closing gestures, the narrator names his exile from black social life as his greatest personal disappointment; it is his want for black sociality that marks his black interiority, even as the protagonist comes to live in the world after his mother's death as ex-colored. As in *Up from Slavery*, the death of the mother produces a desire to incorporate what the black maternal engenders for the construction of an interiority not wholly given by antinomic forces, which produce blackness in a social world structured by antiblackness.

Being, Black and Modern: A Trans Phenomenon

Blackness, as a condition of possibility that made transness conceivable in the twilight of formal slavery, would require "revision" to engender itself as modern. This reconstitution of blackness signaled a return to the scene of "female flesh ungendered" to create blackness anew. From the named and unnamed "patients" captured and obscured in James Marion Sims's archive to the mothers that animate *Three Negro Classics,* black women have been made to reproduce and remediate myriad borders—anthropomorphic and semiotic ones, as well as in matters of expiration and vitality. Masculinist sensibilities that would figure Afromodernist literature, according to the tenets of manhood rights, necessitated a symbolic rearrangement of black women's figurations. From this view, "black modernity," a phrase that adjoins modernity to its defining negation, constructing blackness as antimodern and as its capacitating void, also carries a distinctly trans dimension, revealing how gender for the black and blackened takes on an anagrammatical quality, subject to reiterative rearrangement. Reading invocations of the black maternal in *Three Negro Classics* highlights the transitivities of blackness, "sex," and "gender" in the afterlives of slavery, even as it also indexes the persistent relevance of flesh within modernity's "cruel ruse" in which, as Alexander Weheliye has argued with regard to modern law, "subjects must be transformed into flesh before being granted the illusion of possessing a body."[121] In another sense, these instances of "saying yes to the 'female' within," as they occur in the literary treatments of the black maternal in *Up from*

Slavery, The Souls of Black Folk, and *The Autobiography of an Ex-Colored Man,* underscore what L. H. Stallings explains are the generated effects of transaesthetics, which, as they relate to matters of being and becoming, "disturb forms, biological and otherwise" so as not to privilege "the human or one specific reality."[122] To examine *Three Negro Classics* according to what these works articulate about being and becoming and for what they reveal about the anatamopoiesis of black literary modernism is to encounter again the transitivity and transversality of blackness and transness, wherein making (sense of) the text requires contravening commonsense notions of the body.

PART III
BLACKOUT

Present and unmade in presence, blackness is an instrument in the making.

—FRED MOTEN, "Blackness and Nothingness
(Mysticism in the Flesh)"

4

A NIGHTMARISH SILHOUETTE
RACIALIZATION AND THE LONG EXPOSURE OF TRANSITION

[The] shadows linger and leak. They seep from mottled grey and scaffold scalar recollections. They assure our potential, securing it by ways and means at once penumbral and exquisite. They instantiate things remembered past their time, promised beyond situation.

—KARLA F. C. HOLLOWAY, *Legal Fictions: Constituting Race, Composing Literature*

THE DECEMBER 1, 1952, *New York Daily News* front-page story "Ex-GI Becomes Blonde Beauty" ignited a media fascination with Christine Jorgensen that would make her, according to trans theorist and historian Susan Stryker, "arguably the most famous person in the world for a few short years."[1] Though Jorgensen's was not the first media story to pivot on transgender concerns—such stories appeared sporadically throughout the early twentieth century—her narrative, as it played out in the contemporary press and in subsequent trans historiographical accounts, produced Jorgensen as an exceptional figuration of trans embodiment. The contours of Jorgensen's narrative were variable and manifold, beginning in the mainstream press in a spectacular story about personal triumph, scientific transformation, and confessional ideality. The *Daily News* initial report, for example, included excerpts from a letter Jorgensen had sent to her parents, which, David Serlin argues, functioned by way of a "'confession' of innocence and . . . [a] presumption of authenticity" to describe her travels to her ancestral home of Denmark for a surgical correction for "nature's mistake."[2] In keeping with the news treatments of spectacular inventions for man's undoing, a recurrent narrative during the postwar, early Cold War period, early media reports of Jorgensen's "sex change" cast her story as another testament to the magnitude of modern science. In this sense, as Stryker has argued, Jorgensen's story dramatized "the pervasive unease felt in some quarters that American manhood, already under siege, could literally be undone and refashioned into its seeming opposite through the power of modern science."[3]

In the black press, Jorgensen was often discussed in terms of her success as an entertainer, with frequent attention paid to the financial trappings of her celebrity. In early coverage in the *Chicago Defender*, an article noted that although she "became a woman only a short while ago . . . she already has learned to say 'no' to Hollywood offers."[4] Alvin Chick Webb wrote for the *New York Amsterdam News,* in his review of Jorgensen's popular show at the New York City nightclub Latin Quarter, "[W]hatever you may think about Christine as a person or as a performer, the fact remains she [is] pulling in plenty pieces of silver."[5] Amid the flurry of responses to her public figuration, the Jamaica-based Rhythm record label released in the Caribbean, the United Kingdom, and the United States what would be a hit song, "Is She Is, or Is She Ain't?" for its writer and composer, Calypso Gene the Charmer, now better known as Nation of Islam leader Louis Farrakhan. The song's refrain, "But behind that lipstick, rouge, and paint / I gotta know—is she is, or is she ain't?," discussed Jorgensen's significance as a transsexual celebrity in ways that riffed on the crisis of visuality that Jorgensen's deviant body evoked, as it signified upon a set of sedimented ideas about where one locates the truth of a body (on its surface? as an essence?) and the degree to which "reality" is sutured to the privileging of sight.[6]

Even as a spectacular application of an American liberal edict of self-invention, Jorgensen could not withstand the burdens of representation, illustrated in the shift in mainstream media coverage five months after her emergence. In April 1953, the *New York Post* published a six-part "exposé" entitled "The Truth about Christine Jorgensen," which claimed that she had not achieved womanhood through surgery and hormonal treatment; *Time* quickly followed suit, declaring, "Jorgensen was no girl at all, only an altered male."[7] Although Jorgensen would later be reclassified as "transsexual" after undergoing vaginoplastic procedures, "Jorgensen's doctors in Denmark," as Joanne Meyerowitz explains, "seemed to confirm the [*Post's*] 'exposé' . . . [when] they described Jorgensen's case as one of 'genuine transvestism'" in the *Journal of the American Medical Association.*[8] Though America's initial romance with Jorgensen soured, her story narratively consolidated an understanding of transsexuality as the outcome of surgical implementation and other medicalized treatments aimed to address gender as an anatomical and biological proposition.[9]

Jorgensen's rise to fame and descent into ill repute hinged on questions of authenticity, scientific certitude, and the seeming limits of self-invention, but her story also raised, as she wrote in a letter to friends in Denmark in 1950, the matter of "life and the freedom to live it."[10] This aspect of Jorgensen's story figured prominently for those acutely aware of how unfreedom—in the forms of criminalization, colonialism, imperial conquest, internment, Jim Crow, and other modes of repressive, quotidian violence—figured black life in the United States and around the world. In a letter written to Jorgensen's parents, one woman wrote, "I am a Negro . . . [and] find many obstacles that must be overcome. [Jorgensen also] . . . belonged to a minority group but she [broke] through its limitations. If more people would face the brunt of the battle I am sure we would all live in a much more pleasant world."[11] The letter's invocation of the rhetoric of war to describe the forms of violent limitation that defined blackness as a matter to "overcome" exposes how Jorgensen's spectacularized trans embodiment carried with it an illusory promise of freedom within a landscape of structural, textual, and physical violence of varying scales. Jorgensen, in other words, as Emily Skidmore has argued, was instrumental to the construction of the "good transsexual," whereby she and other white trans women "were able to articulate transsexuality as an acceptable subject position through an embodiment of the norms of white womanhood, most notably domesticity, respectability, and heterosexuality."[12] This maneuver, Skidmore notes, "was only possible through the subjugation of other gender variant bodies[;] as the subject position of the transsexual was sanitized in the mainstream press and rendered visible through whiteness, other forms of gender variance were increasingly made visible through nonwhiteness."[13] Jorgensen's story of circumventing conventional bodily logics became a vehicle for expressing "freedom" as a mode of technological manifest destiny—rife with racial meaning—articulated as a prerogative for persons and nation-states.

This chapter reads Jorgensen's spectacular mediation as an allegory for transnational body politics in the postwar, early Cold War period. Viewing her media coverage as another instantiation of an American fascination with light and dark that figured Jorgensen as a silhouette, which took shape in relation to a national narrative of somatechnical advancement and might, "A Nightmarish Silhouette" provides an analytical context for how and why Jorgensen's Danish American whiteness mattered contemporaneously and in subsequent iterations of trans historiography, as a peculiar emblem of national freedom, not beloved but somehow incorporable. As Serlin has written with regard to Jorgensen and the period of her emergence, "[F]reedom was [and still is] malleable enough in its time to appeal to religious zealots, civil rights activists, political ideologues, and aspiring transsexual people alike."[14] Yet if Jorgensen's media figuration came to represent a form of freedom, it also signified upon the various kinds of unfreedom that marked and continue to animate black and trans temporalities. News media's initially romantic treatment of Jorgensen's story is instructive here, for, as Toni Morrison has argued, romance, as a genre, has been a critical language for exploring Americans' fears "of being outcast, of failing, of powerlessness . . . of the absence of so-called civilization; their fear of loneliness, of aggression both external and internal. In short, the terror of human freedom."[15] From this vantage point, Jorgensen not only exemplified what some men could potentially lose, she also portrayed an ability to transgress national and somatic borders that were simultaneously counterindexical and intrinsic to a set of racial logics (an ordering arrangement of dark and light) that would maintain Jim Crow regimes within U.S. borders and rationalize antiblack and white-supremacist imperialist policies and military interventions abroad.

As an exploration of the racial order of things that gave rise to the first transsexual celebrity, this chapter focuses on the mediated narratives of black trans figures that occurred within the decade before and after the advent of Jorgensen's celebrity to illuminate the critical role that her "spectacle of male-to-female transsexual re-embodiment" played in figuring America's national racial identity for a global audience.[16] As Viviane

Namaste has argued, gender often becomes "a vehicle that functions to displace the material and symbolic conditions of race and class."[17] This chapter, in its provision of a shadow history, engages the narratives of Lucy Hicks Anderson, Georgia Black, Carlett Brown, James McHarris / Annie Lee Grant, and Ava Betty Brown as different ways to narrate trans embodiment in the postwar, early Cold War period, as they reflect upon the violent and volatile intimacies of darker to lighter bodies amid the global dispersal of refugees following World War II and in the spectacular forms of mediation of the Long Civil Rights Movement.[18] The narratives of Hicks Anderson, Black, the Browns, and McHarris/Grant illustrate how trans figures were positioned by the black press to meditate on intramural black life, not simply as it related to matters of gender and sexuality but also as it pertained to the concept of value and shifting notions of human valuation.

The figures under primary review here, as Hortense Spillers has argued with regard to black women and the dominative symbolic of sexuality, "do not live out their destiny on the periphery of American race and gender magic, but in the center of its Manichean darkness."[19] Spillers's description of black gendered life in the center of "Manichean darkness" informs this chapter's mobilization of the transversal visuality of silhouettes and shadows as associated pictographic phenomena that emerge in relation to sources of light. Whereas silhouettes outline in bold, general strokes the contours of their subject matter, shadows appear by way of obstruction. Regarding the media narratives of Hicks Anderson, Black, the Browns, and McHarris/Grant as "shadows"—as narratives that disrupt the teleology of medicalized transsexuality as corporeal freedom—is also an incitement to rethink the classic formulation of the "center and the margins" in order to identify and contest the ways that convention of language obscures how power operates through defining what Nicholas Mirzoeff aptly describes as the "seeable" and "sayable."[20] As Spillers contends, "The fact of domination *is* alterable only to the extent that the dominated subject recognizes the potential power of its own 'double-consciousness.' The subject is certainly seen, but she also *sees*. It is the return of the gaze that negotiates at every point a space for living, and it is the latter that we must willingly name the counterpower, the counter-mythology."[21] What Spillers claims as a countermythology finds fictive elaboration in Ralph Ellison's *Invisible Man,* which was initially published in 1952 and received the U.S. National Book Award for fiction in 1953, at the height of Jorgensen's celebrity. In the book's prologue, the narrator explains that he has acquired the ability to see "the darkness of lightness"—not as an awakening to a supernatural gift but as a consequence of having been repeatedly struck across the head by a "boomerang" more commonly known as History. The narrator's ability emerged, then, from his lived experiences within the contradictions of power that dictate, according to him, "how the world moves."[22] Viewed through the "darkness of lightness," the media stories of Hicks Anderson, Black, McHarris/Grant, and the Browns are not merely a matter of excavating forgotten narratives, or of offering up presence over absence. Rather, they, as countermythologies, become ways to read the imbrications of race and gender as indexes of power's circulation and as instantiations of the ways discourse recursively presses flesh into bodies of meaning over time.

Although each of the figures examined in this chapter has elements of narrative distinction, they occupy a similar position in the archives of transsexuality. Positioned in the shadows of History, perhaps existing there even in their moments of notoriety, they lay the groundwork for understanding trans/gender embodiment in relation to the kinds of violence that inflect black and trans life, only one of which is the violence of erasure, and for which that erasure is about not an absence but a persistent and animating presence. Viewing Jorgensen's story in relation to the ones related here as mediated arrangements of light and dark, which is to say, as proxies for a series of meaningful political conversations that manifested as domestic struggles around Jim Crow and other forms of violence inflicted upon black and blackened figures in the United States and on a global scale illustrates a chasm between the United States and allied countries' attachment to democracy and capitalism against the darkened specters of communism, socialism, and fascism. In this broader context, Jorgensen's figuration allays as many fears as it evoked, as she represented the ability to find a scientific solution to lay one body—or, as this chapter bears out, numerous bodies—to rest in order to make room for a "new" iteration of U.S. exceptionalism.

Before proceeding, allow me to make a few notes about methodology, which could serve simultaneously as my idiosyncratic reflections on the ethics of engaging this archive. Because journalism is simply another genre of writing, I have not treated the stories that follow as if they might produce the "truth" of the figures I discuss. Rather, this archive is akin to what Saidiya Hartman described, in a riff on Foucault, as existent by "an act of chance or disaster," to produce "a divergence or an aberration from the expected and usual course of invisibility . . . [to the] surface of discourse."[23] As news, these stories are biased and partial, structured by contemporaneous modes of thought that engendered a figure "newsworthy." More often than not, media treatments of Hicks Anderson, Black, McHarris/Grant, and the Browns were framed as jokes, as indications of their supposedly essential disposability. Also, in many instances, these stories did not produce conventionally satisfying endings, and I have chosen not to ameliorate any feelings of dissatisfaction for the reader by endeavoring to "complete" the stories originally produced. I have also declined to reproduce some aspects of the stories that might read as reasonable within contemporary journalistic standards, such as the name the person was given at birth, or a detailed account of when and how that person came to identify as differently gendered. These details, which are fairly commonplace in discussions of trans people, perform gender as teleology, an approach which I ask my reader to suspend. Although the media stories discussed here occurred within the decade before and after Jorgensen's spectacular emergence, what follows is not exclusively, or even primarily, a chronology of each figure's temporary emergence to the surface of discourse; it is a series of arguments about the potential of shadows to refigure trans historiography, necessarily redirecting focus on occasions of unbecoming as well as becoming, of disappearance, of haunting, and of political deployments of ambulatory time (that is, History).

"Sometimes Sovereignty Is More Precious Than Liberty": The Trials of Lucy Hicks Anderson

On February 18, 2011, the *Tom Joyner Morning Show* aired the segment "Little-Known Black History Fact," which described Lucy Hicks Anderson as "the first transgendered black to be legally tried and convicted in court for impersonating a woman."[24] The following year, a version of her story appeared alongside others', including those of Carlett Brown, Sir Lady Java, Miss Major, and Marsha P. Johnson, in a feature on black trans trailblazers in *Ebony* magazine, written by trans advocate and blogger Monica Roberts.[25] Her biography was made into a short documentary, *We've Been Around—Lucy Hicks Anderson,* released on Advocate.com and Essence.com in 2016. Her name is often attached to the history of Oxnard, California, including in Jeffrey Maulhardt's *Oxnard: 1941–2004* and in a *Los Angeles Times* article focused on the impending closure of a restaurant that enjoyed the patronage of Oxnard's "old-timers."[26] This degree of documentation has provided greater access to the details of her existence: that she was born in 1886 in Waddy, Kentucky, and arrived in Oxnard, California, in 1920; that she was married twice, first to Clarence Hicks and then to Ruben Anderson; that she was a domestic worker and a madam; that she was tried twice, first locally, in Ventura County, California, and later by the federal government; that she went to prison; that she was barred from returning to Oxnard after serving her sentence lest she risk further prosecution; and that she died in Los Angeles in 1954. Most of these details are gleaned from articles written about her from 1945 to 1946, when her trials received national media coverage.

An image still of Lucy Hicks Anderson, from the Focus Features docuseries *We've Been Around* (2016).

In the November 5, 1945, issue that introduced a version of Lucy Hicks Anderson's story to a national audience, *Time* magazine ran as its cover an image of then U.S. ambassador to Argentina Spruille Braden. Situated to the right of Braden's face was an illustration of South America, rendered in banana leaves with swastikas overlaying the part that an atlas would label Argentina. In the bottom left-hand corner, directed toward the figurative pestilence of fascism, appeared a pesticide can, which greatly resembled a fighter aircraft. A quotation from Braden underneath the composition read, "Sometimes sovereignty is more precious than liberty."[27] Though meant as an affirmatory illustration of U.S. interventionist strategies in Argentinian electoral politics and of the nation's prerogative to combat and squelch the popularity of future president of Argentina Juan Domingo Perón, Braden's temporally qualified valuation of sovereignty over liberty also described the politics of Hicks Anderson's various encounters with local and federal criminal procedures. The question, as it pertained both to matters of U.S. foreign policy and to the legal apprehension and adjudication of Hicks Anderson's gender, was, What conditions would give rise to that particular revaluation?

Published after an editor "found the bones of the story tucked obscurely away in a Pacific Coast paper," *Time*'s feature, "California: Sin and Souffl," told "the story of Lucy Hicks, leading cook, confidante, philanthropist, and bordello-boss of Oxnard, Calif.," and garnered more mail from its readership than any other article in recent history.[28] The report focused as much on the town of Oxnard as it did on Hicks Anderson: "The town was newly rich on sugar beets, and its Chinese and Mexican laborers blew their pay nightly on light ladies, gambling, whiskey and opium." Weaving her story through that of the development of the town, it exclaimed that "in Ventura County she became as well known as Oxnard's huge American Crystal Sugar Co. refinery," describing how the growth of Oxnard allowed Hicks Anderson to expand her "lone bawdyhouse" to a sprawling half block of brothels. According to the article, "Lucy was accepted by easygoing Oxnard as commercially, not personally, involved in the operation of her bordellos." In addition to her role as the proprietor of several brothels, Hicks Anderson was known as one of the best cooks in town, working for most of Oxnard's political and business elites. Her proximity to the powerful carried certain benefits:

"When the sheriff arrested her one night, her double-barreled reputation paid off—Charles Donlon, the town's leading banker, promptly bailed her out. Reason: he had scheduled a huge dinner party which would have collapsed dismally with Lucy in jail." In sardonic tones, the feature described how Hicks Anderson gave "expensive going-away parties for the sons of prominent families"; provided local commentary alongside that of "churchmen and other civic leaders" for the Oxnard papers; contributed regularly to the Red Cross, the Boy Scouts, and other charities; and had purchased almost $50,000 in war bonds.[29]

"Sin and Souffl" included one quotation from Hicks Anderson— a response to her role as a philanthropist, which included the editorial description of her "cackling happily": "Jist don't ask where the money came from."[30] Its final sentence, a punch line, "Lucy was a man," conclusively signaled to *Time*'s readership that she was someone to laugh at. In a letter to subscribers a few months later, *Time*'s new publisher, James A. Linen, described Hicks Anderson's story as one of "astonishment and embarrassment [for] her fellow townsmen" as he noted the number of letters from the magazine's readership that nominated her for *Time*'s "Man of the Year" for 1945.[31] Although the initial feature failed to mention how her story was brought to their attention, namely, that she was being brought up on perjury charges, as an update to the story and alongside a doodle-like illustration of a bearded, big-busted figure in a dress, Linen wrote, "But there is one more chapter to add now to the story of Lucy's trials and tribulations: the U.S. Army is after 'her' for evading the draft." Indicative of the symptomatic treatment of Hicks Anderson in *Time*, Linen's quip brings to the surface the serious subtext of a joke shared between the magazine's staff and its readers. Delivering the news of Hicks Anderson's criminalization for humorous effect, his additive elaboration also recast Hicks Anderson's narrative in terms of personal hardship rather than as cause for Oxnardians' chagrin. The editorial decision to tell her story in the form of a joke brings into sharper focus *Time*'s cover image. Just as interventionist strategies in Argentina were illustrated as a necessary extermination of a scourge of phantasmatic fascism, Hicks Anderson's racially caricatured speech and the article's deployment of gender–as–punch line similarly rationalized the violent temporalities that would privilege to sovereignty over liberty within a prosecutorial logic.

When, on December 12, 1945, *The Afro-American* ran the front-page article "Night Life Queen Guilty of Perjury in Sex Case," it chronicled Hicks Anderson's first encounter with criminal proceedings as it invited its readership to participate in a theater of suspicion, visually reinforced by an accompanying illustration of a woman standing next to a sign that read, "Beware. Not what you think it is."[32] Facing perjury charges for signing her marriage application, Hicks Anderson and her weeklong trial in the Ventura County court were the primary foci of the D.C.-based black newspaper's two-page account. Beginning with the declaration that she had been "adjudged a man in the eyes of the law by a jury . . . and convicted on a charge of perjury," the article focused on the trial so as to also provide readers Hicks Anderson's defense. In response to the prosecutor's lines of questioning, for example, Hicks Anderson described her aesthetic sensibilities ("Asked if 'she' often wore a wig, Lucy said: 'If I think I look better with a wig, I do'"), her past romantic relationships ("When asked if Hicks [Hicks Anderson's first husband] were a man, Lucy replied: 'Well, he's supposed to be'"), and her understanding of her body ("Asked what part of 'her' body 'she' considered feminine, 'she' said: 'For one thing, my chest,' which she bared forthwith to the jury, revealing a very masculine chest").[33] Hicks Anderson's reported testimony underscores how black trans life was subjugated but not completely subjectified by criminal and carceral logics. The inclusion of Hicks Anderson's courtroom testimony did more than provide "color" to the article's prose, as her interjections, which also pivoted on humor sometimes, identified and intervened in the flow of the normative discourses that placed her on trial. To view Hicks Anderson's responses as instances of counterpower requires acknowledging the discursive contradictions that shape "how the world moves" and therefore as illustrations of the ways norms and normativity function as capillaries of power that can sometimes be obstructed.

The *Afro-American* article also mentioned the inclusion of five doctors' testimonies, all attesting that Hicks Anderson "was definitely a man."[34] It was a statement that, in the arc of the narrative of the trial, was meant to show an overwhelming preponderance of evidence against her claim to womanhood but that simultaneously revealed a concern and consequent overcompensation for the role of medical expertise in legal proceedings. In response to the prosecutorial strategy, her defense attorney offered the theory that Hicks Anderson had "hidden organs," which would not be discoverable "until an autopsy [could be made] after her death."[35] In exchange for an unincarcerated life, Hick Anderson's "hidden organs" defense offered up her corpse to be put to indefinite institutional use, indexing the medical industry's sustained practice of experimentation on black bodies in the United States, as I have discussed in chapter 1.[36] Though Hicks Anderson's defense comprised a critique of medical wisdom as a science of the surface, it also highlighted how black flesh had long been central to medical professional knowledge.

The "hidden organs" argument was also a plea for time, and at face value it seemed to cast time as a linear process, which would enable Hicks Anderson to live (freely) before pursuing the question of her gender, as a matter of biology. Yet, as a proposal, it also positioned the act of postmortem medical discovery in ways that disrupted normative temporalities, indexing a rupture that brought the medical industry's "past" into its future. In Deleuzian terms, Hicks Anderson's "hidden organs" might be understood as constituting a "field of experience beyond (or, rather, beneath) the constituted reality."[37] As "virtualities," which Gilles Deleuze defines as matters of perception, positioned alongside the "reality" of her body, and as a discursive imprint made by the sedimentation of perception over time, her "hidden organs" carried a supposition for an approach to history focused on matters of becoming, which is to say that her imperceptible organs provided a counternarrative for a body that had yet to appear. In this sense, Hicks Anderson's "hidden organs" are both a shadow and a foreshadow of transsexual corporeality, as her first trial's defense staged the difficulties in assessing the "truth" of trans bodies in anatomical terms as well as the potential for transsexuality to emerge as a matter of medical invention.

The final installation of coverage on Hicks Anderson in the *Afro-American,* "Allotment for 'Wife' Fatal," focused on Sgt. Reuben Anderson's federal trial on April 20, 1946. Anderson was facing "a maximum of ten years in a Federal prison and top fine of $10,000 not because he married another man—but because he had the Government send his male wife $950 in allotment checks."[38] Similarly focused on the prosecutorial and defense strategies exhibited on trial, but written after Hicks Anderson was convicted and sentenced for perjury at the federal level, the article reported that she took the stand by way of a writ of habeas corpus that brought her east to testify at her husband's trial. She was "lodged in the men's section of the Federal House of Detention, but has been wearing women's clothes because, prison officials say, he has no others."[39] In contrast to the repartee that figured prominently in the *Afro-American*'s reportage of the Ventura County courtroom scene, this article depicted Hicks Anderson as a recalcitrant witness: "Lucy refused to answer the question: 'Do you have male sex organs?' The question [was] rephrased in several ways but Lucy Hicks steadfastly refused to reply."[40] Hicks Anderson's refusal, her unwillingness to cooperate with or to corroborate prosecutorial logics, represents another deployment of the polyvalence of shadows, namely, that sometimes—on those occasions when "sovereignty is more precious than liberty"—silence becomes countermythological.

"Black People Die Differently": Georgia Black and Value's Sleight of Hand

Blurbed on the issue's cover, just above a photo of boxer Ezzard Charles and his wife, Gladys, *Ebony*'s feature "The Man Who Lived 30 Years as a Woman," first published in October 1951 and republished in *Ebony*'s thirtieth-anniversary edition, in November 1975 (and reprised in *Jet* in 1989), was the first of a series of media stories focused on trans concerns to appear in Johnson Publishing Company's imprints, *Ebony* and *Jet*. Typically advertised in the top right-hand corner, *Ebony* covered a number of stories of intramural black life throughout the 1950s, including "exposés" on nudism and dwarfism, as well as reports of racial and gender "passing." *Ebony*'s feature on Georgia Black exhibited many of the conventions of the exposé, although it is not particularly clear what exactly was being uncovered. Even as the headline suggested its subject matter, the article, in its treatment of how Black *lived*, embedded a counterimpulse within its sensationalizing prose such that, "despite all the evidence, official statements and pictures" that figured Black as "one of the most incredible stories in the history of sexual abnormalities," *Ebony* reporters could not help but tell how she was beloved by various and disparate communities in Sanford, Florida.[41] Reporting that when she died, in June 1951, "lining the sidewalks of the Dixie town that once barred Jackie Robinson from its stadium, Negro and white mourners rubbed elbows, bowed heads and shed genuine tears." This was a remarkable gesture of desegregation occasioned by a person who, the feature describes in its opening line, "[b]y every law of society . . . should have died in disgrace and humiliation and been remembered as a sex pervert, a 'fairy' and a 'freak.'"[42]

On September 8, 1951, a few weeks before *Ebony*'s feature on Black hit newsstands, representatives of forty-eight nations signed the Treaty of San Francisco, marking the official end of World War II. Japan and the United States also signed the Security Treaty on the same day, allowing the United States to establish its first military base in East Asia, operating on Japanese soil. Even as the American government extended its military presence and reach in Asia, under the banner of protecting and maintaining freedom and democracy throughout the world, with equal fervor it protected and maintained racist repressive regimes within its national borders. *Ebony*'s feature reflected that seeming contradiction in global American policy, which was not a contradiction at all but rather a paradox that conveyed shifting conceptions of value. As the late cultural theorist Lindon Barrett explained, "Value denotes domination and endurance in a space of multiplicity. Its presence and performance entail the altering, resituating, and refiguring of the Other, or many Others, in margins, in recesses—indeed, paradoxically, outside a self-presence (defined by a fetishized boundary) that nonetheless aspires to be everywhere."[43] Barrett's description of value and its denotations also pronounced the values of the United States as an imperial nation-state, embroiled in the Korean War, a bloody declaration of the country's militaristic investment in opposing communism wherever it seemed to be advancing around the world.[44]

In relation to violence and volatility domestically and abroad, Georgia Black's story was, according to *Ebony*'s reporters, a "bizarre and moving drama which had its finale in a simple grave at Sanford's Burton Cemetery."[45] In an effort to portray how humanness, as a contested and exclusionary praxis, was conferred through the rites and rituals of death, the article exposed value's denotations, which are transitively expressed in Karla F. C. Holloway's description of shadows as "penumbral and exquisite" in reference to those things that are "promised beyond [their] situation."[46] Black's narrative obstructed the dominant valuation of black life as an extractable calculation of black death. Describing Black as a mother, a widow, a church leader, and a domestic worker, *Ebony*'s story began by explaining that it was only after she died that her story could be told in full, rendering "Georgia Black's incredible history" from the perspectives of "Negro and white physicians who had examined Black, . . . neighbors of both races, and [as] heard from Black's own lips a death bed recital."[47] The timing of the article was a consequence of various actors—her pastor, employers, family, and friends—who blocked sensational media coverage of her life as she was dying.

The article's accompanying images of Black visually explore the imbrications of black life and death. Taking up more than half of the first page, the lead photograph did not clearly announce itself as occurring before or after Black's death. The caption clarified some but not all of the temporal ambiguity: "On death bed, Georgia Black smells fragrance of rose from bouquet brought by neighbor during fatal illness. Man who lived as a woman for 30 years had funeral cortege of more than 30 cars, was buried in woman's clothes. Death certificate had no stipulation of sex. Georgia Black was leader of Women's Missionary Society."[48] The series of photographs that accompanied Black's feature also alerts readers to the position she held in Sanford, Florida, as seen in the lead caption's inclusion of details about her funeral cortege, burial garments, and position in the church. The lack of stipulation on Black's death certificate might further indicate the degree to which she experienced an unexpected (at least to the *Ebony* journalist[s]) relation to power. In its content and by the conventions of photojournalism, the lead photograph would be regarded as an example of the genre of the "about-to-die image," which, as Barbie Zelizer explains, contravenes typical conventions of photojournalism, as an expression of documentary realism, to convey "the subjunctive voice of the visual."[49] In other words, photojournalistic images of the dying, whether in media stories about ecological disasters, the terminally ill, or captures of the ravages of war, produce a different kind of relationship between that which is being mediated and its viewer, as each portrayal invites spectators to extend their imaginative capacities, consequentially creating speculative relations between life and death, the living and the dead.[50] It should be noted, as Susan Sontag has written, that photojournalism in the United States came "into its own in the early 1940s—wartime."[51] Rationalizing the U.S. and allied forces' military activity in World War II, photojournalism, in its depiction of wartime deaths, emerged through an articulation of its contradiction: the subjunctive and the objective. Yet Black's image must have also reminded *Ebony*'s readers of the long history of representations of black death around the world, mediations that conveyed, as Rinaldo Walcott has argued, how "the historical relations that produced black peoples are the same relations that produce their deaths" and how "black death is constantly framing black peoples' everyday livability."[52]

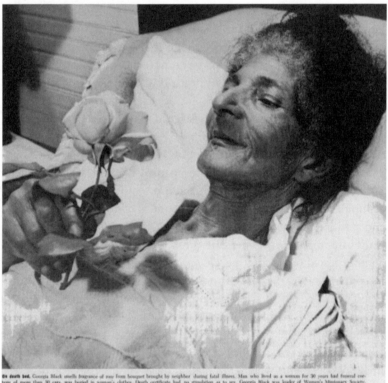

On death bed, Georgia Black smells fragrance of rose from bouquet brought by neighbor during fatal illness. Man who lived as a woman for 30 years had funeral cortege of more than 30 cars, was buried in woman's clothes. Death certificate had no stipulation as to sex. Georgia Black was leader of Women's Missionary Society.

The lead photograph of Georgia Black, the composition of which heightens the visual ambiguity of the subject's status as alive or dead. As the feature notes, when the local daily newspaper carried a front-page story on Black's gender "reveal," "Pastor James Murray of the Trinity Methodist Church phoned the Herald editor, protesting. . . . The editor apologized and forthwith ended local publicity on the case." This detail in reporting might also relate to why *Ebony* published Black's story after her death, which also distinguishes Black from her contemporaries.

As Rinaldo Walcott maintains, in an analysis of black life and death as it was forged through the violence of the transatlantic slave trade and as it was instrumentalized in the formation and maintenance of the ordering logics of the New World, "If modern blackness is thus founded in death, it is not so as a coming to terms with what it means to be human or even with a desire for freedom from human worldliness, but rather comes into being through an inability to lay its dead to rest in the throes of unfreedom."[53] The various forms of unfreedom that would give shape

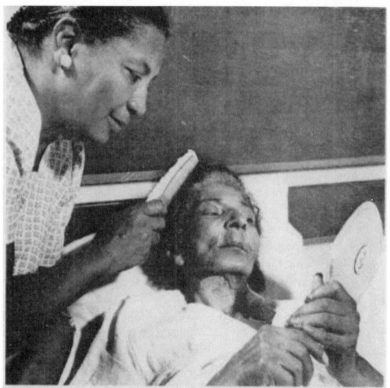

Combing Georgia Black's hair, Lugenia Black, sister of one of homosexual's late husbands, demonstrates that revelation of Black's true sex made no difference to her. Rumor in town is that Hollywood is thinking of movie about Georgia.

Alongside photographs of other residents of Sanford, Florida, that were taken at the time of reporting, this image of Black, pictured with her sister-in-law Lugenia, brings into sharper focus an ethics of care that arose around Black's imminent death. *Ebony*, October 1951.

to Black's life and black life engendered a reading of the images of her dying among *Ebony*'s readership as a remediation of the question of freedom as a concept forged through burial rites. Another image of Black included with the story (pictured with her sister-in-law Lugenia) was poised to address what Christina Sharpe frames as the urgent question of "What does it look like, entail, and mean to attend to, care for, comfort, and defend those already dead, those dying, and those living lives consigned to the possibility of always-imminent death, life lived in the presence of death; to live this imminence and immanence as and in the 'wake'?"[54]

Even as the article suggested that it was recounting Black's history, it was also showing, by way of the relations promoted in the inclusion of "about-to-die" imagery, routes to new forms of black life in an imagined not too distant future, in which the virulence of Jim Crow might be dampened and black life might be identified and valued, even if through the pathway of black dying and death. As the feature suggested in its opening line, the question of Black's gender identity pivoted not on the issue of her "true sex" but on the fact that she was somehow valorized, valued by black and white residents of Sanford, Florida, to the extent that they all came to mourn her death and, in so doing, made hers a "grievable life."[55] Perhaps more shocking than Black's story of gender transformation, Black's death did what for many black and blackened peoples felt unattainable; as Sharon Holland has discussed in her work on the constitutive role of death in the construction of black subjectivity, Black attained, "in the eyes of others, the status of the 'living.'"[56]

This is not to suggest that the images upended the textuality of "The Man Who Lived 30 Years as a Woman" or even that they significantly altered an understanding of the dimensions of the narrative, which represented Black as an agent of deceit, bringing to mind for some of its readers a relation, albeit on a different scale and register, between her story and contemporaneous media coverage of Soviet spies and accused communist sympathizers embedded in the federal government.[57] This is also not to imply that some readers did not think of Black as simply another figuration of passing, and therefore that she assumed an identity of a woman in order to attain greater life chances, such as financial security and increased mobility, that might have been denied to her if she were a gay man. This understanding of Black was certainly present, expressed in the "Letters to the Editor" section of *Ebony* even after its 1975 reprint.[58] Rather, the focus on the visual elements becomes a way to make sense of the article's conclusion, which, following Black's declaration of innocence ("I never done nuthin wrong in my life"), read, "People in Sanford, where Black lived and died, loved and was loved, agree."[59] As a reflection on value and its meanings, the feature's final lines subtend an alternative, although not wholly incompatible, hermeneutic for reading the article, in which value is conveyed not merely through the hegemonic ordering of the center and its margins but also in a poetics of relation that had the potential to disrupt that very paradigm.[60]

"Mimicry Is at Once Resemblance and Menace": On the Decolonial Temporalities of Carlett Brown and Ava Betty Brown

By the time the narratives of Carlett Brown and Ava Betty Brown emerged in the black press, Christine Jorgensen's story of gender transformation had already taken root in the public imagination. Both Browns were cast in a diminutive relation to Jorgensen, largely described as latecomers to a conversation already established. Their characterization as mimetic figures finds some explanation in Homi Bhabha's work on colonial mimicry and the desire "for a reformed, recognizable Other, *as a subject of a difference that is almost the same, but not quite.*"[61] For Bhabha, mimicry is constituted by ambivalence and contradiction: "[I]n order to be effective, mimicry must continually produce its slippage, its excess, its difference."[62] Mimicry, as it inflects and reflects colonial and imperial power, exhibits itself as a paradoxical formulation whereby on the one hand, it is required to confirm the official colonial, imperial discourse as superlative, and, on the other, it demonstrates, by revealing its constitutive disavowals, the violent ways such discourse is invested as and with colonial-imperial authority. As mimicry pertains to the stories of Carlett Brown and Ava Betty Brown, their media construction as Jorgensen's imitators illustrated, within a teleology of medicalized transsexuality, the impossibility of a "black Jorgensen" as they simultaneously exposed how anti-blackness has been a critical paradigm for making sense of Jorgensen's figuration.

Often footnoted in trans historiographical accounts as the first black American to plan a sex change, Carlett Brown began receiving episodic treatment in *Jet* magazine on June 18, 1953. Appearing in the "Mr. and Mrs." section of the magazine, which frequently featured the violent outcomes of relationships gone wrong, the first installment of *Jet's* coverage emerged under the headline "Male Shake Dancer Plans to Change Sex, Wed GI in Europe." Described as "a 26-year-old shake dancer and professional female impersonator," Brown "told *Jet* he has arranged with doctors in Bonn, Germany, for an operation that will make him female" before marrying U.S. Army sergeant Eugene Martin. "'We'll be married as soon as I am legally a woman,' said Brown."[63] Undoubtedly aware of how Jorgensen's story was playing out in the press at the time, Brown framed her decision to pursue sexual-reassignment surgery in response to a previously diagnosed intersex condition; *Jet* reported that one doctor "diagnosed his condition as due to the . . . existence . . . of female glands." Opposing the doctor's recommendation to remove the glands, Brown stated that she preferred to have her "male sex organs removed by surgery." After writing surgeons in Germany, Denmark, and Yugoslavia for assistance, Brown was told that that she must give up U.S. citizenship in order to undergo the procedure. Brown's response, according to *Jet*: "I'll become a citizen of any country where I can receive the treatment I need and be operated on."[64]

In a subsequent article, *Jet* reported that Brown had renounced her American citizenship at the Danish consulate in Boston, Massachusetts, in order to receive treatment from Dr. Christian Hamburger, the supervising physician for Jorgensen's procedure and chief hormone specialist at Riges Hospital in Copenhagen, Denmark. Brown announced plans to board the S.S. *Holland* on August 2, 1953, with a new passport that reflected her name change to Carlett Angianlee Brown, telling *Jet* reporters, "I regret leaving the United States, but after the Christine Jorgensen affair, the United States refuses to give an American citizen permission to alter his sex."[65] *Jet* would publish two additional stories on Brown in the coming weeks, the first reporting that Brown was "virtually destitute in Boston," unable to raise five dollars for bail when imprisoned for wearing "female garb" in public. The second, appearing on August 6, four days after her scheduled departure for sexual-reassignment surgery, explained that Brown had postponed plans to go to Denmark, opting

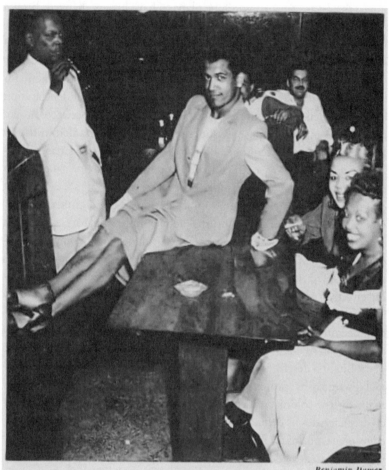

Benjamin Dames

▶ **Leg Technique:** Charles Brown, 26-year-old male shake dancer who plans to go to Germany for an operation which will make him a "woman," shows friends in a Boston night club "correct technique" for displaying legs. Later Brown, who had hair set before visiting club, was arrested for wearing women's clothes, fined $5.

This photograph was cropped for headshots that appeared in early articles on Carlett Brown in *Jet*. The full image appeared as part of a longer feature in *Jet* on April 15, 1954, under the headline "Are Homosexuals Becoming Respectable?"

instead to have facial-feminization surgery in the United States. According to the *Jet* article, "Although he plans to have his sex changed, Brown will keep his ties with female impersonators. Said he: 'I feel that impersonators are being denied their right of life, liberty and the pursuit of happiness when they are arrested for wearing female clothes—especially when they are minding their own business.'"[66] Brown's argument for the rights of female impersonators via the language of the Declaration of Independence pronounces an experiential distance between Brown and Jorgensen, her supposedly superlative double. As framed in the *Jet* article, Brown's comment here also reveals police harassment as a structuring condition that would continue to tether a future post-op Brown to those described as "female impersonators" and, in doing so, casts doubt on sexual-reassignment surgery's ability to transform her future encounters with the police. Brown and the "female impersonators" she names are figured as outside—in excess of—the "American womanhood" paradigm through which Jorgensen emerged. As cultural outsiders, they, as Roderick Ferguson notes, are made to "represent the socially disorganizing effects of capital, play[ing] a powerful part in past and contemporary interpretations of political economy."[67] In one sense, Brown's declaration becomes a portal for understanding the double-barreled feature of transsexuality's definitional authority.

Bhabha describes the effect of mimicry on "the authority of colonial discourse" as "profound and disturbing." As he writes, "[F]or in 'normalizing' the colonial state or subject, the dream of post-Enlightenment civility alienates its own language of liberty and produces another knowledge of its norms."[68] Brown's use of "life, liberty, and the pursuit of happiness" to articulate the forms of unfreedom experienced by "female impersonators" signals a rupture in Jorgensen's figuration, particularly as the Jorgensen story was instrumentalized into a narrative about personal triumph and individual freedom in the United States. Brown's mimetic difference, then, illustrates how, in matters of trans historiography, Jorgensen's spectacularized transsexual "freedom" was tethered to equally robust representations of racialized unfreedom, not only as they pertained to Brown and the vulnerabilities of "female impersonators" but also as they were playing out in imagistic expressions of the U.S.'s ever-expanding interventionist Cold War ideology and in the density of images of decolonial struggles around the world. As an exposure of the ways U.S. colonial-imperial authority is shored up by whiteness and a constitutive disavowal of the nation's foundational logic of white supremacy, Brown's expression gave discursive form to mimicry's disturbing relation to the language and logics of colonial-imperial authority, as it pointed to the constitutive shadow that obstructed the U.S.'s expressed commitment to democracy and freedom.

In the final installation of coverage, on October 15, 1953, *Jet* reported that Carlett Brown had postponed plans to go to Europe indefinitely, as she was ordered by the federal government not to leave the United States until after she paid $1,200 in owed income tax. Brown told *Jet* that she "took a $60-a-week temporary job as a cook at Iowa State College's Phi Kappa House" to begin repayment.[69] Never again to return to the surface of public discourse, and rendered stateless, like so many others figured as refugees during the postwar, Cold War period, Brown's figuration is an incomplete narrative—defined, as Bhabha has argued, by the colonial need to script its subjects as "partial," and as such to "represent [them] as the strategic limitation or prohibition within the authoritative discourse."[70] But Brown's "estrangements are not hers to own."[71] As Ferguson explains in his reading of the depiction of the drag queen prostitute in Marlon Riggs's *Tongues Untied*, "They are, in fact, the general estrangements of African American culture . . . [in] its distance from the ideals upheld by epistemology, nationalisms, and capital that culture activates forms of critique."[72] Brown's story is, for its readers, an exploration of the racial and gender magic that lies in the "heart of Manichean darkness," which is to say that it narrates the experience of being embedded in the contradictions of power that dictate "how the world moves" and that consequentially, through its movement, fixes certain objects in its path.

Carlett Brown's aside—"especially when they are minding their own business"—names the conditions that gave rise to Ava Betty Brown's representation, in April 1957. Described by the *Chicago Daily Defender* as "a Chicago version of the Christine Jorgensen story," Ava Betty Brown appeared in the local black press under the headline "'Double-Sexed' Defendant Makes No Hit with Jury," featured alongside a collection of news briefs, including an announcement of the start of Operation Plumbbob, the name given to the series of twenty-nine nuclear tests conducted by the U.S. military later that year. According to the article,

"Brown was arrested on March 14 . . . [while] standing on the corner of Oakley and Madison waiting" for her boyfriend. Though minding her own business, Brown was arrested for wearing women's clothes on Chicago's West Side that day, taken to a police precinct, and "undressed and found to be physically a man."[73] She was charged with female impersonation. Less than a month later, Ava Betty Brown testified in court that she was "double-sexed," announcing plans to go to Denmark for an operation to correct her condition. By this time, the Danish government had prohibited such plans; in January 1954, Danish parliament member Dr. Viggo Starcke told U.S. reporters, "Don't let the prospective Christines come to Copenhagen any longer."[74] Brown's defense attorney, George C. Adams, described Brown's arrest as unconstitutional, citing that it infringed on her rights as a private citizen and contending that the police were "picking" on her.

In excess of the logics of law and medicine for which she was made to account, Brown shared with the court the critical detail that her friends and business acquaintances all knew her as Ava Betty Brown, adding, "'Everything I own is in the name of Betty Brown. . . . If I am a man, I don't know it."[75] Here, in this rhetorical maneuver, which also invoked the previously circulating narratives of Hicks Anderson and Black, Brown offered an alternative set of relations—that of black sociality—as the site for her gender articulation, and, like Carlett Brown, she enunciated a mimetic difference from Jorgensen that simultaneously exposed the set of logics to which Jorgensen's figuration was made to confirm. In the provision of a description of life beyond the court and the clinic, Brown's declaration disturbed the contemporaneous common sense of transsexuality as a development narrative that put forth gender transformation as exclusively attainable by way of certain medical surgeries and legal recognition; instead, she provided an answer to a question Judith Butler later raised: "How can one refer to a given sex or gender without first inquiring how sex and/or gender is given [and] through what means?"[76] Thus, if Ava Betty Brown is Jorgensen's "partial" double, according to a colonial logic, then Brown's articulation here also points to how knowledge systems unrecognized by colonial authority have given rise to her mimetic form of being. Put differently, Brown's declaration—"If I am a man, I don't know it"—suggests a different, and perhaps decolonial, understanding of the body she inhabited.

Accompanying the *Chicago Daily Defender*'s 1957 article "Double-Sexed Defendant" is this photograph of Ava Betty Brown, taken at the courthouse. Reprinted with permission of the *Chicago Defender*.

As the initial article's headline suggested, the jury found Brown guilty of female impersonation, and she was fined one hundred dollars. The *Daily Defender* also reported her home address, a further intrusion on her privacy that Brown would note in the next and final installment of the *Defender's* coverage, more than twelve years later. On Monday, October 13, 1969, on the heels of the Stonewall Rebellion, an old publicity photograph of "A. B. Brown" appeared on the front page of the *Chicago Daily Defender* with the caption headline "Brutality 'Twist.'"[77] Now forty-four years old and a domestic worker, Ava Betty Brown resurfaced in the news for filing an official complaint with the Police Internal Inspections Division after being attacked by two Wabash District policemen three days earlier. According to the accompanying article, "'A patrol car containing two black officers passed by and then backed up,' Brown recalled. One officer, later identified as a Ptl. Hicks, reported[ly] called out, 'Come over here.' When Brown asked 'for what?' the officer allegedly retorted, 'Don't make me get out of the car. If you do it will be too bad.'" This was Brown's description of her second arrest that day, and she told *Daily Defender* staff writer Toni Anthony that her earlier protests of treatment while in lockup likely spurred the attack. Emblematic of the journalistic edict "two sides to every story," Anthony included the police's version of the event as well: "A Wabash District spokesman told Anthony that Brown's second tangle with the police was sparked because he struggled violently when Hicks and Hunter tried to arrest him." "'But since I abhor violence in any form, shape or fashion,' Brown responded, '(whenever I am arrested) I go meekly with the arresting officers. More times than not they are nasty and try to excite me to the point of saying something (obscene).'" She told Anthony that she had been "arrested and convicted several times on various vice raps," even after she was able to legally change her name, and that she still planned to obtain surgery.[78] More than fifteen years after Carlett Brown called for the right to life, liberty, and the pursuit of happiness for "female impersonators" in *Jet*, Ava Betty Brown was sharing her continuing struggles with the police, and, as in Carlett's case, surgery—and all the privileges it could but probably would not afford—was constructed as an indefinitely deferred proposition.

As mimetic narratives that expose more official histories of the United States, including the constitution and consolidation of a set of

Images accompanying the *Chicago Daily Defender*'s update article on Ava Betty Brown in October 1969. Reprinted with permission of the *Chicago Defender*.

discourses known as "transsexuality," the Browns—though both figured as "partial" (à la Bhabha)—reveal the mechanisms by which the nation and its histories constituted (and disavowed) the frailty of its own narratives (for example, with Jorgensen) in order to represent with authority a version of progress over time. In one sense, as Barrett related, the Browns' media narratives demonstrate how "as much as they are affirmative, value and authority are at every point oppressive, from absent or unknown vantages." From this point of view, "the negative, the expended, the excessive invariably form the ground of possibilities for value."[79] However, the Browns' stories also provide a glimpse into a decolonial temporality of transsexuality, one in which the press, the courts, the clinics, and the police could not lay claim to or make sense of their gender expressivities or the various contexts in which their black and trans lives were conferred and affirmed. Made to represent the impossibility of a "black Jorgensen" in the contemporaneous press, each Brown, in the "pleasure of her existence," articulated a "critique of commonplace interpretations of her life."[80] As Ferguson notes, "Doubtless, she knows that her living is not easy. But that's a long way from reducing the components of her identity to the conditions of her labor."[81]

"Still Restive": The Shadow Theater of McHarris/Grant

Emerging between the media narratives of Carlett and Ava Betty Brown, James McHarris / Annie Lee Grant splashed across the pages of *Ebony* and *Jet* in the summer and fall of 1954. According to Serlin, by the time articles about McHarris/Grant appeared, "the Christine Jorgensen phenomenon . . . had already peaked—and to a certain extent fizzled out."[82] On July 29, 1954, tucked away at the bottom of a page in the national news section, *Jet* began coverage of McHarris/Grant with a paragraph-length article under the headline "Mississippi Woman Poses as Man for 8 Years." According to the article, "When Kosciusko, Miss., police arrested husky James McHarris for driving a car with improper lights, they made an astonishing discovery: James McHarris was really 30-year-old Annie Lee Grant, a 175-pound woman who had been posing as a man for eight years, doing heavy-duty male work as a garage mechanic. Explained Miss Grant: 'I posed as a man to earn more money.'"[83] Tacitly raising for *Jet*'s readership a feminist labor concern about how gender unequally structures pay, McHarris/Grant's explanation, which reads more as a defense, confirms the conventional logic of passing as a performance of false identity. The context of the "astonishing discovery" here is the scene of an arrest for a traffic violation—an instance of "driving while black"—and, as an added irony, the article includes details about McHarris/Grant's "heavy-duty male work as a garage mechanic." *Jet*'s initial foray differed from *Ebony*'s more detailed account in terms of temporality, scope, and rationale for McHarris/Grant's gender permutations. In November of the same year, *Ebony* printed a five-page feature, replete with images of McHarris/Grant, under the headline "The Woman Who Lived as a Man for 15 Years." The contrast between the uses of "poses," as an affected assumption of manhood, in *Jet*'s headline, and "lived," as an index of gender as a context for inhabitation, in *Ebony*'s, illustrates key differences in coverage across Johnson Publishing Company's imprints. The discrepancy in the articles' number of years may have been a function of more careful research on the part of the *Ebony* reporters. It is also plausible, however, that McHarris/Grant provided different information to various reporters—a conjecture that also dovetails with other techniques McHarris/Grant used to avoid being pinned down.

The *Ebony* feature began with an explication of the scene of McHarris/Grant's capture: "Into the small, bare office of the mayor of Kosciusko, Mississippi, a policeman walked with a husky prisoner." According to the article, the police agent told mayor and city court judge T. V. Rone, "When I tried to search him, he protested and told me: 'Take it easy, I'm a woman.'" Within the confines of the mayor's office, which also served as the courtroom, McHarris/Grant went into a closet, emerging some minutes later having discarded a "shirt, pants and male underwear."[84] Convicted—it is unclear from the articles whether the charges were traffic- or gender-related—and sentenced to thirty days in jail or a fine of one hundred dollars, McHarris/Grant left the courthouse with the intention of serving the time. With numerous editorial flourishes, *Ebony* represented for its audiences how "the domain of gender" is, as Eric Stanley describes, one of "the most volatile points of contact between state violence and [a] body."[85] The interplay of race and gender here, in which a racially motivated form of police surveillance gave way to a gender-related court conviction, produced a tripartite formulation, as jail time was but one of McHarris/Grant's modes of disciplining.

Annie Lee Grant, alias Jim McHarris, lights cigarette in typical masculine gesture on front porch of house where she lived as a man in Kosciusko. Says she: "I've posed as a man, off and on, most of my life."

Published on the first page of *Ebony*'s feature, McHarris/ Grant is pictured with the quotation "I've posed as a man, off and on, most of my life." *Ebony*, November 1954.

Following Rone's decision, "word of the sensational unmasking of Jim McHarris quickly got around Kosciusko" and, according to the article, "jarred the quiet small town."[86] In addition to producing McHarris/Grant's gender as spectacle, McHarris/Grant was sent to the men's prison facility, in which McHarris/Grant was "treated as a woman."[87] Sarah Haley's analysis of "carceral gendering" is instructive here, revealing, as she argues, "that gendered knowledge is produced not merely through male/female binaries but through a complex of material and discursive knowledge projects" in which "normative female gendering was produced through the spectacular cultural and legal production of the black female invert."[88] In this sense, one should understand how Mississippi's penal system was particularly equipped to "make sense" of McHarris/Grant's gender according to a "neither/nor" logic, which is to say that McHarris/Grant's legal assessment and carceral treatment were part of a longer history of gendered racial terror, knowledge, and discipline.[89]

To the right of *Ebony*'s opening scene, occupying more than half of the page, was a full-body photograph of McHarris/Grant with the accompanying caption "Annie Lee Grant, alias Jim McHarris, lights cigarette in typical masculine gesture, on front porch of the house where she lived as a man in Kosciusko. Says she: 'I've posed as a man, off and on, most of my life.'"[90] The use of "alias"—ordinarily referring to people who assume a different name to engage in criminalized activities but also harking back to the various names people employed to escape enslavers before the ratification of the Thirteenth Amendment in the United States—amplified the tone of the feature's opening, in which McHarris/Grant is also described, presentencing, as a "prisoner." Yet the use of "alias" also rhetorically figures McHarris/Grant's gender—the moving "off and on" between man and woman—in a manner that the article would later describe as "restive," using a paradoxical word that means to be both obstinately motionless and willfully unable to be still.

The story of how Annie Lee Grant became known as James McHarris, particularly because McHarris/Grant was raised only seventy-eight miles away from Kosciusko, in the town of Meridian, Mississippi, loomed as one of the major questions for the article to address. As a form of visual "proof," *Ebony* included an image of McHarris/Grant, on the top of the second page of the feature, in a moment of partial undress; the caption read, "Displaying bust compressor, a homemade band of white

Working at gas station, Annie Lee lubricates a customer's car. Husky woman, who stands 5-foot-5 and weighs 175 pounds, worked at a Kosciusko gas station for almost three months. At time of exposure, she was working as a short-order cook.

Working on prison farm, Annie Lee swings milk buckets as she leaves barn and heads for kitchen where she was head cook. On prison farm, Annie Lee wore men's clothes, but was treated as woman. Farm head said she was a "hard worker."

Part of a couplet of pictorial illustrations of McHarris/Grant's labor, the lower image portrays McHarris/Grant at work on the prison farm. *Ebony*, November 1954.

cloth, Annie Lee reveals gimmick which helped her to fool thousands." As textual evidence, the article "explained" that before taking residence in Kosciusko, McHarris/Grant lived and worked in Memphis, Chicago, and other midwestern cities, where "she threw herself wholeheartedly into the male masquerade, seeking the hardest jobs," including as a cook, a taxi driver, a gas station attendant, and a preacher.[91] Although McHarris/Grant's movement from city to city was put forward as a context for McHarris/Grant to practice and "perfect" life as a man, the movement itself was also explained as the outcome of McHarris/Grant's "talent for avoiding situations which would have revealed her true sex," such as by "quit[ting] jobs whenever medical examinations were scheduled."[92]

In an anecdote meant to dramatize the distance between McHarris/Grant's adolescent presentation and appearance as an adult, *Ebony*

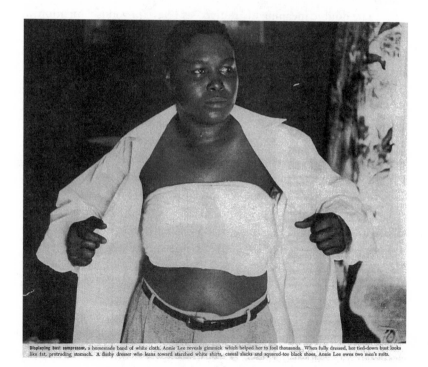

Displaying bust compressor, a homemade band of white cloth, Annie Lee reveals gimmick which helped her to fool thousands. When fully dressed, her tied-down bust looks like fat, protruding stomach. A flashy dresser who leans toward starched white shirts, casual slacks and squared-toe black shoes, Annie Lee owns two men's suits.

Described in the caption as the revelation of a "gimmick," McHarris/Grant shows bound chest in a gesture that mimics the details of the proceedings of the trial. *Ebony*, November 1954.

opined, "But Annie Lee was still restive. Though an attractive youngster with long pretty hair, she was happier wearing overalls. . . . [According to Bishop Jones, who is described as a childhood friend of McHarris/Grant,] 'But something . . . happened to her long before she started wearing men's clothing only.'"[93] Invoking sexual violence as a possible catalyst for McHarris/Grant's "change," the article's use of "still restive," presumably deployed as a disparaging characterization of McHarris/Grant's gender comportment, opens onto a schema for understanding how McHarris/Grant's various movements and gendered ways of being were negotiation points in what Spillers describes as a "space for living."[94] As counterpolitical gestures, they form an alternative assemblage of evidence—not of teleological gender transformation but of the possible positions one can occupy within contradictory, itinerant circuits of power.

The double meaning of "restive," as I have previously mentioned, in one sense describes the adverse behavior of the discontented, an inability to remain still, silent or submissive, and in another characterizes a person "stubbornly refusing to advance . . . intractable, refractory . . . fixed in an opinion or course of action"; both refer, whether by fixedness or by movement, to a person intent on resisting control.[95] The term's multiple meanings also give context for McHarris/Grant's impermanent gender identifications, providing a more precise alternative to passing's narration to suppose how a figure may inhabit various gender positions with a sense of sincerity and intransience until otherwise moved. Here, gender restivity names again the transitive and transversal relations between fungibility and fugitivity expressed in fugitive slave narratives, discussed in chapter 2, as McHarris/Grant finds space for maneuvering in and through gender in the afterlives of slavery. This sense of "restive" also becomes a way to read the article's accompanying images differently, that is, to read them less in terms of Ebony's curation of photographic evidence in support of an argument about McHarris/Grant's deceitfulness and more in terms of how the imaged figure returns the viewer's gaze.

As the image that accompanied the article's shift in focus to townspeople's reactions to the news of Jim McHarris's other life/lives, Ebony included a shot of McHarris/Grant posed in a dress. The caption read, "Dressed as a woman, Annie Lee assumes a hand-in-hand feminine pose. Annie Lee, who does not own any women's clothes, borrowed dress, hat

Dressed as a woman, Annie Lee assumes a hand-in-hand feminine pose. Annie Lee, who does not own any women's clothes, borrowed dress, hat for pictures, urged photographer: "Hurry up, man, so I can get out of this stuff. This is a drag!"

Posed in borrowed clothes, McHarris/Grant is quoted as describing the experience as a "drag." *Ebony,* November 1954.

for pictures, urged photographer: 'Hurry up, man, so I can get out of this stuff. This is a drag!'"⁹⁶ The caption's emphasis on McHarris/Grant's lack of preparedness for the photo, in conjunction with the inclusion of the quotation "This is a drag!," reveals the transitivity of McHarris/Grant's representation of a collapsed and naturalized coupling of femmeness and femaleness, in ways that remediate theories of gender as drag (à la Butler) with what Elizabeth Freeman terms "temporal drag," as the "counter-genealogical practice of archiving culture's throwaway objects" that "gestures toward the past's unrealized futures."⁹⁷ As a restive performance, the hurried photograph that is meant to confirm McHarris/Grant's gender as a woman and that is staged entirely through acquired props offers an understanding of gender's multiple, that is, restive temporalities, in which "drag" might function at once as a fugitive impulse to move around or to reflect a common social-movement strategy of "sitting in" or standing still. Here, McHarris is not Grant's future, nor is McHarris Grant's past, but rather McHarris/Grant's restive gender appears as a matter of bursts and lags in and on time, which is to say, McHarris/Grant's gender took shape in response to what Ellison's narrator described as the "boomerang" of History.

The feature's closing vignette staged the final exchange between McHarris/Grant and the prison superintendent at the moment of McHarris/Grant's release: "Bidding her goodbye Superintendent Eakin advised: 'Girl, you get you a dress now and the things a woman oughta do!'" In response, McHarris/Grant was quoted as saying simply, "I don't see it like that." *Ebony*'s story, bookended by scenes of McHarris/Grant's capture and release, ultimately concluded in the way it began: "At 30, after a lifetime of heartbreaks and deception, Annie Lee made an incredible decision: she decided to remain a 'man,' though exposed and publicized as a woman . . . determined to hold onto the strands of a way of life which makes her happy."⁹⁸ In other words, McHarris/Grant remained restive.

Inhuming a Body: Blackness and Trans Historiography

Situating Jorgensen's silhouette alongside a series of media narratives that were overshadowed by her celebrity contemporaneously in the press is at once a willful rereading of Jorgensen in relation to blackness and an attempt to think otherwise about the fact(s) of transsexuality that

Jorgensen's figuration was made to consolidate in matters of trans historiography. There is a growing consensus in transgender studies that trans embodiment is not exclusively, or even primarily, a matter of the materiality of the body. Where one locates a "transsexual real," whether phenomenologically, in the practices (social, medical, legal, and so on) of transition, in narrative, via the cinematic, or even in the unspeakable and unrepresentable aspects of imaging transness, shifts in relation to racial blackness.[99] In apposition with transness, blackness, as, among other things, the capacity to produce distinction, has come to structure modes of valuation through various forms, producing shadows that precede their constituting subjects/objects to give meaning to how gender is conceptualized, traversed, and lived. As the media narratives of Hicks Anderson, Black, the Browns, and McHarris/Grant shed light on the negativity of value, exposing how the notion is produced in an alchemy of black criminalization, violence, disappearance, and death, they also illustrate—albeit circumscribed in their partiality—other ways to be trans, in which gender becomes a terrain to make space for living, a set of maneuvers with which blacks in the New World had much practice.

5

DEVINE'S CUT
PUBLIC MEMORY AND THE
POLITICS OF MARTYRDOM

The nagging question of blood hounds me.
How do I honor it?

— ESSEX HEMPHILL, "The Father, Son, and Unholy Ghosts"

IN AN ENVIRONMENT SATURATED with images of black and trans death, it feels unnecessary to review the details of how Brandon Teena, Lisa Lambert, and Phillip DeVine were killed at the hands of John Lotter and Marvin Thomas Nissen in Lambert's farmhouse in Humboldt, Nebraska, on New Year's Eve 1993. Most readers are no doubt familiar with the killings through some encounter with their mediations: in international news coverage, as the subject of Aphrodite Jones's work of creative nonfiction *All S/he Wanted: The True Story of "Brandon Teena"* (1996), or as they appeared in filmic treatments, most notably in Susan Muska and Gréta Ólafsdottir's documentary *The Brandon Teena Story* (1998) and Kimberly Peirce's full-length feature *Boys Don't Cry* (1999).[1] These constitute a few of the major touchstones in what J. Jack Halberstam has described as the "Brandon archive," referring to a repository of materials that assemble "a resource, a productive narrative, a set of representations, a history, a memorial, and a time capsule."[2] One could infer by its name—the Brandon archive—how such materials have been laboriously organized to produce meaning about a particular life.

Put in filmic terms, as its cinematic iterations convey to supreme effect, the Brandon archive has been edited to produce Brandon Teena as a kind of secular martyr, his death consecrated by way of a particular iteration of queer and transgender politics. Referring to the ethical and aesthetic implications of DeVine's erasure from the feature film, Jennifer Devere Brody explains that "*Boys Don't Cry* is emblematic of the way in which the radical erasure of blackness makes queer stories queerer."[3] The absence of DeVine from Peirce's feature is so complete that, as Shana Agid notes in the longer description of his screen-printed poster "The Disappearance of Phillip DeVine," DeVine's name is not even included in the memorial text at the end of *Boys Don't Cry*, precipitating a question for the artist: "[W]hat sacrifices are made to construct lesbian, gay, bisexual, and transgender stories for mass consumption?"[4] Agid's concern for how the machinations of capitalism attenuate the narrative of the Humboldt killings subtends my broader interest in the nature of archives as repositories of value, in which one might read a double meaning of negativity as a resource in the creation of value and in the production of space in the cinematic and the televisual.

Highlighted in the *20/20* segment "The Truth behind *Boys Don't Cry*," their deaths were told in a narrative that hinged upon questions about what kinds of difference were permissible in rural Nebraska: "In this conservative community, they were three misfits: Lisa, a single mom, Phillip, a black man in a nearly all white town, and Brandon, even more of an outcast."[5] While noting DeVine's racial difference, this brief description fails to include that Phillip was also an amputee, an omission of a personal detail that animated the logics of the killings. The use of "conservative" to frame various forms of disparagement and violence in individualistic, stratified terms—apparently measured on a scale of inarticulability—underscores what Halberstam has argued about Brandon Teena's posthumous liberal subjectification, a process that, beginning at the moment of his death, constructed his life as a "true tragedy and an indictment of backward, rural communities."[6] Even as Christine Jorgensen had captured the public imagination approximately forty years earlier, news outlets spectacularly represented Brandon Teena as America's *first* glimpse into the world of transgender people. In a retrospective on the killings ten years later, the *Lincoln Journal Star* provided a summation that typified media coverage, asking, "Was Brandon killed

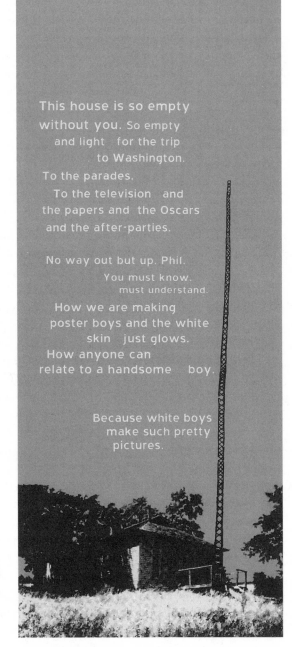

This house is so empty
without you. So empty
    and light   for the trip
            to Washington.
To the parades.
    To the television   and
the papers and the Oscars
and the after-parties.

No way out but up. Phil.
            You must know.
                must understand.
How we are making
poster boys and the white
        skin   just glows.
How anyone can
relate to a handsome   boy.

        Because white boys
        make such pretty
        pictures.

"The Disappearance
of Phillip DeVine."
Courtesy of
Shana Agid.

for dressing like a man? . . . [T]he question remains unanswered, but one fact has become certain: Brandon's death gave rise to a first-ever national transgendered movement."[7] In addition to the article's mendacious claim—one could point to any number of prior events, including the Compton Cafeteria riot (1966) and the Stonewall rebellion (1969), as examples of actions (led by black and brown trans people)—its designation of "first-ever" illustrates how news coverage of Brandon Teena's death is symptomatic, referring in Marxist and psychoanalytic terms to a kind of hermeneutical sleight of hand, in which a narrative, formally and as a vehicle of ideology, accrues its meaning by constructing other forms of knowledge as unthought.[8]

In an explanation that casts DeVine as a casualty of a more concentrated aggression aimed at Brandon Teena, DeVine's death is figured as an instance of "wrong place, wrong time." Ungeographical and untimely, DeVine appears within a rhetorical maneuver that situates his existence in the Brandon archive by evacuating DeVine's constitutive presence to and place within the archive's construction. The passage of the Hate Crimes Sentencing Enhancement Act (HCSEA) in 1994 ensured that Brandon Teena's death and the public memory of the Humboldt killings would accrue much of their political meaning in relation to criminal law, with several queer and trans groups seizing upon spectacularized mediations of Brandon Teena's death to discuss the merits of hate-crimes legislation. HCSEA and its predecessor the Hate Crimes Statistics Act, signed into law by George W. Bush in 1990, politicized Brandon Teena's death through the logic of visibility and inclusion, whereby his interred body could be symbolically reanimated and restored through the pageantry of the criminal court procedure and spectacularized punishment.[9] In this sense, HCSEA could be read as another symptom, in which a narrative of "expanded categories of protection" masks the links between criminalization, carcerality, and death that produce blackness and transness as objects of necropolitical valuation. Prosecutors in Nissen's trial, for example, disclosed the defendant's membership in the Ku Klux Klan as part of their case; even so, as Aphrodite Jones explains, "jurors believed that the killing of DeVine was just some weird coincidence. One African-American juror said Phillip was just a 'bonus' for Nissen, that DeVine's race didn't make a damn bit of difference."[10] It would seem that Jones's inclusion of the juror's race is meant to color a reception of the sentiment expressed, yet the comment also demonstrates the centrality and spec-trality of antiblackness in U.S. criminal law, as it invoked DeVine's death as a bonus—presumably "for the good" of white supremacy—while simultaneously figuring DeVine's blackness as inconsequential to the antiblack machinations (of racial capital, among other things) that would construct his death in terms of extractible value.

The ascription of DeVine's death as "wrong place, wrong time" is instructive for a reading of the symptomatically disavowed coarticu-lations of antiblack and antitrans violence, as it engenders a way to perceive how those mechanisms which contributed to Teena's symbolic significance to trans historiography simultaneously posited DeVine's fig-uration as always and already untimely, assigned to a conversation per-petually deferred. As David M. Jones has written, noting a few exceptions that "filmmakers and academics alike have hesitated to examine," Phil-lip DeVine's erasure from historical memory to "hegemonic whiteness" is responsible for shaping the construction of an assemblage of materials and narratological strategies that constitute the Brandon archive.[11] In queer and trans criticism, the Brandon archive has been fodder for numer-ous debates regarding the dynamics of rural queer life, the problems of writing transgender biography and historiography, the conventions of queer cinema, and the politics of transgender martyrdom.[12] Yet, as Jones relates, the "tragedy remains a missed opportunity" to examine the imbri-cations of antitrans and antiblack violence, alongside, among other things, "anti-queer and compulsory heterosexuality . . . hegemonic whiteness, social class, and masculinity from a rural Midwestern perspective."[13]

In prosecutor James Elworth's closing argument at the Nissen trial, his injunction to the jury included these words: "Consider Phillip DeVine. If you can imagine the terror of Phillip DeVine sitting in that room, this young amputee, sitting in that other room listenin[g] to two people die and knowing—he had to know—he—he was next." Here, one encounters an evocation and description of DeVine as a figure in *wait* of his ultimate and untimely demise, a condition which Fanon aptly defined as a consequence of colonial violence, wherein waiting is the resultant expression of a "history that others have compiled."[14] Within New World grammars, blackness was defined as somehow always out of time, out of place, wrong anyplace and anytime. As such, the "wrong place" also signifies upon the various ways blackness is figured by way of a "colonial fiction" that, as Katherine McKittrick has explained, renders black geographies "ostensible impossibilities."[15] "Wrong time," then, as it articulates a Fanonian formulation of blackness-as-waiting, also expresses what Hortense Spillers has referred to as the hegemony of "mythical time," under which "the human body becomes a defenseless target for rape and veneration . . . [rendered as] a resource for metaphor."[16]

The symptomatic disavowal of blackness and antiblackness in the Brandon archive traces back (and forward) at least as far as the moment when DeVine's dead body was apprehended in Lisa Lambert's home, illustrated in Lambert's mother, Anna Mae's, discussion of her discovery of the killings: "[At] first I think I denied there was anything wrong. I just seen this Negro sitting on the floor with a coffee table over his lap. And I thought, this is strange, but yet you know, I knew then there was something there wrong, but yet, I just kept telling myself there wasn't and I just walked right on through the house."[17] In her description, which reverberates across accounts in the Brandon archive and which attends not to whether DeVine was alive or dead but to his presence as "strange" and as an indication of something "wrong," DeVine—"this Negro"— becomes an evil omen. Here, Lambert's language configures DeVine as a "spooky black," or what David Marriott defines as a "blackness that haunts," whose "existence reveals a residue of the human that cannot be incorporated."[18] Other narratives linking blackness and death emerged simultaneously. In an instance of how the law functions by way of constitutive exemptions of black (and black trans) people from the state's political grammar of protection, DeVine's dead body was apprehended as a source of criminality in the moment the farmhouse became a crime scene. As Aphrodite Jones relates, when one of the first responders to Anna Mae Lambert's 911 call arrived on the scene, upon finding Phillip's body, the police officer "looked very carefully for a gun, thinking it could have been a murder/suicide."[19]

The title of this chapter, "DeVine's Cut," signals how its narration emulates the form of a "director's cut"—a rearrangement of materials previously constituted as *the* narrative. However, this chapter is not a plea to add DeVine as another martyr to the visual pantheon of black and trans figures who, by their exposure to "state-sanctioned or extralegal" modes of violence, have met premature death.[20] I am also not interested in representing DeVine's life by soliciting pathos or making recourse to sentimentality, which is to say that this is not another scene of sub-jection wherein violence becomes the naturalized way to subjectify DeVine, simultaneously offering up his death as a psychic place for those who are understood within other identificatory rubrics to imag-ine, through his dying, other modes of freedom and vitality.[21] Rather, this chapter enacts in language a pivotal transitivity of blackness and transness, as it takes expression in the form of a question about inven-tion. Constructing DeVine's life in the context of the Humboldt kill-ings, which are viewed as a necessarily unfinished geography of human praxis, this chapter, following Sylvia Wynter's work, asks, What aspects of DeVine's figuration, as a matter of sociogenesis, constitute a usable history for more livable black and trans lives?

The archive here, as in previous chapters, is both extensively doc-umented and underdeveloped for the questions I seek to address. To focus the discussion on DeVine requires nothing short of invention, which is to say that what follows is a narrative composed from fiction, as fiction, and as fiction as "facts." This chapter thus proceeds as a biomythogra-phy, an invention of the life of Phillip DeVine—who, like Audre Lorde, is figured as an outsider.[22] Their shared cohabitation of the liminal—or what Fanon described as "the Damned"—necessitates a reading of biomythography as a formal enactment of what Wynter has otherwise named the "sociogenic principle," a "science" aimed at studying "the rhetoricity of . . . human identity."[23] Wynter turns to this principle as a hermeneutical experiment purposed for the possible disarticulation of the governing codes that give rise to what it means to be human, or, as McKittrick has succinctly explained, toward the development of a "sci-ence" that "*feels and questions* the unsurvival of the condemned."[24]

The task of writing invention is beset with difficulties, surrounded and beseeched by failure, which is to say that a litany of failure some-times feels more readily accessible than a litany for survival. As Wynter has asked, how does one escape "the self-evidence of the order of con-sciousness that is everywhere the property of each culture's sociogenic principle, and of the mode of nature-culture symbiosis to which each principle gives rise?"[25] Put differently, how does one access a language outside of and in contradistinction to the governing codes that cur-rently determine human definition such that it gives rise to new mean-ings, forms of life, and genres of being? Moreover, as Marriott adds,

"[W]hat can this rhetoric do if the governing codes lie beyond history[?]," and "[O]n behalf of whom or what is the biological conception of the human no longer absolute?"[26] One might find answers to these questions in Lorde's *Zami: A New Spelling of My Name,* in its scripting of the "dreams/myths/histories" of black life in order to consider how blackness, as it has been given meaning by antiblackness, could acquire new spellings to engender itself (and queerness and transness) as symbolically and materially livable, which is perhaps what Lorde meant in the book's preface about "coming out blackened and whole."[27]

As Elizabeth Alexander has argued, Lorde's biomythography offers vast possibilities for rethinking "questions of identity" in its ability to formally dissemble identities' "static limitations."[28] Biomythography is both a genre of literature and an invitation to create different discursive structures for human identification, ones that contravene colonial modes of cataloging difference in favor of the possibility of engendering ways of life and genres of being based on the specificities of lived experience.[29] As Michael Benton has observed, "[B]iomythography dissolves the distinction between 'actual life' and 'posthumous life'" in a "process of gathering and organizing the scattered fragments of the past to meet the needs of the present." Biomythography, then, is a praxis of invention that erupts as a question about (past and present) temporalities in the register of the future imperfect, in which past and future give rise to a set of conditions and responses in the present, and which, as Marriott suggests, finds form in "a moment of inventiveness whose introduction necessarily never arrives and does not stop arriving, and whose destination cannot be foreseen, or anticipated, but only repeatedly traveled."[30] To presence DeVine—to invent his/a life—then, is to approach phenomenologically the interstitialities of black and trans life and black and trans death, particularly as they bear upon the current conjuncture of black trans life and spectacularized black trans death and their routes of public circulation in Transgender Days of Remembrance/Resistance and in the Trans Lives Matter (TLM) and Black Trans Lives Matter (BTLM) movements.

As sociogenesis involves an invention in language that figures language against itself, this chapter has infinite opportunities for misreading. Then again, this chapter is a misreading, or at least a misappropriation, of the genre of scholarly composition, as it performs a kind of writing that is typically regarded as a matter of fiction. Yet theory, at its best, is nothing more than "dreams/myths/histories" aimed at giving expression to ways of seeing and ways of being in the world. What follows, then, is a meditation on the porousness of a supposed distinction between anti-blackness and antitrans violence, or perhaps a consideration of the ways that antitrans violence is also and always already an articulation of anti-blackness. This chapter's focus on DeVine's life also opens onto another set of questions about sociogeny, as it relates to genres of being and matters of time, but also as it gives expression to forms of life. Against the biocentrism and linear temporality that constructs "life" in univer-sal terms, I explore in this chapter the question, How does one think about and express genres of life that are reiteratively, transitively, and transversally related to death?

Black study has provided numerous meditations on this point. The conditions of blackness and queerness have given names to modes of living that have been described as "social death," as "the social life of social death," or as "near life."[31] Christina Sharpe attends to "the wake" as a condition and location for thinking through the meanings of care and disaster as problems for thought in relation to black non/being.[32] In conversation with Agamben's notion of "bare life," Achille Mbembe describes "raw life" as "a place and time of half-death—or, if one prefers, half life . . . a place where life and death are so entangled that it is impos-sible to distinguish them, or to say what is on the side of the shadow or its obverse."[33] Alexander Weheliye works through the writings of Spill-ers and Wynter to add flesh to "bare life" and biopolitical discourse.[34] In all of these instances, life and death function as schemata for systems of social valuation. In addition, numerous black diasporic spiritual prac-tices are firmly rooted in a belief in the enmeshment of life and death, giving expression to a continuity of black sociality in the form of com-muning with the ancestors or in the afterlives. In what follows, my con-sideration is not concerned with producing a new philosophy of life so much as with naming a condition of possibility for black and trans life through sketching a temporality of emergence for DeVine in the Bran-don archive. Doing this, which is also an exercise in what Fanon described as "introducing invention into existence," is to contend with "still life" and the even-so and as-yet of living.[35]

Still Lives

Nine months prior to Phillip's birth, a one-minute seismic event shook communities near Sylmar, California, in the San Fernando Valley, claiming sixty-five lives, injuring more than two thousand people, and creating an estimated $505 million in property damage.[36] At the time, the DeVines—Paul Jr., Paul III, and Aisha (then named Phyllis) lived a thirty-minute drive away, in Pasadena. Phillip's paternal grandparents, Paul Sr. and Edith, lived on the other side of town. They would welcome Phillip as the newest addition to their family on October 8, 1971, two months before he was expected.

Accounts of Phillip DeVine often include some mention of his untimely birth, relating his mother's intake of diethylstilbestrol (DES), a "synthetic estrogen" marketed to reduce morning sickness, to his infant medical conditions and disabilities. The Food and Drug Administration, in response to research indicating higher correlations of vaginal and cervical cancer among adults prenatally exposed to DES, issued a bulletin a few weeks after Phillip's birth advising physicians to stop prescribing the drug to pregnant people.[37] In a twist of the biocentric knot, and in a proliferative gesture of Spillers's formulation of the "'female' within"— in this case, the mother being inside the son and, through her presence, the son becoming her daughter—the same drug that purportedly caused DeVine's disabilities would also become a biochemical explanation for trans and intersex existence, as medical researchers linked prenatal exposure to DES and other "endocrine disrupting chemicals" to "gender-related disorders."[38]

Mel Chen's work on animacies is instructive here, to explain how queer and trans forms of subjectivation are reanimated in a "womb," which is here constructed as an environment of toxicity.[39] Chen's argument also brings to mind Jared Sexton's discussion of the "black womb" as it has been constructed in contemporary pro-life rhetoric and in the co-articulation of Black Lives Matter (BLM) and reproductive-justice movements, wherein black wombs function as a rhetorical and material site for the production of an "unbearable blackness," by which "racial blackness reappears as an affected, fetal way of being alive, both unborn and undead"—perhaps one way to describe DeVine's presence within the Brandon archive.[40]

Phillip's mother described his condition at birth as "touch and go, touch and go." She related to Aphrodite Jones, "They wanted to put Phillip into an institution because they felt he would never be able to function. . . . His lungs were scarred like he had been smoking for fifty years, he had a tracheotomy, and he had a heart problem, so he was on digitalis."[41] Phillip would have two surgeries during infancy: one on his eyes, for congenital strabismus; and a removal of "two toes and part of a heel," in order to fit a prosthesis for his right leg.[42] Both surgeries were considered successful, and Phillip was eventually weaned off the digitalis and breathing implements, as they became unnecessary for regulating his life function.

Accounts such as the closing testimony at Nissen's trial referred to Phillip as an amputee, bringing to mind Fanon's discussion of the lived experience of the black as one of "amputation"—in which blackness is dis/figured as a "corporeal malediction" placed "by the other, the white man, who had woven [the black] out of a thousand details, anecdotes, stories."[43] Troping on the power dynamics that structure the hegemony of doctors over patients, Fanon formulates blackness as a symbolic amputation of being within antiblack rationality. In this formulation, which regards amputation as a form of loss, Fanon characterizes blackness-as-amputation as an uncauterized wound that signifies upon the violence of colonial fantasy. In other moments, Fanon categorically denies a relationship between blackness and disability, as if compulsory able-bodiedness is not also part of a colonial fantasy.[44]

Phillip's amputation of toes and a partial heel for the fitting of a prosthesis—an object typically defined as an artificial device for the replacement of a missing body part but that can also mean, as Uri McMillan notes, "a morphological surplus"—maps and allegorizes his life as both a cut and an excess in meaning.[45] Without further risk of rendering Phillip's blackness and disabilities in pure metaphor, let me flag how biomythography is not unlike a prosthesis, which is to say, it is a practice of symbolic surrogation, not as a supplemental thing but through supplementarity. Put differently, invention is not about completion; it does not perform or propose reconciliation.

According to Aphrodite Jones, caring for Phillip's infant medical conditions compelled Aisha, his mother, to explore transcendental meditation (TM), a consciousness-based education that offered a technique described by some of its practitioners as capable of "transforming lives through silence."[46] Aisha began commuting to attend meetings in Los Angeles and eventually became a TM teacher, opening a center in Pasadena, where she worked without pay. During a several-week trip to Ethiopia in association with her instruction, she chose her name Aisha, which in Arabic roughly translates to "She who lives." She wanted to change her sons' names as well, but didn't. Financial difficulties and divergent worldviews were cited when the DeVines decided to divorce. At the time, Phillip was a toddler.

Nikki Giovanni's poem "Nikki-Rosa" begins, "childhood remembrances are always a drag / if you're Black," which signals a few things as it relates to what directly follows here.[47] Recalling the preceding chapter's discussion of drag and the ways blackness remediates the supposed distinctions between gendered and temporal performativities in the case of McHarris/Grant, one should read Giovanni's stanzas as an opening salvo in a war on the racial politics of memory, which is to say that time, like money, is funny—eccentric even and not at all teleological in its circumnavigations within blackness.

With the encouragement of Phillip's paternal grandparents, Paul DeVine Jr. sued for permanent custody of his two sons. Edith and Paul Sr. viewed TM as a way for Aisha to avoid spending time with her children. Paul Sr. told Jones, "My own opinion is that Phyllis in a sense, rejected her son Phillip. . . . She would always take Paul [III] with her, but she wouldn't want this little handicapped boy with her." Aisha, however, described the current custody agreement as a way to secure a more financially stable life for her children: "I didn't have a refrigerator to keep my baby's milk cold. I'd go around to restaurants to get hot food because I was cooking on a hot plate, and Paul [Jr.] wasn't giving me any money. . . . So I thought, maybe he'll take care of his kids. I was living off AFDC [Aid to Families with Dependent Children], and I needed to be able to go out and find work. He was remarried at the time, he was stable, he had a big house, and I didn't have anything." It was only since the 1960s that federal aid to families with dependent children was available to people in need. Political organizing and legislation associated with Lyndon B. Johnson's War on Poverty made AFDC more accessible to black people, who previously had been structurally barred from participation.[48] On the heels of this policy shift came new regulatory measures touted as welfare reform, including the Work Incentive Program (WIN), enacted in 1967. By the early 1970s, welfare was a hot-button national issue. In the year of Phillip's birth, 1971, Congress passed WIN II, which strengthened sanctions against "nonworking" participants in AFDC, placing greater emphasis on immediate job placement.[49] Simultaneously, media coverage of poverty and AFDC overwhelmingly constructed welfare as a national problem associated with the black urban poor.[50]

Phillip and Paul III moved in with their father and stepmother, Henrietta, and spent every weekend with their paternal grandparents. They had little to no contact with their mother during this time. As a child, Phillip was encouraged by his grandparents to go outside and play: "We told him, 'You're no different from anyone else. You can ride a bike or do anything you want to do.' And he did all that." Playing was an instruction for Phillip on the capacities of his growing body, as the injunction to play is instructive to us for gleaning his family's views on his disabilities.

Recalling the way blackness has frequently been figured as an obstacle to "overcome" and the ways disability recurs in an examination of blackness and transness, Phillip's grandparents' encouragement to their grandson to "go play" also opens onto a discussion of assimilation and the various orders minoritized people are given to perform, as if they are no different from anyone else, which is to say, no different from white people. This, on the one hand, might be regarded as a "survival strategy," but, on the other hand, it maps the colonial promise of assimilation as the always deferred possibility that one might live into as a way to contend with one's current condition.

In 1984, after another divorce, Paul Jr. moved his sons across the country, to Maryland, to start over and to be close to their aunt, Denise. While in Maryland, Denise sent Paul III and Phillip to private schools and found tutors to work with Phillip on his learning disabilities. Phillip would thrive there; he would also fall in love.

At seventeen, Phillip and his girlfriend were expecting a baby and looking for an apartment, and Phillip was determined to support his new family on his McDonald's wages. In less than three years, their relationship dissolved, and Phillip resolved to do something new. He called his mom and decided to move to Iowa. By the time Phillip reconnected with his mother, she had remarried and relocated to Fairfield, Iowa, to be near the Maharishi University of Management, then named the Maharishi International University. Paul III had already spent a year with his mother there, but left because he felt ostracized and because he was experiencing some problems with his peer group because of his romantic interest in a young local white woman. Phillip, however, liked Fairfield. He started a job at the fast-food chain Hardee's and did self-directed studies on religion. Aisha told Jones, "Phillip got to know me. Phillip's joy was cooking, and he'd be at home in Fairfield, trying these recipes. He thought about becoming a chef and owning his own restaurant at one time. . . . He also used to study a lot about spiritual life; he wanted to study the Bible in its original text and the original of the Koran and meld the two. He wanted to show people that they worship the same God. They're just looking at different angles." Phillip developed a fascination with the Virgin Mary. He once told his mother he had seen an image of her in a tree outside their house in Fairfield, and for his twenty-second birthday, in 1993, Aisha took him to Golden, Colorado, to the Mother Cabrini Shrine. He happened to be home that fall, recuperating from an injury to his left leg, which he broke during a game of touch football at the Job Corps campus in Denison, Iowa.

When Aisha McCain testified at Nissen's trial, then assistant attorney general James Elworth asked her to tell the court which of Phillip's legs had been recently broken. According to the *Omaha World Herald News*, "[T]he corners of Ms. McCain's mouth nudged upward. 'It was hard to tell,' she said. 'Phillip was so good with both of them.'"[51] She would tell reporters covering the trial how Phillip climbed countless stairs with a cast on one leg and a prosthetic implement for the other during their recent pilgrimage to the Mother Cabrini Shrine. "'He walked up a hundredsomething steps with a cast on his leg, and this is his good leg,' Aisha recalled. 'It was an ordeal for him to go to the top of the shrine. I was really surprised. He really had to go through a lot of effort to get up there. We took a picture of the two of us at the top.'"

By 1993, Phillip was already completing his curriculum at Job Corps, a free education and training program administered by the U.S. Department of Labor for young people at least sixteen years of age who qualify as low income. He was the Business Club president at the Denison, Iowa, location and represented the center at a national event held in Washington, D.C.[52] As Aphrodite Jones relates, "His Job Corps family was ever so proud of him for that and Dick Knowles, the town's newspaper editor and one of the people responsible for bringing Job Corps to Denison, encouraged DeVine to consider running for mayor." Job Corps officer Ike Johnson spoke of DeVine as "the kind of student a lot of other students would like to emulate because he had those leadership qualities. People were just drawn to him." Outgoing and good-looking, Phillip, according to Jones, "had his choice of girls on campus, and having been there a while, had dated plenty." Officer Johnson recalled, "He used to take out very nice looking girls, very nice intellectual girls, and along came this lady who was different." Had it not been for his broken leg, Phillip may have never met Leslie Tisdel. He was planning to transfer to a Job Corps center in Colorado that fall.[53] By all accounts, the attraction between Leslie and Phillip was immediate. Jones writes, "Almost from the moment Leslie met DeVine, she couldn't help but notice him—he was one of those people who stand out in a crowd. Being just a year older than her . . . she was already thinking of him as marriage material. He was the right age, the right size, the right color for her." By "right color," it should be noted that Jones is referring to the fact that Leslie had a daughter with a black man; she and Phillip developed plans to regain custody and raise the child together in Colorado Springs.

It is unclear whether and how the matter of paternity was addressed in Phillip's earlier romantic relationship in D.C., bringing to mind Sherley Williams's short story "Tell Martha Not to Moan," which opens with a question and response:

> "Who's the daddy?"
> "Time."[54]

This matter of paternity, as it also signifies a relation to time, must be kept in mind, as it pertains to the narration of romance between Phillip and Leslie Tisdel in the Brandon archive. At the very least, there are inferences to draw here about how the two relationships—in D.C. and in Falls City—articulated Phillip's vision for fatherhood in/as his future.

Phillip and Leslie had not been dating for more than a few weeks before Leslie left Job Corps and returned to Falls City, Nebraska. Phillip made plans to spend the holidays with her, arriving by bus in the nearby city of Omaha on December 14, 1993. Leslie, Lisa Lambert, and Brandon Teena had all gone to pick him up from the station. According to Jones, upon Phillip's arrival in Falls City, "Leslie and Phillip were at odds, and Phil realized he had made a mistake." Among the many guests and residents at Leslie Tisdel's family home was "her buddy" Lenny Landrum, whom Phillip, as Aphrodite Jones relates, "thought . . . should leave."

Aphrodite Jones writes that Lenny and Phillip would eventually become friendly with one another. They would find common topics for discussion, "like Salt-N-Pepa, Boyz II Men, Michael Jordan and the Chicago Bulls" and their mutual experiences in gangs—Lenny was in the Crips, and Phillip "had once been part of the Bloods." This detail about gang affiliation emerges seemingly out of nowhere in Jones's discussion of Phillip DeVine. Yet for it to appear alongside black pop-cultural references suggests a crucial constitutive absence in Phillip's narration, namely, his position and participation within black communities, or that which I have previously described as the vexed appearance of black sociality, which, as it has emerged across the book, has figured various sites of animating abjection. To consider these two figures, Lenny—described as "a person of color" and "only half black"—and Phillip—who, according to all records, was "one of a few" blacks, if not the only black, in Humboldt (at the time of the killings)—is to contend with how the epistemic rupture of gang life in Jones's narrative foreshadows Phillip DeVine's figuration as a tear in the Brandon archive, as Phillip's minimized, singular form proliferates into incalculable and maximal forms of blackness. His presence in Falls City, and later Humboldt, also indexes the larger presence of blackness that is positioned out of view and characterized as out of place within those geographies.

There is an auxiliary claim to make here about the supposed disrespectability of gang life as a mode of black sociality. I am attempting not to rescue it from its disrespectable position so much as to signal how the term "gang life" further emphasizes the ways black assemblages are constructed as animating abjections and, perhaps more importantly, to emphasize that the narrative of DeVine is not one of "innocence," precisely because black assembly—and the individuated presence of blackness—is regarded as suspicious and is framed through a grammar of criminality.

Leslie perceived Phillip's initial dislike of Landrum's presence as a sign of his jealousy; there would be a number of breakups and reconciliations over the winter break. They would fight and have sex and make future plans, but before New Year's Eve they broke up for good. On December 30, Leslie drove Phillip to Lisa Lambert's house, the first stop in Phillip's plans to leave Nebraska and head back home to his mom's house in Fairfield. He had already called his mom, "saying he needed money for a bus ticket home as soon as possible. Arrangements were made, but DeVine didn't live until the next bus left."⁵⁵

According to the prosecution's closing statement at the Nissen trial, "He's [Nissen's] the one that goes to get Phillip DeVine, and in his own words he's sayin' 'I knew then nobody was gettin' out alive.' And he goes and gets Phillip DeVine, who is a member of a minority race that he doesn't much care for to begin with, and he brings Phillip DeVine into that living room where he can be shot. And the gun jams." Though not emphasized in the closing statement, DeVine's being moved into the living room, where his body was later found by Anna Mae Lambert, was a way of staging the crime in relation to a disapprobation of interracial sexuality. Both historically and as a matter of the recent past (with regard to his relationship with Leslie), but also into the future (such that his presence would not be read as an indication of potential sexual involvement with Lisa or Brandon), in this way, Phillip's death figured a fold in time that brings his particular experience of execution into relation with the history and ongoing practices of lynching.

"And the gun jams."

It is seductive but perhaps too easy to read the gun as a failure of the white phallus. Surely, white cisheteropatriarchy is not infallible, as it remains lethal. Rather than thinking about the jamming of the gun as a moment of white cis-heteropatriarchal fallibility, I would underscore here what that moment signified in DeVine's life, which is to focus on the moments in which the gun was pointed at his head and fired, and yet he survived. He survived in the richness of that word's meaning, that is, he lived a life that exceeded life—*super vivere*—and yet black survival here, as elsewhere, mitigates the supposed distinction between "super" and "sub," such that one might suggest that black life subverts—*sub vere*—the meaning of life as it has been constructed through Western epistemology. In Lorde's "litany for survival," she described such a moment as "in the hours between dawns / looking inward and outward / at once before and after," revealing the ways that living beyond life also arranges, or perhaps exposes, time as outside of time and self, beyond self, which is to say that the "self" is itself a rupture, particularly with regard to the dominant epistemic, ethical, and ontological conceptions and codes that give rise to the overrepresentation of Man as human.[56]

As it relates to the temporalities of sociogenic invention, "the gun jams" signals a disruptive intrusion of the future's incrementalized past, which includes the now, which is to say, and as Dionne Brand has written, DeVine's survival in this moment is a "tear in the world," "a rupture in history, a rupture in the quality of being."[57]

DeVine's posthumous life began a few moments later. DeVine's presence portended, for Lisa's mother, the reality of her daughter's death: "As she stepped inside, seeing the young man dead on the floor, she could only think the worst. *Lisa is probably dead in the bedroom,* she thought." Leslie and her sister, Lana Tisdel, arrived at the crime scene on December 31, 1993, asking to speak to Phil; they told the police that Phillip owed them gas money. DeVine was invoked—usually in passing—in news coverage of the case, which was then interred in the Brandon archive. As it relates to these passing invocations that work as erasing gestures, one might ask the same question posed by Sonia Sanchez in a poem: "Did they search for pieces of life / by fingerprinting the ash?"[58]

Perhaps I should have let DeVine rest. As Fred Moten reminds, "What is often overlooked in blackness is bound up with what has often been overseen."[59] And as Brand explains, "The self which is unobservable is a mystery. It is imprisoned in the observed. It is constantly struggling to wrest itself from the warp of its public ownerships. Its own language is plain yet secret. Rather, obscured."[60] Sociogenic invention, though, is not concerned with ownership, and the mystery I have painstakingly attempted to solve is perhaps too plain—namely, that Phillip DeVine had a life, however sutured to death, and that he still lives in the even-so and as-yet of living, as black and trans life does.

By "inventing a life" for Phillip DeVine, I am not attempting to make a case for a new martyr from the materials of the Brandon archive. There are too many names listed on the impossibly long ledger of black and trans deaths, and this is not a story that equates national memory with national restoration. Rather, at least in part, I am proposing that DeVine's biomythographical life disrupts and reshapes the dominant view of the Humboldt killings, unsettling and upending the ways that archive has been put toward claims for a juridical grammar for trans inclusion. From this vantage point, Elworth's instruction to the jurors—"Consider Phillip DeVine"—takes on different meanings as one is faced with how racial terror animated the scene of spectacularized (and exemplarized) anti-trans violence, just as one confronts how blackness and antiblackness undergirded the logics of the three killings and the recurrent, reiterative circulations of meaning about their deaths into the contemporary.

These considerations find enunciation in the #SayHerName movement, which, following the death of Sandra Bland, has given expression to the ways antiblack violence affects black women and girls, finding sonic elaboration in Janelle Monae's anthemic song "Hell You Talmbout (Say Their Names)." Because Say Her/Their Name(s) functions both as a digital repository and a catalog of those whose exposure to violence has precipitated their premature deaths, it is worthwhile to reflect on what assumptions and politics about memory are fomented within various political movements, including Black Lives Matter, Trans Lives Matter, and Black Trans Lives Matter, which are invested in securing the existence of black and trans people in the present and into the future. The practice of remembering and saying their names is also a demand for new structures for naming that evince and eviscerate the conditions that continually produce black and trans death.

It is also worth noting here that the variation Black Trans Lives Matter highlights an impetus to specify and make explicit black trans life, even as movement leaders have attested to "a fundamental belief that when we say Black Lives Matter, we mean all black lives matter."[61] In his musings on BLM, which he describes as, "from its inception, a feminist and queer proposition," Jared Sexton provides a list of names, curated to demonstrate a range of figures beyond and alongside black cisgender men, that constitute part of the rhetorical landscape of the movement— "Jordan Davis *and* Renisha McBride *and* Eric Garner *and* Aiyana Stanley-James [*sic*] *and* Sean Bell *and* CeCe McDonald *and* Jonathan Ferrell *and* Rekia Boyd *and* . . ."—before he arrives at the "overriding question": "[H]ow do we create a world were black lives matter to everyone?"[62]

It is a worthy and weighty question that I will attend to momentarily. However, before that—or perhaps as a way to begin to address Sexton's "overriding question"—it is necessary to linger on the catalog of figures he invokes. Amid his necessarily incomplete list of whose lives matter in the BLM movement, CeCe McDonald's name emerges as an anomaly of sorts, as she is both the only trans person on Sexton's list and the only figure who remains alive. McDonald made national headlines in 2012 when, after being verbally attacked with racist, sexist, antiqueer, and anti-trans epithets as well as physically assaulted, she accepted a plea deal for second-degree manslaughter for the death of Dean Schmitz. Although journalists and advocates pointed to the incident as a clear matter of self-defense, McDonald was sentenced to forty-one months in a men's prison in Minnesota. As journalist Akiba Solomon noted in an article about the case in *Ebony*, CeCe McDonald was, for all intents and purposes, being "punished for *surviving*."[63] She was released from prison on January 13, 2014.

Perhaps McDonald's encounter with the prison industrial complex explains how she would find inclusion on Sexton's list. As numerous scholars have discussed in different ways, carceral life is the new Jim Crow (à la Michelle Alexander); it is neo–slave life (see Ruth Wilson Gilmore, and Dennis Childs, among others) and a form of social death, produced, as Lisa Marie Cacho succinctly explains, by "racism [as] a killing abstraction . . . [that] creates spaces of living death."[64] Maybe what Eric Stanley refers to as "near life," a kind of "death-in-waiting" that "constitutes for the queer that which is the sign of vitality itself," serves as an interpretive frame that would encompass McDonald in a list of those whose lives have found different significations in and through death.[65] Although it remains unclear from Sexton's list whether this was the point of interring McDonald's name among the cissexual dead, it does seem that her anomalous inclusion gets to the heart of Afropessimism, as Sexton has defined it; in other words, McDonald's "still life" conveys how "Black life is not lived in the world that the world lives in, but it is lived underground, in outer space. . . . [It] is not social . . . [but] *lived* in social *death*."[66] On McDonald's own terms, as conveyed in her prison letters, she seems to live in what L. H. Stallings, drawing on the work of Alvin Plantinga, describes as a "trans-world identity," a human praxis that actualizes in "the ability to think of whatever one acknowledges as possible in the spatio-temporal world."[67] As McDonald wrote, "One thing I've learned, which was brought to my attention by a close friend, was that throughout this case, from the beginning to end, all of us have played a part in this 'mirroring effect,' where we see each other as we saw ourselves, giving to each as we would, or have wanted to, for ourselves. And in each of us was that struggle, and that was also seen, so like we would have tried for ourselves we uplifted and encouraged each other to go beyond our natural selves."[68] In a sociality that traverses carcerality and a genre of being human that goes "beyond our natural selves," McDonald's letter describes a life that she had only recently begun to imagine from prison and in regard to which she remained "unsure of where [her] future lies."[69]

Still life, as it describes the interface of survival as that form of life that exceeds life's meanings and posthumous life wherein black and trans life continues to accrue meaning after the event of death, gives expression to black and trans ghosts that persist and linger, as if they are not from the past but from the not-so-distant future. I use "still life" here not only to bring McDonald into direct conversation with DeVine but also as a gesture to the subterranean convergence between blackness and transness that have been submerged in the Brandon archive as well as in particular iterations of transgender historiography and black studies. But this is not an indictment of absences or even of inclusions, which are made by way of exception. Put simply, this is not about content (and attending arguments about presence and absence) but about context (and the positionality of subterranean and submersed thought), which is also how I approach Sexton's "overriding question," namely, not as a matter of which lives are included in the BLM movement but under what conditions—and particularly in which temporalities—do black lives matter.

Suppose that BLM, TLM, and BTLM are not present-tense or presentist formulations. Rather, as rhetorical enactments, they evince a different conception of history and therefore necessarily a different rubric for valuation, recalling how, as Édouard Glissant explained, "history is destined to be pleasure or distress *on its own terms*."[70] Glissant's emphasis on history's "own terms" elicits an engagement with sociogeny and the sociogenic principle as concepts through which to explore the temporal registers of BLM, TLM, and BTLM. In the future imperfect, which is to say, in that commingling of temporalities wherein the past is brought forth to the future to give rise to the present, Black (Trans) Lives Matter provides a conceptual framework to understand the ongoing struggle in the present by way of a future (aspiration) in which black lives *will have mattered* to everyone. For some, including and following Fanon, that future effectively means the end of the world. And perhaps black and trans lives' mattering in this way would end the world, but worlds end all the time; Sun Ra and his Intergalactic Research Arkestra already told us by way of their album produced in the year of DeVine's birth that "it's after the end of the world." Even so and as yet, there is still life.

ACKNOWLEDGMENTS

This book is especially for you who have made new names and found new modes of naming.

It is for you who have forged different ways of being and methods for inhabiting the world.

It is for our collective survival.

This is for Monica and Andrea and Kai and Dora and Enoch and Cecilio and Heath and Matt and Treva and Trystan and Kye and Mayowa and CeCe and Miss Major and Oluseyi and Olivia and Jevon and Maddox and Missta and Bryanna and Laverne and Marquise and Janet and Tiq and Seven and Sasha and L.L. and Kortney and Dex and Kim and Cris and Andre and Eli and Zerandrian and Mykki and Kylar and Che and Phillip and R.J. and Phillipe and Juliana and Qui and Jamal and Kokumo and D'Jamel and Day and Cazembe and Imani and Ramona and Louis and Nic and LaTony and Sir Lady Java and Kiara and Tristan and Isis and Dee Dee and Angelica and D'hana and Van and Sydney and Simone and Tyree and Precious and Myles and Luc and Tanika and Naim and D'Lo and Renae and Marie and Omari and Storme and T.J. and Monica and Niv. This is for Marsha and Sylvia and Amber and Cheryl and Leslie and Blake and Gwen and Carlett and James and Tyra and Lucy and Jazz and Georgia and Ava and Yaz'min and Mia and Marcela and Deshawnda and Demarkis and Mercedes and T.T. and Dee and Skye and Letecia and Bianca and Keyonna and Shante and London and Zella and Elisha and Islan and Evon and Dominique and Ashley and Kelly and Brandi and Kendra.

As I was completing this book, Kendra Adams, a black trans woman, was murdered by her lover in Ithaca, New York. Some weeks later, her drag house held a memorial and celebration. Many thanks to Carrie Freshour for inviting me to the event, as it provided an opportunity for me to see another version of still life and the ways black and trans life persists—even after death—in places that feel devoid of black and trans life. I never met Kendra, but I am grateful that I, along with others, was able to honor her life. This book is for Kendra and Chyna and Kenneth and JoJo and Mesha and Ebony and . . . for all of us who mourn and celebrate and fight and resist and survive and ensure the survival of others.

The completion of this study would not have been possible without the opportunity to spend a year in the Scholar-in-Residence program at the Schomburg Center for Research in Black Culture, underwritten by the generous support of the National Endowment for the Humanities and Cornell University's Office of Faculty Diversity and Development. Under the direction of Farah Jasmine Griffin, who is among the most generous and gracious examples of genius I have had the privilege to know, I was able to develop the ideas expressed in this book with a cohort of amazing thinkers, colleagues, and friends, including Sylvia Chan-Malik, Tanisha Ford, Soyica Diggs Colbert, Kaima Glover, Tsitsi Jaji, Caree Banton, Nicole Wright, Jeff Diamant, and Andreana Campbell. It was also during my time at the Schomburg that I was able to write and think alongside the inestimable Sister Sonia Sanchez. I would be remiss without naming the support and encouragement of Khalil Gibran Muhammad, Aisha Al-Adawiya, Steven Fullwood, Melay Araya, and Kelsie Mason.

Thank you to my editor at the University of Minnesota Press, Jason Weidemann; my editorial collaborator, Dani Kasprzak; and Erin Warholm-Wohlenhaus, Tammy Zambo, and Laura Westlund for additional editorial assistance. Thank you to the anonymous reviewers, who provided critical and generative feedback on earlier versions of this manuscript, and much gratitude to everyone at the University of Minnesota Press for supporting this project as well as my first, *Nobody Is Supposed to Know.* This project benefited greatly from the close and generous readings of my two writing groups. Thank you to the members of SPACE and to my New York City media studies clan of Michael Gillespie, Jonathan Gray, and Paula Massood. I am grateful for the opportunities I had to present aspects of this work while in progress. Many thanks to Trish Salah and the University of Winnipeg; Mel Chen and Juana Maria Rodriguez at the University of California, Berkeley; Kyla Wazana Tompkins at Pomona College; Erica Edwards, Sherie Randolph, and my fellow collaborators at the Black Feminist Think Tank; Felice Blake at the University of California, Santa Cruz; L. H. Stallings and Julius Fleming at the University of Maryland; Treva Lindsey at the Ohio State University; R. Cassandra Lord at the University of Toronto; Tavia Nyong'o, Lisa Duggan, Kelli Moore, Hentyle Yapp, E. Francis White, and Ann Pellegrini at New York University; Monica Miller at Lehigh University; Camilla P. Benbow and Joseph Diorio at Vanderbilt University; Robert Reid-Pharr at City University of New York Grad Center; Amy Billingsley, Megan Burke, and the University of Oregon; Perry Zurn and the University of Pennsylvania; Susan Stryker and Arizona State University; Lyndon Gill at the University of Texas at Austin; Ara Wilson and Gabe Rosenberg at Duke University; Wallace D. Best and Princeton University; Britnay Proctor, Shoniqua Roach, and Chelsea Frazier at Northwestern University; Michael X. Delli Carpini and the Annenberg School for Communication at the University of Pennsylvania; Grace Hong and the very dear Sarah Haley at the University of California, Los Angeles; Angie Willey at the University of Massachusetts Amherst; Aliyyah Abdur-Rahman, Chad Williams, and Brandeis University; and Phanuel Antwi and Denise Ferreira da Silva at the University of British Columbia at Vancouver.

The things that are useful about this book are in great part the result of the labor and encouragement of those I think of as friends of my mind, to make plural a phrase in Toni Morrison's *Beloved*. Whether they know it or not, they have indelibly shaped my thinking through conversations and through my encountering their work. Some are listed elsewhere in this brief, imperfect genre for the expression of gratitude. Yet I am particularly grateful for Christina Sharpe, Rinaldo Walcott, Hortense Spillers, Saidiya Hartman, Alondra Nelson, Cheryl Clarke, Kara Keeling, John L. Jackson Jr., Matt Richardson, Enoch Page, Roderick Ferguson, Alexander Weheliye, Daphne Brooks, Thadious Davis,

Sylvia Wynter, Darieck Scott, Cathy Cohen, Fred Moten, Katherine McKittrick, Siobhan Somerville, Jack Halberstam, the late Richard Iton, and the late Lindon Barrett. I am also grateful to a larger collective of thinkers and friends, mentors and colleagues who helped me—in deed and word—to develop this work. Many thanks to Shana Redmond, Amber Musser, Autumn Womack, Dan Berger, Nicole Fleetwood, Kandice Chuh, Joseph M. Pierce, Ashon Crawley, Scott Poulson-Bryant, Nijah Cunningham, Cecilio Cooper, Gayatri Gopinath, Houston Baker, Candice Jenkins, Ricky Rodriguez, Deb Vargas, Darius Bost, Marlon Moore, Angelique Nixon, Elias Krell, Meiver De la Cruz, Andrew Brown, Tim Tamez, Alexis De Veaux, Ann Cvetkovich, Dana Luciano, E. Patrick Johnson, Jafari Allen, Vanessa Agard Jones, Rizvana Bradley, Aimee Cox, Jin Haritaworn, Uri McMillan, Eric Stanley, Robin Bernstein, Jennifer Tyburczy, Cáel Keegan, Erica Rand, Jayna Brown, Moya Bailey, Keeanga-Yamahtta Taylor, Trystan Cotten, Ren Hwang, Alexis Pauline Gumbs, Jessica Marie Johnson, Jasmine Johnson, Shante Smalls, Therí Pickens, Kai Green, Treva Ellison, Karma Chavez, Ivan Ramos, Omise'Eke Natasha Tinsley, Marlon Bailey, Mireille Miller-Young, Marcia Ochoa, Miriam Petty, A. J. Christian, Marsha Nicole Horsley, Idil Abdillahi, and Josh Chambers-Letson.

My colleagues at Cornell University have been very generous and supportive, including Karen Jaime, Samantha Sheppard, Gerard Aching, Dagmawi Woubshet, Noliwe Rooks, Lyrae Van Clief-Stefanon, Margo Natalie Crawford, Carole Boyce Davies, Ella Maria Diaz, Kathleen Perry Long, Oneka LaBennett, Judith Byfield, Ananda Cohen Suarez, Mostafa Minawi, Naminata Diabate, Sara Warner, Sabine Haenni, Nick Salvato, Amy Villarejo, Lucinda Ramberg, Dehanza Rogers, Saida Hodžić, N'Dri Thérèse Assié-Lumumba, Kevin Gaines, Siba Grovogui, Riché Richardson, Olúfẹ́mi Táíwò, Locksley Edmondson, Judith Peraino, and Camille Robcis. Thank you to the archivists and librarians at the Cornell University Library, particularly Brenda Marston and Eric Acree, for all of their expertise; and for the ongoing collaborations, I owe an additional debt of gratitude to Lyrae, Karen, Gerard, Dag, and Margo, who consistently made time to hear me talk through nascent ideas and who make me a better thinker each time we converse. I would also like to thank the students with whom I work and from whom I learn: Dora Silva Santana, Marshall Smith III, Amaris Brown, Mayowa Willoughby, J. Michael

Kinsey, Marquise Bey, Rae Langes, Dave Molina, Nicholas Caldwell, Natalia Santiesteban, Kristen Wright, Sadé Ayorinde, S. Tay Glover, and Mlondolozi Zondi; a special thanks to Kristen and Mayowa for their assistance with the manuscript in its final stages. A few people read earlier stages of this book from cover to cover: Candice (CB/CF) Lin, Nayan Shah, Kai, Treva, and Dora. Your willingness to generously read this as a project in process was of incalculable value to me.

To two of my dearest friends with whom I speak nearly every day, Jasmine Cobb and Mecca Jamilah Sullivan, who made graduate school bearable and professional life possible, I am so glad to have had you in my life for the past decade (and change) and for your willingness to think with me all along the way. Thank you to LeiLani Dowell, who has read every page, heard every idea, witnessed every complaint and fit of doubt, and cared for me through all of it: you are my family. Thank you to my siblings, Joe Jr., Hannah, and Emuel; to my sister and one of my closest friends with whom I also had the fortune to grow up, Dorcas Wilson; to my mom, Lois Wilson; and to my grandfather Luther Riley. My grandmother Bertha Elmore and my grandfather remain my ongoing inspiration in all things.

NOTES

Preface

1. Laverne Cox, interview by Robin Roberts, *Good Morning America,* ABC News, August 18, 2015.

2. Nicole Hensley, "Transgender Woman Repeatedly Run Over, Killed in Missouri Church Parking Lot," *New York Daily News,* August 19, 2015, http://www.nydailynews.com/news/national/trans-woman-repeatedly-ran-killed-mo-parking-lot-article-1.2330892.

3. Glenn E. Rice and Brian Burnes, "Transgender Woman Killed in Northeast Kansas City Attack Felt 'Freedom' in America, Friends Say," *Kansas City Star,* August 18, 2015, http://www.kansascity.com/news/local/crime/article31397231.html.

4. Enoch H. Page and Matt U. Richardson, "On the Fear of Small Numbers: A Twenty-First-Century Prolegomenon of the U.S. Black Transgender Experience," in *Black Sexualities: Probing Powers, Passions, Practices, and Policies,* ed. Juan Battle (New Brunswick, N.J.: Rutgers University Press, 2010), 60.

5. Dawn Ennis, "Victim Number 17: Trans Woman of Color Murdered in Missouri," Advocate.com, August 18, 2015, http://www.advocate.com/transgender/2015/08/18/victim-number-17-trans-woman-color-murdered-missouri. Also see Mitch Kellaway and Sunnvie Brydum, "The 21 Trans Women Killed in 2015," Advocate.com, January 12, 2016, http://www.advocate.com/transgender/2015/07/27/these-are-trans-women-killed-so-far-us-2015?page=full.

6. Katherine McKittrick, "Mathematics Black Life," *Black Scholar* 44, no. 2 (2014): 17.

7. Dagmawi Woubshet, *The Calendar of Loss: Race, Sexuality, and Mourning in the Early Era of AIDS* (Baltimore: Johns Hopkins University Press, 2015), 4.

8. Walter Benjamin, *Illuminations,* ed. Hannah Arendt, trans. Harry Zohn (New York: Harcourt Brace Jovanovich, 1968), 257 (emphasis added).

9. Homi Bhabha, "Remembering Fanon: Self, Psyche, and the Colonial Condition," foreword to the 1986 ed. of *Black Skin, White Masks,* new ed. (London: Pluto Press, 2008), xxiv (emphasis in original).

10. Kara Keeling, "Looking for M——: Queer Temporality, Black Political Possibility, and Poetry from the Future," *GLQ: A Journal of Lesbian and Gay Studies* 15, no. 4 (2009): 579.

11. Frantz Fanon, *Black Skin, White Masks* (New York: Grove Press, 1967), 11.

12. Keeling, "Looking for M——," 565.

13. Cathy J. Cohen, "Punks, Bulldaggers, and Welfare Queens: The Radical Potential of Queer Politics?," *GLQ: A Journal of Lesbian and Gay Studies* 3, no. 4 (1997): 437–65.

14. Kai M. Green and Treva C. Ellison, "Tranifest," *Transgender Studies Quarterly* 1, nos. 1–2 (2014): 224.

15. This insight is also embedded in the title of director Kortney Ryan Ziegler's award-winning documentary *Still Black: A Portrait of Black Transmen* (Blackstarmedia, 2008), which linguistically encapsulates the persistence of blackness in making sense of the politics and practices of transition.

16. Mitch Kellaway, "Trans Teen Activist, Former Homecoming King, Dies in Charlotte, N.C.," Advocate.com, March 24, 2015, http://www.advocate.com/obituaries/2015/03/24/trans-teen-activist-homecoming-king-dies.

17. Ibid. See also Mothering across Continents, http://www.motheringacrosscontinents.org/.

18. Katya Lezin, "Transgender People in Charlotte Struggle to Find Tolerance," *Charlotte Observer,* January 5, 2015, http://www.charlotteobserver.com/living/health-family/article9252857.html.

19. Michael Gordon, Mark S. Price, and Katie Peralta, "Understanding HB2: North Carolina's Newest Law Solidifies State's Role in Defining Discrimination," *Charlotte Observer,* March 26, 2016, http://www.charlotteobserver.com/news/politics-government/article68401147.html. See also Rick Glazier, "18 Questions, 18 Answers: The Real Facts behind House Bill 2," prepared for the North Carolina Justice Center, at http://www.ncjustice.org/?q=18-questions-18-answers-real-facts-behind-house-bill-2.

20. Lezin, "Transgender People in Charlotte."

21. *BrocKINGton* (2014), produced by Jason Sklut, Sergio Ingato, and Maggie Sloane, Vimeo video, https://vimeo.com/95884282.

22. Hortense Spillers, "Mama's Baby, Papa's Maybe: An American Grammar Book," *Diacritics* 17, no. 2 (1987): 65.

23. Ibid.

24. See, e.g., Sylvia Wynter, "Unsettling the Coloniality of Being/Power/Truth/Freedom: Towards the Human, after Man, Its Overrepresentation—An Argument," *CR: The New Centennial Review* 3, no. 3 (2003): 257–337.

25. Lezin, "Transgender People in Charlotte."

26. Kimberly Juanita Brown, *The Repeating Body: Slavery's Visual Resonance in the Contemporary* (Durham, N.C.: Duke University Press, 2015), 13.

27. Kellaway, "Trans Teen Activist."

28. "Death of Blake Brockington," Wikipedia.org, accessed September 25, 2016, at https://en.wikipedia.org/wiki/Death_of_Blake_Brockington.

29. C. Riley Snorton and Jin Haritaworn, "Trans Necropolitics: A Transnational Reflection on Violence, Death, and the Trans of Color Afterlife," in *Transgender Studies Reader 2*, ed. Susan Stryker and Aren Aizura (New York: Routledge, 2013), 67.

30. Ibid., 67, 74.

31. Yasiin Bey, "Mathematics," *Black on Both Sides* (Rawkus Records, 1999).

32. Janet Mock, *Redefining Realness: My Path to Womanhood, Identity, Love, and So Much More* (New York: Atria, 2014), xvii.

33. Keeling, "Looking for M——," 571–72.

34. Fanon, *Black Skin, White Masks,* 229.

Introduction

1. *Speaking of Sex,* Hirshland Exhibition Gallery, Carl A. Kroch Library, Cornell University, February 14–October 11, 2014; online exhibit accessed February 22, 2016, at http://rmc.library.cornell.edu/speakingofsex/exhibition/perform/index.html.

2. These details were gleaned through personal correspondence with San Francisco–based antiquarian book dealer, collector, and historian Gerard Koskovich on October 30, 2014.

3. Saidiya Hartman, "Venus in Two Acts," *Small Axe* 12, no. 2 (2008): 13.

4. Daphne Brooks, *Bodies in Dissent: Spectacular Performances of Race and Freedom, 1850–1910* (Durham, N.C.: Duke University Press, 2006), 271.

5. *Dictionary of Caribbean English Usage,* ed. Richard Allsopp (New York: Oxford University Press, 1996), s.v. "cake-walk."

6. James Weldon Johnson, *The Autobiography of an Ex-Colored Man,* in *Three Negro Classics* (New York: Avon Books, 1965), 440.

7. Brooks, *Bodies in Dissent,* 272, 274.

8. See Brent Hayes Edwards, "The Practice of Diaspora," in *American Studies: An Anthology,* ed. Janice A. Radway, Kevin Gaines, Barry Shank, and Penny Von Eschen (Hoboken, N.J.: Wiley-Blackwell, 2009), 33–40, for more on the First Pan-African Conference; and Havelock Ellis and John Addington Symonds, *Studies in the Psychology of Sex,* vol. 1, *Sexual Inversion* (Watford, U.K.: University Press, 1897), x. See also Siobhan Somerville, *Queering the Color Line: Race and the Invention of Homosexuality* (Durham, N.C.: Duke University Press, 2000), for a cogent analysis of the relationship between the concept of homosexuality and scientific racism in nineteenth-century sexological texts and in the production and circulation of the "homosexual" throughout the twentieth century. Somerville, too, turns to Du Bois and Ellis and Symonds to think about the imbrications of racialization and sexual nonnormativity and is one of my interlocutors throughout the book.

9. Nadia Ellis, *Territories of the Soul: Queered Belonging in the Black Diaspora* (Durham, N.C.: Duke University Press, 2015), 3; and Brooks, *Bodies in Dissent,* 273.

10. Fred Moten, "Blackness and Nothingness (Mysticism in the Flesh)," *South Atlantic Quarterly* 112, no. 4 (2013): 746.

11. Claire Colebrook, "What Is It Like to Be a Human?," *Transgender Studies Quarterly* 2, no. 2 (2015): 228 (emphasis in original).

12. Ibid. (emphasis in original).

13. *Oxford English Dictionary Online,* December 2015, s.v. "transitive," http://www.oed.com/.

14. Bill Brown, "Thing Theory," *Critical Inquiry* 28, no. 1 (2001): 4 (emphasis added).

15. In *The Order of Things,* Foucault attends to the sites of discursivity that give rise to Man and (continue to) position Man as the center of what Sylvia Wynter would describe as a colonial nexus of "being/power/truth/ freedom." See Michel Foucault, *The Order of Things: An Archaeology of the Human Sciences* (New York: Routledge, 2002); and Sylvia Wynter, "Unsettling the Coloniality of Being/Power/Truth/Freedom: Towards the Human, after Man, Its Overrepresentation—An Argument," *CR: The New Centennial Review* 3, no. 3 (2003): 257–337.

16. Nancy Farriss, foreword to *The Social Life of Things: Commodities in Cultural Perspective* (New York: Cambridge University Press, 1988), ix.

17. Frantz Fanon, *Black Skin, White Masks* (New York: Pluto Press, 2008), 176.

18. José Esteban Muñoz, "Ephemera as Evidence: Introductory Notes to Queer Acts," *Women and Performance: A Journal of Feminist Theory* 8, no. 2 (1996): 6.

19. Wynter, "Unsettling the Coloniality," 331. See also Wynter, "Towards the Sociogenic Principle: Fanon, the Puzzle of Conscious Experience, of 'Identity' and Its Like to 'Black'" (paper presented in advance of the publication of "Towards the Sociogenic Principle: Fanon, Identity, the Puzzle of Conscious Experience, and What It Is Like to Be 'Black,'" in *National Identities and Sociopolitical Changes in Latin America*, ed. Mercedes F. Durán-Cogan and Antonio Gómez-Moriana (New York: Routledge, 2001), 11.

20. The concept of valorizing without redemption is indebted to Kara Keeling's "Looking for M——: Queer Temporality, Black Political Possibility, and Poetry from the Future," *GLQ: A Journal of Lesbian and Gay Studies* 15, no. 4 (2009): 565–82.

21. Susan Stryker, Paisley Currah, and Lisa Jean Moore, "Trans-, Trans, or Transgender?," introduction to special issue, *Women's Studies Quarterly* 36, nos. 3–4 (2008): 13.

22. Ibid., 11, 15.

23. Neil Roberts, *Freedom as Marronage* (Chicago: University of Chicago Press, 2015), 29 (emphasis in original). For notable exceptions, see, e.g., Matt Richardson, *The Queer Limit of Black Memory: Black Lesbian Literature and Irresolution* (Columbus: Ohio State University Press, 2013); L. H. Stallings, *Funk the Erotic: Transaesthetics and Black Sexual Cultures* (Urbana: University of Illinois Press, 2015); Janet Mock, *Redefining Realness: My Path to Womanhood, Identity, Love, and So Much More* (New York: Atria Books, 2014); and Trystan Cotten, ed., *Transgender Migrations: The Bodies, Borders, and Politics of Transition* (New York: Routledge, 2011), as a few examples of scholarly and popular book-length projects that explore the relationships between blackness and transness.

24. W. E. B. Du Bois, *The Souls of Black Folk* (Chicago: McClurg, 1903), 5.

25. Ibid. After all, in *Stone Butch Blues,* this is how Ed, a black working-class gender-variant character, explains to the novel's protagonist, Jes, the decision to begin hormone treatment, telling Jes about *The Souls of Black Folk*: "There's this paragraph I marked for you. I carry it in my wallet. Read it. That's how I feel. I couldn't say it any better." Leslie Feinberg, *Stone Butch Blues* (New York: Alyson Books, 1993), 263.

26. Tavia Ochieng' Nyong'o, *The Amalgamation Waltz: Race, Performance, and the Ruses of Memory* (Minneapolis: University of Minnesota Press, 2009), 11.

27. Fanon, *Black Skin, White Masks*, 179.

28. David Marriott, "Inventions of Existence: Sylvia Wynter, Frantz Fanon, Sociogeny, and 'the Damned,'" *CR: The New Centennial Review* 11, no. 3 (2011): 49.

29. Félix Guattari, *Chaosmosis: An Ethico-Aesthetic Paradigm*, trans. Julian Pefanis (Bloomington: Indiana University Press, 1995), 117, 132.

30. Troy Rhoades and Christoph Brunner, "Transversal Fields of Experience," *Inflexions* 4 (2010): iii.

31. Dionne Brand, *A Map to the Door of No Return: Notes to Belonging* (Toronto: Vintage Canada, 2002), 4–5.

32. Nyong'o, *Amalgamation Waltz*, 18.

33. Édouard Glissant, *Caribbean Discourse: Selected Essays*, trans. J. Michael Dash (Charlottesville: University Press of Virginia, 1989), 66–67 (emphasis in original).

34. Ibid, 67.

35. Brand, *Map to the Door*, 1.

36. *Oxford English Dictionary Online,* December 2015, s.v. "transversal," http://www.oed.com/. The language of "afterlives of slavery" is drawn from Saidiya Hartman, *Lose Your Mother: A Journey along the Atlantic Slave Route* (New York: Farrar, Straus & Giroux, 2007).

37. Glissant, *Caribbean Discourse,* 190.

38. Rizvanna Bradley and Damien-Adia Marassa, "Awakening to the World: Relation, Totality, and Writing from Below," *Discourse* 36, no. 1 (2014): 122.

39. Ibid.

40. Hortense Spillers, *Black, White, and in Color: Essays on American Literature and Culture* (Chicago: University of Chicago Press, 2003), 156.

41. *Oxford English Dictionary Online,* s.v. "transversal."

42. Stallings, *Funk the Erotic,* 224.

43. Saidiya Hartman, *Scenes of Subjection: Terror, Slavery, and Self-Making in Nineteenth-Century America* (New York: Oxford University Press, 1997), 12; Hortense Spillers, Saidiya Hartman, Farah Jasmine Griffin, Shelly Eversley, and Jennifer Morgan, "'Whatcha Gonna Do?': Revisiting 'Mama's Baby, Papa's Maybe: An American Grammar Book'; A Conversation with Hortense Spillers, Saidiya Hartman, Farah Jasmine Griffin, Shelly Eversley, and Jennifer Morgan," *Women's Studies Quarterly* 35, nos. 1–2 (2007): 308.

44. See Heather Russell Andrade's discussion of Du Bois's "manhood rights" in "Revising Critical Judgments of *The Autobiography of an Ex-Colored Man*," *African American Review* 40, no. 2 (2006): 259.

45. I became aware of this term through conversation; however, one also finds application in Sharpe's work on Aunt H/Ester in *Monstrous Intimacies: Making Post-slavery Subjects* (Durham, N.C.: Duke University Press, 2010).

46. Hortense Spillers, "Mama's Baby, Papa's Maybe: An American Grammar Book," *Diacritics* 17, no. 2 (1987): 80.

47. See the anthology *Sylvia Wynter: On Being Human as Praxis,* ed. Katherine McKittrick (Durham, N.C.: Duke University Press, 2014), for a critical genealogy of Wynter's work on the human as a sociogenic genre of being.

1. Anatomically Speaking

1. According to Nicole Ivy, "Sims carried out operations on 12 to 17 enslaved women." Cited in Lauren Sausser, "'Savior of Women' or Medical Monster? The Fraught Legacy of South Carolina's Most Infamous Physician," *Charleston (S.C.) Post and Courier,* April 7, 2017, https://data.postandcourier.com/saga/jmarionsims/page/1.

2. J. Marion Sims, *Silver Sutures in Surgery: The Anniversary Discourse before the New York Academy of Medicine* (New York: Samuel S. & William Wood, 1858), 54.

3. Ibid., 52, 54.

4. Achille Mbembe, *On the Postcolony* (Berkeley: University of California Press, 2001), 215.

5. I come to the phrase an "unethical grammar of suffering" through Frank Wilderson's discussion of the relation between ethics and suffering and "the violence that underwrites the modern world's capacity to think, act, and exist spatially and temporally." Frank Wilderson, *Red, White, and Black: Cinema and the Structure of U.S. Antagonisms* (Durham, N.C.: Duke University Press, 2010), 2.

6. Lindon Barrett, *Blackness and Value: Seeing Double* (New York: Cambridge University Press, 1998), 35.

7. Hortense Spillers, "Mama's Baby, Papa's Maybe: An American Grammar Book," *Diacritics* 17, no. 2 (1987): 68.

8. Sims, *Silver Sutures in Surgery,* 52.

9. The supposition of "flesh in objects" is shaped by Sarah Haley's paper "Materialized Scene(s): Paradox, Prison, and Protection," presented at The Flesh of the Matter: A Hortense Spillers Symposium, Ithaca, N.Y., March 19, 2016.

10. L. L. Wall, "The Medical Ethics of Dr. J. Marion Sims: A Fresh Look at the Historical Record," *Journal of Medical Ethics* 32 (2006): 347.

11. Durrenda Ojanuga, "The Medical Ethics of the 'Father of Gynecology,' Dr. J. Marion Sims," *Journal of Medical Ethics* 19 (1993): 29. Deborah Kuhn McGregor also notes in her study of the professionalization of gynecology that the World Health Organization lists poor living conditions and malnutrition as chief causes for vesicovaginal fistula. Deborah Kuhn McGregor, *From Midwives*

to Medicine: The Birth of American Gynecology (New Brunswick, N.J.: Rutgers University Press, 1998), 112.

12. Havelock Ellis, *Studies in the Psychology of Sex,* vol. 2, *Sexual Inversion* (2004), e-text prepared by Juliet Sutherland and the Project Gutenberg Online Distributed Proofreading team, http://www.pgdp.net/c/.

13. Sander L. Gilman, *Difference and Pathology: Stereotypes of Sexuality, Race, and Madness* (Ithaca, N.Y.: Cornell University Press, 1985), 90.

14. W. O. Baldwin, "Sketches and Reminiscences: Of the Life of Dr. J. Marion Sims, as Given at the Late Memorial Meeting of the Medical and Surgical Society of Montgomery," in *Tribute to the Late James Marion Sims, M.D., LL.D.* (Montgomery, Ala.: W. D. Brown, Steam Power Printers and Book Binders, 1884), 9.

15. Saidiya Hartman, *Scenes of Subjection: Terror, Slavery, and Self-Making in Nineteenth-Century America* (New York: Oxford University Press, 1997), 101.

16. Spillers, "Mama's Baby, Papa's Maybe," 68.

17. J. Marion Sims, *The Story of My Life* (New York: Appleton, 1884), 227. Subsequent references to this source in this passage appear parenthetically in the text.

18. Marie Jenkins Schwartz, *Birthing a Slave: Motherhood and Medicine in the Antebellum South* (Cambridge, Mass.: Harvard University Press, 2010), 287.

19. Gilman cites W. H. Flower and James Murie's "Account of the Dissection of a Bush-Woman," in the opening volume of the *Journal of Anatomy and Physiology* 1, no. 2 (1867): 189–208. See Gilman, *Difference and Pathology,* 88–89.

20. Andrew S. Curran, *The Anatomy of Blackness: Science and Slavery in an Age of Enlightenment* (Baltimore: Johns Hopkins University Press, 2013), 176.

21. Petra Kuppers, "Remembering Anarcha: Objection in the Medical Archive," *Liminalities: A Journal of Performance Studies* 42, no. 2 (2008): 5, http://liminalities.net/4–2/anarcha. For additional disability analysis of Sims's experiments, see Rachel Dudley, "Toward an Understanding of the 'Medical Plantation' as a Cultural Location of Disability," *Disability Studies Quarterly* 32, no. 4 (2012), http://dsq-sds.org/article/view/3248/3184. See also Dierdre Cooper Owens, *Medical Bondage: Race, Gender, and the American Origins of Gynecology* (Athens: University of Georgia Press, 2017).

22. Sims, *Story of My Life,* 235–36.

23. Harriet Washington, *Medical Apartheid: The Dark History of Medical Experimentation on Black Americans from Colonial Times to the Present* (New York: Doubleday, 2006), 66.

24. Sims, *Silver Sutures in Surgery,* 52–53.

25. Ibid.

26. Seale Harris, with the collaboration of Frances Williams Brown, *Woman's Surgeon: The Life Story of J. Marion Sims* (New York: Macmillan, 1950), 88.

27. Sims, *Story of My Life,* 237–38.

28. Harris, *Woman's Surgeon,* 89.

29. Sims, *Story of My Life,* 240.

30. William Ian Miller, *The Anatomy of Disgust* (Cambridge, Mass.: Harvard University Press, 1997), 1–2.

31. Ibid., 247–48.

32. Harris, *Woman's Surgeon,* 90.

33. L. H. Stallings, *Funk the Erotic: Transaesthetics and Black Sexual Cultures* (Urbana: University of Illinois Press, 2015), 14. See also Jasmine Cobb, *Picture Freedom: Remaking Black Visuality in the Early Nineteenth Century* (New York: New York University Press, 2015).

34. Stallings, *Funk the Erotic,* 14.

35. See, e.g., McGregor, *From Midwives to Medicine;* and Wall, "Medical Ethics of Dr. J. Marion Sims," 346–50.

36. McGregor, *From Midwives to Medicine,* 35.

37. Sianne Ngai argues that affects such as paranoia, envy, or animatedness produce an "obscuring of the subjective-objective boundary," while disgust functions to strengthen and regulate the distinction between subject and object. Sianne Ngai, *Ugly Feelings* (Cambridge, Mass.: Harvard University Press, 2005), 335. Disgust is perhaps also expressed in Sims's use of "this kind," which Rebecca Wanzo flags through a series of questions: "What does 'this kind' mean? Patients suffering from vesicovaginal fistulae? Or patients who are hearty enough to live and suffer?" Rebecca Wanzo, *The Suffering Will Not Be Televised: African American Women and Sentimental Political Storytelling* (Albany: State University of New York Press, 2009), 154.

38. Harris, *Woman's Surgeon,* 90.

39. Sims, *Story of My Life,* 242.

40. Harris, *Woman's Surgeon,* 95.

41. American Medical Association, *Code of Medical Ethics of the American Medical Association: Originally Adopted at the Adjourned Meeting of the National Medical Convention in Philadelphia* (Chicago: American Medical Association Press, 1847).

42. Sims, *Story of My Life,* 241–42.

43. Harris, *Woman's Surgeon,* 91.

44. Ibid., 92.

45. Sims, *Story of My Life,* 246.

46. Ibid.

47. Ibid., 259.

48. J. Marion Sims, "On the Treatment of Vesico-vaginal Fistula," *American Journal of the Medical Sciences* 45 (1852): 63.

49. Although Sims never mentions the race, age, or status of the vesico-vaginal fistula cases, he concludes the essay with an account of a "negro woman (aged 27)" who experienced a postsurgical injury on her thumb (ibid., 82).

50. Ibid.

51. Ibid., 60.

52. Foucault first used "polyvalent mobility" in his 1976 lectures at the Collège de France. Ann Laura Stoler explicates Foucault's notion of the phrase in *Race and the Education of Desire: Foucault's "History of Sexuality" and the Colonial Order of Things* (Durham, N.C.: Duke University Press, 1999), 55–94, as well as in *Carnal Knowledge and Imperial Power: Race and the Intimate in Colonial Rule* (Berkeley: University of California Press, 2002). As she writes in *Race and the Education of Desire,* "[F]or Foucault, this polyvalent mobility does more than describe [race's] etymology; it critically accounts for the nature of modern racism and the sustained power invested in it. Racial discourses are not only righteous because they profess the common good; they are permeated with resurrected subjugated knowledges, disqualified accounts by those contesting unitary power and by those partisan voices that speak for the defense of society" (69).

53. Sims, "On the Treatment of Vesico-vaginal Fistula," 68.

54. *Oxford English Dictionary Online,* 3rd ed. (2007), s.v. "speculum," http://www.oed.com/.

55. Sims, "On the Treatment of Vesico-vaginal Fistula," 68.

56. Ibid.

57. Maria Lugones, "The Coloniality of Gender," *Worlds and Knowledges Otherwise* 2, no. 2 (2008): 12.

58. Harris, *Woman's Surgeon,* xviii.

59. Elaine Scarry, *The Body in Pain: The Making and Unmaking of the World* (New York: Oxford University Press, 1987), 182.

60. Michel Foucault, *Abnormal: Lectures at the Collège de France, 1974–1975* (New York: Picador, 1999), 52.

61. *Oxford English Dictionary Online,* 3rd ed. (2007), s.v. "catheter," http://www.oed.com/.

62. Sims, "On the Treatment of Vesico-vaginal Fistula," 80.

63. Ibid. The term "pornotropic" is derived from Hortense Spillers's use of the phrase "potential for pornotroping" as a form of imposed meaning on captive bodies. She relates: "1) the captive body becomes the source of an irresistible, destructive sensuality; 2) at the same time—in stunning contradiction—

the captive body reduces to a thing, becoming being for the captor; 3) in this absence from a subject position, the captured sexualities provide a physical and biological expression of "otherness"; 4) as a category of "otherness," the captive body translates into a potential for pornotroping and embodies sheer physical powerlessness that slides into a more general "powerlessness," resonating through various centers of human and social meaning" ("Mama's Baby, Papa's Maybe," 67). See also Keguro Macharia's analysis of the implications of pornotroping for queer studies in "Queer Genealogies (Provisional Notes)," *Bully Bloggers* (blog), January 13, 2013, https://bullybloggers.wordpress.com/tag/hortense-spillers/; and Alexander Weheliye, "Pornotropes," *Journal of Visual Culture* 7, no. 1 (2008): 65–81.

64. J. Marion Sims, "Two Cases of Vesico-vaginal Fistula, Cured," *New-York Medical Gazette and Journal of Health* 5, no. 1 (January 1854): 1.

65. Ibid., 2.

66. Ibid.

67. Ibid., 3.

68. Ibid., 5.

69. Ibid.

70. Ibid.

71. Sims, *Story of My Life,* 300.

72. Ibid., 299.

73. Ibid., 301.

74. "History of the Department," Department of Obstetrics and Gynecology, Mount Sinai Roosevelt and Mount Sinai Saint Luke's, New York, accessed June 21, 2016, at http://www.nywomenshealth.com/history-obstetrics-gynecology-st-lukes-roosevelt-hospital-new-york.htm.

75. Harris, *Woman's Surgeon,* 207.

76. Ibid.

77. Sims, *Story of My Life,* 364–65.

78. Ibid., 365.

79. Harris, *Woman's Surgeon,* 214.

80. Ibid., 229.

81. Sims, *Story of My Life,* 366.

82. Ibid., 330–31.

83. Foucault, *Abnormal,* 201–2.

84. Ibid., 51.

85. Greg Thomas, "The 'S' Word: Sex, Empire, and the Black Radical Tradition," in *After Man: Towards the Human,* ed. Anthony Bogues (Miami: Ian Randle, 2006), 78. See also Thomas's *The Sexual Demon of Colonial Power:*

Pan-African Embodiment and Erotic Schemes of Empire (Indianapolis: Indiana University Press, 2007), 30.

86. Nicole Ivy, "Bodies of Work: A Meditation on Medical Imaginaries and Enslaved Women," *SOULS: A Critical Journal of Black Politics, Culture, and Society* 18, no. 1 (2016): 15.

87. Sims, *Story of My Life,* 458.

88. McGregor, *From Midwives to Medicine,* 159–66. See also Jeffrey S. Sartin, "J. Marion Sims, the Father of Gynecology: Hero or Villain?," *Southern Medical Journal* 97, no. 5 (2004), for more on Sims's infamous temper and violent outbursts; available at http://www.medscape.com/viewarticle/479892_2.

89. "Report of the Memorial Meeting of the Medical Society of the District of Columbia, at the National Capital, in Honor of Dr. J. Marion Sims, Held November 21, 1883," in *Story of My Life,* 450 (emphasis added).

90. "Birthplace of Dr. James Marion Sims," plaque erected by Lancaster County, sponsored by the Waxhaws Chapter of the Daughters of the American Revolution, 1848.

91. Wanzo, *Suffering Will Not Be Televised,* 153.

92. Jennifer Morgan, *Laboring Women: Reproduction and Gender in New World Slavery* (Philadelphia: University of Pennsylvania Press, 2004), 8.

93. G. J. Barker-Benfield, *The Horrors of the Half-Known Life: Male Attitudes toward Women and Sexuality in Nineteenth-Century America,* 2nd ed. (New York: Routledge, 2000), 86.

94. Mbembe, *On the Postcolony,* 220.

95. Wanzo, *Suffering Will Not Be Televised,* 159–60.

96. Kuppers, "Remembering Anarcha," 26.

97. Evelynn Hammonds, "Black (W)holes and the Geometry of Black Female Sexuality," *differences: a journal of feminist cultural studies* 6, nos. 2–3 (1994): 138–39.

98. Ibid., 139.

99. See scholar and poet Bettina Judd's poem "The Researcher Discovers Anarcha, Betsey, Lucy," *Meridians* 11, no. 2 (2011): 238–39.

100. "About Johns Hopkins Medicine: Arts as Applied to Medicine," accessed July 10, 2016, at http://www.hopkinsmedicine.org/about/history/history7.html.

101. Thomas S. Cullen, "Max Brödel, 1870–1941: Director of the First Department of Art as Applied to Medicine in the World," *Bulletin of the History of Medicine* 33 (1945): 28.

102. Max Brödel, "How May Our Present Methods of Medical Illustrations Be Improved?," *Journal of the American Medical Association* 49, no. 2 (1907): 138.

103. Max Brödel, "Medical Illustration," *Journal of the American Medical Association* 117, no. 9 (1941): 669.

104. Cullen, "Max Brödel," 6.

105. Ibid., 9.

106. Ranice W. Crosby and John Cody, *Max Brodel: The Man Who Put Art into Medicine* (New York: Springer-Verlag, 1991), 34.

107. Howard A. Kelly, *Medical Gynecology* (New York: Appleton, 1912).

108. Wilderson, *Red, White, and Black,* 325.

109. Washington, *Medical Apartheid,* 131–32.

110. Ibid, 138.

111. See, e.g. Calvin Warren, "Black Time: Slavery, Metaphysics, and the Logic of Wellness," in *The Psychic Hold of Slavery: Legacies of American Expressive Culture,* ed. Soyica Diggs Colbert, Robert J. Patterson, and Aida Levy-Hussen (New Brunswick, N.J.: Rutgers University Press, 2016), 55–68, for more on the violence of metaphysics.

112. Jonathan M. Metzl and Joel D. Howell, "Great Moments: Authenticity, Ideology, and the Telling of Medical 'History,'" *Literature and Medicine* 25, no. 2 (2006): 517.

113. Ibid., 502.

114. Ibid., 517.

115. Ibid.

116. Washington, *Medical Apartheid,* 2.

117. See, e.g., Kuppers, "Remembering Anarcha"; and Washington, *Medical Apartheid.*

118. Washington, *Medical Apartheid,* 2.

119. As Metzl and Howell note, "Thom [frequently] dressed 1950s persons into what he believed to be appropriate costumes, posed them in desired positions, and then painted them—often with a change in skin color—directly into history. . . . Often, characters in Thom's life reappeared in ways ranging from quirky to troubling, suggesting the loose ways in which models were matched with the national origins and ethnicities of the historical figures" ("Great Moments," 511).

120. McGregor, *From Midwives to Medicine,* 43.

121. Sigmund Freud, "The Psychology of Dream Activities," in *The Interpretation of Dreams,* 3rd ed., trans. A. A. Brill (New York: Macmillan, 1913), published August 2010 by Bartleby.com, http://www.bartleby.com/285/7.html, ll. 173–76.

122. Hans-Dieter Gondek, "From the Protective Shield against Stimuli to the Fantasm: A Reading of Chapter 4 of *Beyond the Pleasure Principle,*" in *Lacan in the German-Speaking World,* ed. Elizabeth Stewart, Maire Jaanus, and Richard Feldstein, trans. Elizabeth Stewart (Albany: State University of New York Press, 2004), 226.

123. Judith Butler, *Gender Trouble: Feminism and the Subversion of Identity* (New York: Routledge, 1990), 145 (emphasis in original).

124. Accessed July 8, 2016, at http://biblehub.com/john/1.htm.

125. Butler, *Gender Trouble,* 146.

126. Alexander Weheliye, *Habeas Viscus: Racializing Assemblages, Biopolitics, and Black Feminist Theories of the Human* (Durham, N.C.: Duke University Press, 2014), 44.

2. Trans Capable

1. Henry Colebrooke, *Treatise on Obligations and Contracts, Part 1* (London: Black, Kingsbury, Parbury, & Allen, 1818), 193.

2. Ibid. (emphasis in original). Colebrooke discusses the legal status of the slave in some depth in chapter 3 of the treatise, defining the slave as unable to enter into "contract or agreement, towards any person, whether a stranger or his own master. . . . For the master has a right to all the goods of his slave, and all his labour, work and service, by the very condition of slavery" (30). This description of the "very condition of slavery" also sensitizes my reading of Sims's archive in chapter 1.

3. Saidiya Hartman, *Scenes of Subjection: Terror, Slavery, and Self-Making in Nineteenth-Century America* (New York: Oxford University Press, 1997), 25–26.

4. Hortense Spillers, "Mama's Baby, Papa's Maybe: An American Grammar Book," *Diacritics* 17, no. 2 (1987): 67.

5. Ibid. For a particularly cogent reading of how the attribution of "transition" obscured developing and established relations of power, read Lisa Lowe, *The Intimacies of Four Continents* (Durham, N.C.: Duke University Press, 2015).

6. Fred Moten, *The Feel Trio* (Tucson: Letter Machine, 2014), 65 (emphasis in original).

7. Spillers, "Mama's Baby, Papa's Maybe," 67.

8. William Still, *The Underground Rail Road: A Record of Facts, Authentic Narratives, Letters, &c., Narrating the Hardships Hair-Breadth Escapes and Death Struggles of the Slaves in the Efforts for Freedom* (Philadelphia: Porter & Coates, 1872), 1.

9. Barbara McCaskill, "'Yours Very Truly': Ellen Craft—the Fugitive as Text and Artifact," *African American Review* 28, no. 4 (1994): 510.

10. As Farah Jasmine Griffin notes in her introduction to the Barnes & Noble Classics edition of *Incidents in the Life of a Slave Girl* (New York: Barnes & Noble Books, 2005), xiii–xxvi, the narrative—as transposed by Lydia Maria Child—was published a year later (1862) in the United Kingdom under the title *The Deeper Wrong*.

11. Jonathan Ned Katz notes that the *New York Sun* reported that "Mary Jones also went by the names 'Miss Ophelia,' 'Miss June,' and 'Eliza Smith.'" *Love Stories: Sex between Men before Homosexuality* (Chicago: University of Chicago Press, 2001), 81.

12. The phrase "cross-dressing and theft" appears in Katz's discussion of Jones in ibid.

13. Harriet Jacobs, *Incidents in the Life of a Slave Girl*, ed. L. Maria Child (Boston: Published for the Author, 1861), 83–85.

14. These details are found in various iterations in Timothy J. Gilfoyle, *City of Eros: New York City, Prostitution, and the Commercialization of Sex, 1790–1920* (New York: Norton, 1992), 136–37; Katz, *Love Stories;* and Tavia Nyong'o, *The Amalgamation Waltz: Race, Performance, and the Ruses of Memory* (Minneapolis: University of Minnesota Press, 2009).

15. Katz, *Love Stories*, 81.

16. Nyong'o, *Amalgamation Waltz*, 96.

17. Katz, *Love Stories*, 83.

18. The legal transcript included an exchange between a court official and Jones: "'What is your *right* name?' he was asked. 'Peter Sewally—I am a man,' he answered," quoted in ibid. (emphasis added). As one example of how Jones's responses were shaped by the court, the unsolicited addition of a legally legible gender in response to the question seems to indicate how she was made to capitulate to the logics of the state. For more courtroom description, refer to pp. 82–84.

19. This description is drawn from ibid., 84; and Nyong'o, *Amalgamation Waltz*, 97.

20. Katz, *Love Stories*, 84.

21. Nyong'o, *Amalgamation Waltz*, 98.

22. Erika Piola, "The Rise of Early American Lithography and Antebellum Visual Culture," *Winterthur Portfolio* 48, nos. 2–3 (2014): 130. In his essay "The Unforgivable Transgression of Being Caster Semenya," *Women and Performance* 20, no. 1 (2010): 95–100, Tavia Nyong'o draws attention to the connections between nineteenth-century Jones and twenty-first-century Semenya as they relate to their shared commodification within print culture and the imbrications of blackness and nonnormative gender presentations.

23. Jasmine Nichole Cobb, *Picture Freedom: Remaking Black Visuality in the Early Nineteenth Century* (New York: New York University Press, 2015), 161.

24. Katz, *Love Stories*, 82.

25. "Singular Case," *New York Herald*, December 21, 1844, image 2, accessed from the Library of Congress, https://www.loc.gov/.

26. Katz, *Love Stories*, 84.

27. Nyong'o, *Amalgamation Waltz*, 98–99 (emphasis in original).

28. "Many Gastronomic Records Established," *Virginia Enterprise*, October 2, 1908, image 6, accessed from the Library of Congress, https://www.loc.gov/.

29. Nyong'o, *Amalgamation Waltz*, 99.

30. Vincent Woodard, *The Delectable Negro: Human Consumption and Homoeroticism within U.S. Slave Culture*, ed. Justin A. Joyce and Dwight McBride (New York: New York University Press, 2014), 14.

31. Kyla Wazana Tompkins, *Racial Indigestion: Eating Bodies in the Nineteenth Century* (New York: New York University Press, 2012), 13.

32. Hortense Spillers, *Black, White, and in Color: Essays on American Literature and Culture* (Chicago: University of Chicago Press, 2003), 383.

33. See, e.g., Spillers, "'All the Things You Could Be by Now, If Sigmund Freud's Wife Was Your Mother': Psychoanalysis and Race," in ibid., 381.

34. Tompkins, *Racial Indigestion*, 165–67.

35. See "The World of Harriet Jacobs and *Incidents in the Life of a Slave Girl*," in the Barnes & Noble edition of *Incidents*, xi. See also Jean Fagan Yellin's entry "Harriet Ann Jacobs (1813–1897)," in *The Heath Anthology of American Literature*, ed. Paul Lauter, 5th ed., online edition, http://college.cengage.com/english/lauter/heath/4e/students/author_pages/early_nineteenth/jacobs_ha.html.

36. *Incidents* was purchased twice, first by the Boston publishing company Phillips and Sampson, in 1859, and then by another Boston publishing house, Thayer and Eldridge, in 1860. Both firms went bankrupt before the book was printed. Thayer and Eldridge, according to Yellin, ibid., stipulated that Child provide an introduction to the text for publication.

37. See, e.g., Griffin, introduction, xviii–xix. See also Frances Smith Foster, *Written by Herself: Literary Production by African American Women, 1746–1892* (Bloomington: Indiana University Press, 1993), 108.

38. Valerie Smith, *Self-Discovery and Authority in Afro-American Narrative* (Cambridge, Mass.: Harvard University Press, 1987), 34.

39. Carby also describes how Jacobs rejected Harriet Beecher Stowe's offer "to incorporate her life story into the writing of *The Key to Uncle Tom's Cabin*. This incorporation would have meant that her history would have been circumscribed by the bounds of convention, and Jacobs responded that 'it needed no romance.'" Hazel Carby, *Reconstructing Womanhood: The Emergence of the Afro-American Woman Novelist* (New York: Oxford University Press, 1987), 49.

40. Hartman, *Scenes of Subjection*, 102–3.

41. Spillers, "Mama's Baby, Papa's Maybe," 77.

42. Jacobs, *Incidents*, 84–85.

43. Aliyyah Abdur-Rahman, *Against the Closet: Black Political Longing and the Erotics of Race* (Durham, N.C.: Duke University Press, 2012), 2.

44. Foster, *Written by Herself*, 102. See also Lisa Ze Winters for a careful consideration of the precarity of freedom for "free(d) black women" in *The Mulatta Concubine: Terror, Intimacy, Freedom, and Desire in the Black Transatlantic* (Athens: University of Georgia Press, 2016), 6.

45. Hartman, *Scenes of Subjection*, 9.

46. Christina Sharpe, *Monstrous Intimacies: Making Post-slavery Subjects* (Durham, N.C.: Duke University Press, 2009), 10.

47. Jacobs, *Incidents*, 169.

48. Ibid., 172 (emphasis added).

49. *Oxford English Dictionary*, 3rd ed. (Oxford: Oxford University Press, 2007), s.v. "Pass," available at http://www.oed.com.

50. Cobb, *Picture Freedom*, 47.

51. Nicole R. Fleetwood, *Troubling Vision: Performance, Visuality, and Blackness* (Chicago: University of Chicago Press, 2011), 73.

52. Jacobs, *Incidents*, 171.

53. Ibid., 171–72.

54. Anne Bradford Warner, "Carnival Laughter: Resistance in *Incidents*," in *Harriet Jacobs and "Incidents in the Life of a Slave Girl": New Critical Essays*, ed. Deborah M. Garfield and Rafia Zafar (New York: Cambridge University Press, 1996), 223.

55. John J. Kucich, *Ghostly Communication: Cross-Cultural Spiritualism in Nineteenth-Century American Literature* (Hanover, N.H.: Dartmouth College Press / University Press of New England, 2004), 33.

56. Jacobs, *Incidents*, 240.

57. See Sylvia Wynter, "1492: A New World View," in *Race, Discourse, and the Origin of the Americas: A New World View*, ed. Vera Lawrence Hyatt and Rex Nettleford (Washington, D.C.: Smithsonian Institution Press, 1995), 5–57.

58. Katherine McKittrick, *Demonic Grounds: Black Women and the Cartographies of Struggle* (Minneapolis: University of Minnesota Press, 2006), 130.

59. See Daniel O. Sayers, *A Desolate Place for a Defiant People: The Archaeology of Maroons, Indigenous Americans, and Enslaved Laborers in the Great Dismal Swamp* (Gainesville: University of Florida Press, 2014). See also Wynter, "1492," on the construction of a "subjective understanding" among colonizers.

60. *Encyclopaedia Britannica Online*, s.v. "Great Dismal Swamp: Region, United States," https://www.britannica.com/place/Great-Dismal-Swamp.

61. Jacobs, *Incidents*, 302.

62. "William Wells Brown Describes the Crafts' Escape," *The Liberator*, January 12, 1849, accessed through "Documenting the American South," University Library, University of North Carolina at Chapel Hill, http://docsouth .unc.edu/neh/craft/support1.html.

63. Ibid.

64. Ibid.

65. Daphne Brooks, "Catch Me If You Can: The Art of Escape and Antislavery Performance in the Narratives of William Wells Brown, Henry Box Brown, and William and Ellen Craft," introduction to *The Great Escapes: Four Slave Narratives* (New York: Barnes & Noble Classics, 2007), liii.

66. "William Wells Brown Describes the Crafts' Escape."

67. See, e.g. McCaskill, "'Yours Very Truly,'" 509–29; R. J. M. Blackett, "Fugitive Slaves in Britain: The Odyssey of William and Ellen Craft," *Journal of American Studies* 12, no. 1 (1978): 41–62; and Dorothy Sterling, *Black Foremothers: Three Lives,* 2nd ed. (New York: Feminist Press at CUNY, 1993).

68. Aliyyah I. Abdur-Rahman, "'The Strangest Freaks of Despotism': Queer Sexuality in Antebellum African American Slave Narratives," *African American Review* 40, no. 2 (2006): 229. See also Abdur-Rahman, *Against the Closet.*

69. Barbara McCaskill, *Love, Liberation, and Escaping Slavery: William and Ellen Craft in Cultural Memory* (Athens: University of Georgia Press, 2015), 23.

70. William Craft, *Running a Thousand Miles to Freedom; or, The Escape of William and Ellen Craft from Slavery* (London: William Tweedie, 1860), 2, accessed through "Documenting the American South," University Library, University of North Carolina at Chapel Hill, http://docsouth.unc.edu/neh/craft/craft.html.

71. McCaskill, *Love, Liberation, and Escaping Slavery,* 19.

72. Craft, *Running,* 35.

73. Josephine Brown, *Biography of an American Bondman, by His Daughter* (Boston: R. F. Wallcut, 1856), 76–77, accessed through "Documenting the American South," University Library, University of North Carolina at Chapel Hill, http://docsouth.unc.edu/neh/brownj/brownj.html.

74. McCaskill, *Love, Liberation, and Escaping Slavery,* 25.

75. Craft, *Running,* 61–63.

76. Ibid., 67. Thavolia Glymph provides additional context here in her work on plantation households, as she describes the various ways white women "wielded the power of slave ownership. They owned slaves and managed households in which they held the power of life and death and the importance of those facts for southern women's identity—black and white—were enormous." *Out of the House of Bondage: The Transformation of the Plantation Household* (New York: Cambridge University Press, 2008), 4.

77. Brooks, "Catch Me If You Can," lvii–lviii.

78. Frank B. Wilderson, *Red, White, and Black: Cinema and the Structure of U.S. Antagonisms* (Durham, N.C.: Duke University Press, 2010), 23.

79. Ibid., 38.

80. Spillers, "Mama's Baby, Papa's Maybe," 66.

81. Wilderson, *Red, White, and Black,* 23.

82. Ellen Samuels, "'A Complication of Complaints': Untangling Disability, Race, and Gender in William and Ellen Craft's *Running a Thousand Miles for Freedom*," *MELUS* 31, no. 3 (2006): 19. Samuels quotes Jacques Derrida, *Of Grammatology* (Baltimore: Johns Hopkins University Press, 1976), 163.

83. Samuels, "'A Complication of Complaints,'" 25–26.

84. Ibid., 37.

85. It is not often discussed that the Crafts initially intended to go to Canada but were advised to settle in Boston. Before embarking for England, they lived in Nova Scotia for two weeks, as compared to the four days that receive so much attention in public memory. They began with one night at an inn from which they were pushed out by the white inhabitants and the innkeeper, a woman who found it "impossible to accommodate" them and thus gave them, according to *Running,* "the address of some respectable coloured families, whom she thought, 'under the circumstances,' might be induced to take us. And, as we were not at all comfortable—being compelled to sit, eat and sleep, in the same small room—we were quite willing to change our quarters. I called upon the Rev. Mr. Cannady . . . who received us at a word; and both he and his kind lady treated us handsomely, and for a nominal charge" (106–7). The name Mr. Cannady invokes the traces and presence of black Canadian histories in which the transfigurative politics of black Canada—as the insistence on a place where justice and freedom were possible—was delivered in the face of the failed promises of the Canadian nation-state.

86. The Slavery Abolition Act of 1833 abolished slavery throughout the British Empire, excluding the territories in possession of the East India Company, the island of Ceylon (now known as Sri Lanka), and the island of Saint Helena. The exceptions were eliminated in 1843.

87. McCaskill, *Love, Liberation, and Escaping Slavery,* 56.

88. Craft, *Running,* 108.

89. Ibid., 111.

90. Blackett, "Fugitive Slaves in Britain," 46.

91. Ibid., 47.

92. Ibid.

93. "The Greek Slave," in "Uncle Tom's Cabin and American Culture: A Multi-media Archive," Institute for Advanced Technology in the Humanities,

University of Virginia, accessed November 10, 2015, http://utc.iath.virginia
.edu/sentimnt/grslvhp.html.

94. "Extract of a Letter from Wm. Farmer, Esq., of London, to Wm. Lloyd
Garrison, June 26, 1851—'Fugitive Slaves at the Great Exhibit,'" quoted in
Still, *Underground Rail Road,* 374–75.

95. Ibid., 375.

96. Uri McMillan, *Embodied Avatars: Genealogies of Black Feminist Art and
Performance* (New York: New York University Press, 2015), 81.

97. McCaskill, "'Yours Very Truly,'" 513.

98. Quoted in ibid., 512–13.

99. Cobb, *Picture Freedom,* 53.

100. In many ways, the Crafts seem to have followed the course Black Loyalists forged several decades earlier, as they traveled to Nova Scotia, London, and
British colonial West Africa. See, e.g., Mary Louise Clifford, *From Slavery to
Freetown: Black Loyalists after the American Revolution* (Jefferson, N.C.: McFar-
land Press, 1999); and James W. St. G. Walker, "Myth, History, and Revision-
ism: The Black Loyalists Revisited," *Acadiensis: Journal of the History of the
Atlantic Region* 29, no. 1 (1999): 88–105.

101. See Blackett, "Fugitive Slaves in Britain"; and McCaskill, "'Yours Very
Truly,'" for more details about the commercial success of *Running* and the separate sales of its frontispiece.

102. Blackett, "Fugitive Slaves in Britain," 55.

103. Ibid.

104. Quoted in ibid., 56–57.

105. Dorothy Sterling, *Black Foremothers,* 45.

106. Quoted in Blackett, "Fugitive Slaves in Britain," 57.

107. McCaskill, *Love, Liberation, and Escaping Slavery,* 73.

108. *Report of the British Association for the Advancement of Science, 33rd
Meeting (1863),* 135, accessed through the Biodiversity Heritage Library, http
://www.biodiversitylibrary.org/.

109. "The British Association," *London Times,* August 31, 1863.

110. Ibid. (emphasis in original).

111. Blackett, "Fugitive Slaves in Britain," 58.

112. Ibid.

113. *Report of the British Association,* 140.

114. Ibid.

115. "British Association."

116. Mia Bay, *The White Image in the Black Mind: African-American Ideas
about White People, 1830–1925* (New York: Oxford University Press, 2000),
28–29. Whereas William Craft discussed intraracial difference in ethnological

terms, Ellen Craft was recorded as marking that shift in terms of categorical availability on the U.S. census. As Simone Browne notes, "In the 1850 census, Ellen was listed as residing in Boston and her race is recorded as Black (or rather 'for ditto,' as it was recorded in the column under William's). The 1850 census marked the first time that the federal census included slave schedules for some states in order to enumerate each enslaved person held in a household for dwelling. By the 1890 census, Ellen Craft was recorded as 'M' for Mulatto and her occupation as 'keeping house' in Bryan County, Georgia." Simone Browne, *Dark Matters: On the Surveillance of Blackness* (Durham, N.C.: Duke University Press, 2015), 55.

117. "British Association."

118. Blackett, "Fugitive Slaves in Britain," 59–60.

119. Sterling, *Black Foremothers,* 46–47.

120. Ibid., 47.

121. See Sylvia Wynter, "Unsettling the Coloniality of Being/Power/Truth/Freedom: Towards the Human, after Man, Its Overrepresentation—an Argument," *CR: The New Centennial Review* 3, no. 3 (2003): 257–337.

122. Michael A. Chaney, *Fugitive Vision: Slave Image and Black Identity* (Bloomington: Indiana University Press, 2007), 85.

123. See, e.g., McMillan, *Embodied Avatars;* Samuels, "'A Complication of Complaints'"; Chaney, *Fugitive Visions;* and Ellen M. Weinauer, "'A Most Respectable Looking Gentleman': Passing, Possession, and Transgression in *Running a Thousand Miles for Freedom,*" in *Passing and the Fictions of Identity,* ed. Elaine K. Ginsberg (Durham, N.C.: Duke University Press, 1996), 37–56.

124. McCaskill, "'Yours Very Truly,'" 516.

3. Reading the "Trans-" in Transatlantic Literature

1. Peter Mayer to John Hope Franklin, August 20, 1964, John Hope Franklin Papers, John Hope Franklin Institute, Duke University.

2. Mayer to Franklin, November 7, 1963; Franklin to Mayer, November 12, 1963, John Hope Franklin Papers, John Hope Franklin Institute, Duke University. According to the letters, Franklin refused to write the introduction until after Avon confirmed that Bontemps was not planning to curate the collection of texts.

3. John Hope Franklin, introduction to *Three Negro Classics* (1965; repr., New York: Avon Books, 1999), 21.

4. Ibid., 20.

5. W. E. B. Du Bois, *The Souls of Black Folk,* in *Three Negro Classics,* 213.

6. Franklin, introduction, 21.

7. Heather Russell Andrade compellingly argues that masculinity and racial responsibility are yoked in the works of Washington, Du Bois, and Johnson but most forcefully articulated in Du Bois, when he writes, "To be sure, ultimate freedom and assimilation was [*sic*] the ideal before the leaders [of the abolitionist movement,] but the assertion of the manhood rights of the Negro by himself was the main reliance, and John Brown's raid was the extreme of its logic" (*Souls,* 35). Heather Russell Andrade, "Revising Critical Judgments of *The Autobiography of an Ex-Colored Man," African American Review* 40, no. 2 (2006): 259.

8. Marlon Ross and Martin Summers have both written incisively on the interrelation of race and gender during the period. See, e.g., Marlon B. Ross, *Manning the Race: Reforming Black Men in the Jim Crow Era* (New York: New York University Press, 2004); and Martin Summers, *Manliness and Its Discontents: The Black Middle Class and the Transformation of Masculinity, 1900–1930* (Chapel Hill: University of North Carolina Press, 2004).

9. See, e.g., Hortense Spillers's collection of essays in *Black, White, and in Color: Essays on American Literature and Culture* (Chicago: University of Chicago Press, 2003); Jennifer L. Morgan, *Laboring Women: Reproduction and Gender in New World Slavery* (Philadelphia: University of Pennsylvania Press, 2004); and Saidiya Hartman, *Scenes of Subjection: Terror, Slavery, and Self-Making in Nineteenth-Century America* (New York: Oxford University Press, 1997), which provide generative rubrics for thinking about how and why the dispossession and differential gendering of black women under slavery shape blackness as existential and ontological concerns.

10. Spillers, *Black, White, and in Color,* 217 (emphasis in original).

11. Ibid., 218.

12. Morgan, *Laboring Women,* 77.

13. W. E. B. Du Bois, "The Study of the Negro Problems," *Annals of the American Academy of Political and Social Science,* January 1898, 4–5.

14. Ibid.

15. Frank Wilderson, *Red, White, and Black: Cinema and the Structure of U.S. Antagonisms* (Durham, N.C.: Duke University Press, 2010), 306.

16. Ibid.

17. Laura Doyle, *Bordering on the Body: The Racial Matrix of Modern Fiction and Culture* (New York: Oxford University Press, 1994), 27.

18. David Marriott, *Haunted Life: Visual Culture and Black Modernity* (New Brunswick, N.J.: Rutgers University Press, 2007), 81.

19. Sylvia Wynter, "Towards the Sociogenic Principle: Fanon, the Puzzle of Conscious Experience, of 'Identity' and What It's Like to Be 'Black,'" paper presented in advance of the publication of "Towards the Sociogenic Principle:

Fanon, Identity, the Puzzle of Conscious Experience, and What It Is Like to Be 'Black,'" in *National Identities and Sociopolitical Changes in Latin America,* ed. Mercedes F. Durán-Cogan and Antonio Gómez-Moriana (New York: Routledge, 2001), 11.

20. Frantz Fanon, *Black Skin, White Masks,* trans. Charles Lam Markmann (New York: Grove Press, 1967), 8.

21. It should be noted, as Lewis R. Gordon has argued, that Fanon's emphasis on "want" is distinct from Du Bois's critique of blackness as a "problem." As Gordon writes, "The convergence of the 'black problem' with desire ('want') already marks a distinction in Fanon's analysis. . . . This question of want, of desire, is not as simple as it may at first seem, for the life of desire is pereflective and reflective." Lewis R. Gordon, *What Fanon Said: A Philosophical Introduction to His Life and Thought* (New York: Fordham University Press, 2015), 21.

22. See Wynter, "Towards the Sociogenic Principle," 30–66; and Sylvia Wynter, "Beyond Miranda's Meanings: Un/silencing the 'Demonic Ground' of Caliban's Woman," afterword to *Out of the Kumbla: Caribbean Women and Literature,* ed. Carole Boyce Davies and Elaine Savory Fido (Trenton: Africa World Press, 1990), 355–72.

23. Julia Kristeva, *Powers of Horror: An Essay on Abjection* (New York: Columbia University Press, 1982), 5 (emphasis in original).

24. Hortense Spillers, "Mama's Baby, Papa's Maybe: An American Grammar Book," *Diacritics* 17, no. 2 (1987): 80 (emphasis in original).

25. Lindon Barrett, *Racial Blackness and the Discontinuity of Western Modernity,* ed. Justin A Joyce, Dwight A. McBride, and John Carlos Rowe (Urbana: University of Illinois Press, 2014).

26. Denise Ferreira da Silva characterizes being and interiority as the onto-epistemological grip of the "transparency thesis" of modernity in *Toward a Global Idea of Race* (Minneapolis: University of Minnesota Press, 2007), 4.

27. Spillers, *Black, White, and in Color,* 228 (emphasis in original).

28. Philip Gould, "The Rise, Development, and Circulation of the Slave Narrative," in *The Cambridge Companion to the African American Slave Narrative,* ed. Audrey A. Fisch (New York: Cambridge University Press, 2007), 19–20.

29. Deborah E. McDowell, "Telling Slavery in 'Freedom's' Time: Post-Reconstruction and the Harlem Renaissance," in Fisch, *Cambridge Companion,* 150.

30. Rebecca Carroll, introduction to *Uncle Tom or New Negro? African Americans Reflect on Booker T. Washington and "Up from Slavery" 100 Years Later* (New York: Harlem Moon, 2006), 2.

31. Ibid.

32. Booker T. Washington, preface to *Up from Slavery*, in *Three Negro Classics*, 25.

33. Review of *The Story of My Life and Work*, by Booker T. Washington, *Nation*, April 4, 1901, 281–82.

34. According to Louis R. Harlan, "The *Outlook*'s circulation was more than 100,000, and many copies passed through several hands or were read aloud to the family at the breakfast table or to neighbors in the evening." *The Booker T. Washington Papers*, vol. 1, *The Autobiographical Writings*, ed. Louis R. Harlan (Champaign: University of Illinois Press, 1972), xxviii–xxix.

35. Washington, *Up from Slavery*, 25; and Harlan, ibid., xxii.

36. Harlan, *Autobiographical Writings*, xvi. Harlan suggests, "Sometime in the summer of 1900, Washington began to dictate autobiographical notes to Thrasher as they traveled together on trains or between trains. Washington then wrote a draft of the autobiography from Thrasher's notes and let Thrasher check the manuscript. On occasion, Washington dictated or wrote a rough sketch of a chapter and Thrasher revised it and gave it to the publishers" (xxvi).

37. Ibid., xxix.

38. W. Fitzhugh Brundage, "Reconsidering Booker T. Washington and *Up from Slavery*," in *Booker T. Washington and Black Progress: "Up from Slavery" 100 Years Later* (Gainesville: University Press of Florida, 2003), 1.

39. Robert Gooding-Williams, "Du Bois, Politics, Aesthetics: An Introduction," *Public Culture* 17, no. 2 (2005): 204.

40. Manning Marable argued in his essay "Celebrating *Souls*: Deconstructing the Du Boisian Legacy" that "If Du Bois had not written 'Of Mr. Booker T. Washington and Others,' *Souls* would have been still essentially the same book in its contents, but would probably not have been perceived as a radical challenge to Jim Crow." Manning Marable, "Celebrating *Souls*: Deconstructing the Du Boisian Legacy," in Alford A. Young Jr. et al., *The Souls of W. E. B. Du Bois* (Boulder, Colo.: Paradigm, 2006), 19.

41. Cheryl A. Wall, "Resounding *Souls*: Du Bois and the African American Literary Tradition," *Public Culture* 17, no. 2 (2005): 218.

42. "Criteria for Negro Art," in *W. E. B. Du Bois: "The Crisis" Writings*, ed. Daniel Walden (Greenwich, Conn.: Fawcett Premier Books, 1972), 287–88. Originally published in *The Crisis*, October 1926, 290–97.

43. Ibid.

44. *Oxford English Dictionary Online* (Oxford University Press), s.v. "propaganda," http://www.oed.com/view/Entry/152605?rskey=VMIfPh&result=1.

45. Ross, *Manning the Race*, 42.

46. In this regard, one might trace another connection to be drawn from Alexander Weheliye's *Phonographies: Grooves in Sonic Afro-modernity* (Durham,

N.C.: Duke University Press, 2005), which explores the ways Du Bois prefigured the hip-hop DJ, for example. Du Bois and his intellectual descendants are frequently shaped by black authenticity's figuration of a racialized and gendered real.

47. Du Bois, "Criteria for Negro Art," 285.

48. Du Bois, *Souls,* 241–42.

49. Ibid., 247.

50. Ibid.

51. Erica Edwards, *Charisma and the Fictions of Black Leadership* (Minneapolis: University of Minnesota Press, 2012), 27–28.

52. Jacqueline Goldsby, *A Spectacular Secret: Lynching in American Life and Literature* (Chicago: University of Chicago Press, 2006), 188.

53. Ibid.

54. James Weldon Johnson, *Along This Way: The Autobiography of James Weldon Johnson* (New York: Penguin, 2008), 238–39.

55. "A New Book," review of *Along This Way,* by James Weldon Johnson, *Cleveland Gazette,* June 15, 1912.

56. Ibid.

57. Shana L. Redmond, *Anthem: Social Movements and the Sound of Solidarity in the African Diaspora* (New York: New York University Press, 2013), 75. Redmond is citing Sondra Kathryn Wilson, introduction to Johnson, *Along This Way* (2008), xiv.

58. Johnson, *Along This Way* (2008), 238–39.

59. Dickson D. Bruce Jr., *Black American Writing from the Nadir: The Evolution of a Literary Tradition, 1877–1915* (Baton Rouge: Louisiana State University Press, 1989), 253.

60. Review of *The Autobiography of an Ex-Colored Man,* by James Weldon Johnson, *Chicago Defender,* November 14, 1914.

61. Melvin R. Sylvester, "Negro Periodicals in the United States, an Annotated Bibliography," accessed through Long Island University, December 12, 2014, http://www2.liu.edu/cwis/cwp/library/historic.htm#16.

62. "'Autobiography of an Ex-Colored Man' Appears in German," *Negro Star,* August 9, 1929.

63. James Weldon Johnson, *Along This Way: The Autobiography of James Weldon Johnson* (New York: De Capo Press, 1933), 239.

64. Bruce, *Black American Writing from the Nadir,* 253.

65. Grant Farred, "Autopbiography," *South Atlantic Quarterly* 110, no. 4 (2011): 831–32.

66. Spillers, *Black, White, and in Color,* 217–18.

67. James Weldon Johnson, "The Black Mammy," in *Fifty Years and Other Poems* (Boston: Cornhill, 1917), 12, http://name.umdl.umich.edu/BAD9126.0001.001.

68. Ibid.

69. *Oxford English Dictionary Online* (Oxford University Press), s.v. "mammy," http://www.oed.com/view/Entry/113188?redirectedFrom=mammy.

70. Ibid.

71. Kimberly Wallace-Sanders, *Mammy: A Century of Race, Gender, and Southern Memory* (Ann Arbor: University of Michigan Press, 2008), 2–4.

72. Hartman, *Scenes of Subjection,* 89.

73. Amber Musser, "Masochism: A Queer Subjectivity?," *Rhizomes* 11–12 (2005–2006): para. 4 (emphasis in original). See also Amber Musser, *Sensational Flesh: Race, Power, and Masochism* (New York: New York University Press, 2014).

74. Musser, "Masochism," para. 5.

75. Darieck Scott, *Extravagant Abjection: Blackness, Power, and Sexuality in the African American Literary Imagination* (New York: New York University Press, 2010), 15.

76. Du Bois, *Souls,* 255–57, 300–301.

77. Washington, *Up from Slavery,* 89–90.

78. Patricia Hill Collins, "Shifting the Center: Race, Class, and Feminist Theorizing about Motherhood," in *Representations of Motherhood,* ed. Donna Bassin, Margaret Honey, and Meryle M. Kaplan (New Haven, Conn.: Yale University Press, 1994), 62.

79. Du Bois, *Souls,* 253.

80. Ibid.

81. Ibid., 258–59.

82. Ibid., 259–60.

83. Noliwe M. Rooks, *Hair Raising: Beauty, Culture, and African American Women* (New Brunswick, N.J.: Rutgers University Press, 1996), 26–27.

84. Du Bois, *Souls,* 261, 253–54.

85. Ibid., 259–60.

86. Washington, *Up from Slavery,* 73.

87. Ibid.

88. See Thavolia Glymph, *Out of the House of Bondage: The Transformation of the Plantation Household* (New York: Cambridge University Press, 2008), for a trenchant analysis of white mistresses and plantation households.

89. Washington, *Up from Slavery,* 76–77.

90. Du Bois, *Souls,* 232.

91. Ibid.

92. Du Bois would return to this theme repeatedly in his writings, but he gives sustained treatment on the meaning of menial labor in chapter 5 of *Darkwater*, "The Servant in the House," in which he argues that this kind of service work should be regarded as an anachronism that impedes black people from participating in modernity. *Darkwater: Voices from within the Veil* (Amherst, N.Y.: Humanity Books, 2003).

93. Du Bois, *Souls*, 232.

94. Ibid., 364.

95. Ibid., 366.

96. Ibid., 367.

97. Ibid., 376–77.

98. Ibid. The white and black Johns encounter each other at a concert that foreshadows how racism, violence, and lynching would emerge as prominent events in the narrative.

99. Charles I. Nero, "Queering *The Souls of Black Folk*," *Public Culture* 17, no. 2 (2005): 263.

100. Eve Kosofsky Sedgwick, *Between Men: English Literature and Male Homosocial Desire* (New York: Columbia University Press, 1985), 51; quoted in ibid., 264.

101. Nero, "Queering *The Souls of Black Folk*," 264–68.

102. Tamar Katz, *Impressionist Subjects: Gender, Interiority, and Modernist Fiction in England.* (Urbana: University of Illinois Press, 2000), 3–4.

103. Nero, "Queering *The Souls of Black Folk*," 271.

104. Washington, *Up from Slavery*, 65–66.

105. Ibid., 66.

106. Ibid., 162.

107. Siobhan B. Somerville, *Queering the Color Line: Race and the Invention of Homosexuality in American Culture* (Durham, N.C.: Duke University Press, 2000), 114.

108. C. Riley Snorton, "Passing for White, Passing for Man: James Weldon Johnson's *Autobiography of an Ex-Colored Man* as Transgender Narrative," in *Transgender Migrations: The Bodies, Borders, and Politics of Transition*, ed. Trystan Cotton (New York: Routledge, 2012), 107–18.

109. James Weldon Johnson, *Autobiography of an Ex-Colored Man* in *Three Negro Classics*, 401–2.

110. Jay Prosser, *Second Skins: The Body Narrative of Transsexuality* (New York: Columbia University Press, 2004), 100.

111. Johnson, *Autobiography*, 419.

112. Ibid., 471–72.

113. See, e.g., Robert Stepto, *From behind the Veil: A Study of Afro-American Narrative* (Urbana: University of Illinois Press, 1979); Phillip Bryan Harper, *Are We Not Men? Masculine Anxiety and the Problem of African American Identity* (New York: Oxford University Press, 1996); Somerville, *Queering the Color Line*; Scott, *Extravagant Abjection*; and Cheryl Clarke, "Race, Homosocial Desire, and 'Mammon' in *Autobiography of an Ex-Colored Man*," in *Professions of Desire: Lesbian and Gay Studies in Literature*, ed. George E. Haggerty and Bonnie Zimmerman (New York: Modern Language Association of America, 1995), 84–97.

114. Johnson, *Autobiography*, 472.

115. Ibid., 475.

116. Somerville, *Queering the Color Line*, 121–22.

117. Scott, *Extravagant Abjection*, 124; and Johnson, *Autobiography*, 510.

118. Scott, *Extravagant Abjection*, 124.

119. Matt Richardson, "'My Father Didn't Have a Dick': Social Death and Jackie Kay's *Trumpet*," *GLQ* 18, nos. 2–3 (2012): 362.

120. Johnson, *Autobiography*, 510.

121. Alexander G. Weheliye, *Habeas Viscus: Racializing Assemblages, Biopolitics, and Black Feminist Theories of the Human* (Durham, N.C.: Duke University Press, 2014), 39.

122. L. H. Stallings, *Funk the Erotic: Transaesthetics and Black Sexual Cultures* (Urbana: University of Illinois Press, 2015), 9–12.

4. A Nightmarish Silhouette

1. Susan Stryker, introduction to *Christine Jorgensen: A Personal Autobiography*, by Christine Jorgensen (San Francisco: Cleis Press, 2000), v.

2. David Harley Serlin, "Christine Jorgensen and the Cold War Closet," *Radical History Review* 62 (1995): 154.

3. Stryker, introduction, vii–ix. For more on this, see Stryker on how the interplay of Jorgensen's fantastic and phantasmatic figuration with the availability of newly developing somatic technologies forged a link in representation between the transsexual form and the atomic bomb, in "Christine Jorgensen's Atom Bomb: Transsexuality and the Emergence of Postmodernism," in *Playing Dolly: Technocultural Formations, Fantasies, and Fictions of Assisted Reproduction*, ed. E. Ann Kaplan and Susan Squier (New Brunswick, N.J.: Rutgers University Press, 1999), 157–71.

4. "Tapping the Wires: World and National News Highlights by Teletype," *Chicago Defender*, December 20, 1952.

5. Alvin Chick Webb, "Footlights and Sidelights," *New York Amsterdam News*, January 30, 1954.

6. Louis Farrakhan (aka the Charmer), "Is She Is, or Is She Ain't?," on *The Charmer Is Louis Farrakhan: Calypso Favorites, 1953–1954,* Bostrox Records 9908, CD.

7. "The Truth about Christine Jorgensen," part 1, *New York Post,* April 6, 1953; "The Case of Christine," *Time,* April 20, 1953, quoted in David Serlin, *Replaceable You: Engineering the Body in Postwar America* (Chicago: University of Chicago Press, 2004), 184.

8. Joanne Meyerowitz, "Christine Jorgensen and the Story of How Sex Changed," in *Women's America: Refocusing the Past,* ed. Linda K. Kerber, Jane Sherron De Hart, Cornelia Hughes Dayton, and Judy Tzu-Chun Wu, 8th ed. (New York: Oxford University Press, 2016), 624.

9. As Jay Prosser writes, Jorgensen's popularization of transsexuality coincided with a formula "that continues to trope transsexuality in its medical narrative version, [in which] being trapped in the wrong body has become the crux of an authenticating transsexual 'rhetoric.'" Jay Prosser, *Second Skins: The Body Narratives of Transsexuality* (New York: Columbia University Press, 1998), 69.

10. Jorgensen, *Christine Jorgensen,* 90–91.

11. Meyerowitz, "Christine Jorgensen," 626.

12. Emily Skidmore, "Constructing the 'Good Transsexual': Christine Jorgensen, Whiteness, and Heteronormativity in the Mid-Twentieth Century Press," *Feminist Studies* 37, no. 2 (2011): 271.

13. Ibid.

14. Serlin, "Christine Jorgensen," 156.

15. Toni Morrison, *Playing in the Dark: Whiteness and the Literary Imagination* (New York: Vintage, 1992), 36–37.

16. Stryker, introduction, viii.

17. Viviane Namaste, *Invisible Lives: The Erasure of Transsexual and Transgendered People* (Chicago: University of Chicago Press, 2000), 13.

18. By "Long Civil Rights Movement," I am referring to Jacqueline Dowd Hall's contestation of the typical periodization of the civil rights movement as contained between *Brown v. Board of Education* (1954) and the Voting Rights Act of 1965 to include the years before and after and to unsettle the version of linear progression that the previous chronology implied. Jacqueline Dowd Hall, "The Long Civil Rights Movement and the Political Uses of the Past," *Journal of American History* 91, no. 4 (2005): 1233–63.

19. Hortense Spillers, "Interstices: A Small Drama of Words," in *Black, White, and in Color: Essays on American Literature and Culture* (Chicago: University of Chicago Press, 2003), 174.

20. Nicholas Mirzoeff, "The Right to Look," *Critical Inquiry* 37, no. 3 (2011): 473–96.

21. Spillers, "Interstices," 163.

22. Ralph Ellison, *Invisible Man* (New York: Random House, 1952), 9–10.

23. Saidiya Hartman, "Venus in Two Acts," *Small Axe* 12, no. 2 (2008): 2.

24. Erica Taylor, "Little-Known Black History Fact: Lucy Hicks Anderson," *Tom Joyner Morning Show,* Power 98.9 FM (New York), February 18, 2011.

25. Monica Roberts, "A Look at African-American Trans Trailblazers," Ebony News and Views, *Ebony,* March 1, 2012, http://www.ebony.com/news -views/trans-trailblazers#axzz2KTuytw3m.

26. *We've Been Around—Lucy Hicks Anderson* (webseries), directed by Rhys Ernst, March 1, 2016, http://www.wevebeenaround.com/lucy/; Jeffrey Wayne Maulhardt, *Oxnard, 1941–2004* (Mount Pleasant, S.C.: Arcadia Publishing and the History Press, 2005); Lorenza Munoz, "Last Meal for the Breakfast Club?," *Los Angeles Times,* January 13, 1997, http://articles.latimes.com/1997– 01–13/local/me-18264_1_gloria-stuart.

27. Boris Artzybasheff, *Time* cover illustration of Spruille Braden, November 5, 1945. Running for office in Argentina with the slogan "Braden or Perón," future president Juan Perón's political ideas were described as a form of corporate or "right-wing" socialism, although some scholars have aligned Perón's regime with European strains of fascism, most notably akin to Benito Mussolini. The use of swastikas to characterize and caricature his platform played on *Time*'s readership's anxieties about the prospect of another Axis power near the southern border of the United States.

28. James A. Linen, "A Letter from the Publisher," *Time,* January 14, 1946, 13.

29. "California: Sin & Souffl," *Time,* November 5, 1945, 27.

30. Ibid.

31. Linen, "Letter from the Publisher."

32. "Night Life Queen Guilty of Perjury in Sex Case," *The Afro-American,* December 12, 1945, 1–2.

33. Ibid.

34. Ibid.

35. Ibid.

36. See Harriet Washington, *Medical Apartheid: The Dark History of Experimentation on Black Americans from Colonial Times to the Present* (New York: Doubleday, 2006).

37. Slavoj Žižek, *Organs without Bodies: Deleuze and Consequences* (New York: Routledge, 2004), 4.

38. Michael Carter, "Allotment for 'Wife' Fatal," *The Afro-American*, April 20, 1946, 1–2. It is important to mark here how the language of "male wife" is

a recurrent descriptor of persons in African gender epistemologies. See, e.g., Ifi Amadiume, *Male Daughters, Female Husbands: Gender and Sex in an African Society* (London: Zed Books, 1987); Stephen O. Murray and Will Roscoe, eds., *Boy-Wives and Female Husbands: Studies in African Homosexualities* (New York: Palgrave Macmillan, 1998); and Oyeronke Oyewumi, ed., *African Gender Studies: A Reader* (New York: Palgrave Macmillan, 2005).

39. Carter, "Allotment for 'Wife' Fatal."

40. Ibid.

41. "The Man Who Lived 30 Years as a Woman," *Ebony*, November 1975, 86, 88 (originally printed in October 1951).

42. Ibid., 85.

43. Lindon Barrett, *Blackness and Value: Seeing Double* (New York: Cambridge University Press, 1999), 19–20.

44. An understanding of the U.S. imperative to intervene in "communist expansionism" globally was expressed in A *Report to the National Security Council—NSC 68*, April 12, 1950, President's Secretary's File, Truman Papers, Harry S. Truman Library and Museum, accessed at https://www.trumanlibrary.org/whistlestop/study_collections/coldwar/documents/pdf/10–1.pdf.

45. "Man Who Lived 30 Years."

46. Karla F. C. Holloway, *Legal Fictions: Constituting Race, Composing Literature* (Durham, N.C.: Duke University Press, 2014), 1.

47. "Man Who Lived 30 Years," 85.

48. Ibid.

49. Barbie Zelizer, *About to Die: How News Images Move the Public* (New York: Oxford University Press, 2010), 66.

50. See ibid., 62–66.

51. Susan Sontag, *Regarding the Pain of Others* (New York: Picador, 2003), 34.

52. Rinaldo Walcott, "Black Queer Studies, Freedom, and Other Human Possibilities," in *Understanding Blackness through Performance: Contemporary Arts and the Representation of Identity*, ed. Anne Cremieux, Jean-Paul Rocchi, and Xavier Lemoine (New York: Palgrave Macmillan, 2013), 143.

53. Ibid., 145.

54. Christina Sharpe, *In the Wake: On Blackness and Being* (Durham, N.C.: Duke University Press, 2016), 38.

55. Judith Butler coined "grievable life" in her examination of wartime imagery and its circulation of violence, racism, and methods of coercion. Judith Butler, *Frames of War: When Is Life Grievable?* (New York: Verso, 2010).

56. Sharon Holland, *Raising the Dead: Readings of Death and (Black) Subjectivity* (Durham, N.C.: Duke University Press, 2000), 15. Holland's work

also discusses how black death, in its materiality, troubles the center-versus-margins paradigm. Holland visits this question in her analysis of black life and death in anthropology and literature; I am extending this conversation by making use of the visual and the popular as a way to think about quotidian circulations of black death, particularly as they occur in the intramural spaces of the black press.

57. In April 1951, for example, the adjudication of the death sentence for Julius and Ethel Rosenberg, a couple convicted for conspiracy to commit espionage in relation to sharing information with the Soviet Union about the development of nuclear weaponry in the United States became a national media story. See, e.g., Douglas O. Linder, "Judge Kaufman's Statement upon Sentencing the Rosenbergs," "Famous Trials," University of Missouri–Kansas City Law School, accessed June 22, 2017, at http://www.famous-trials.com/rosenberg/1994-kaufmanstmt.

58. In the February 1976 edition of *Ebony*, editors printed the following letter from Gary McIntire of the People's Gay Caucus: "In your 30th anniversary issue, you had an article about a male who passed as a female for 30 years. Also, in the same issue you had an article about a black person who passed as a white.

"To get to the point it isn't any more 'abnormal' for a gay (man) to pass as a heterosexual (woman) than it is for a black person to pass as a white. In both cases the persons are only trying to get privileges that would otherwise be denied them.

"I think it was sexist of you to classify a very basic desire for human privilege by this gay brother as abnormal. In the future I hope you will be more careful about labeling things 'abnormal' that you don't understand" (18).

59. "Man Who Lived 30 Years," 88.

60. The phrase "poetics of relation," taken up in Rinaldo Walcott's essay "Black Queer Studies, Freedom, and Other Human Possibilities," is inspired by and indebted to Édouard Glissant's *Poetics of Relation*, trans. Betsy Wing (Ann Arbor: University of Michigan Press, 1997).

61. Homi K. Bhabha, *The Location of Culture* (New York: Routledge, 1994), 122–23 (emphasis in original).

62. Ibid.

63. "Male Shake Dancer Plans to Change Sex, Wed GI in Europe," *Jet*, June 18, 1953, 24.

64. Ibid., 25.

65. "Male Dancer Becomes Danish Citizen to Change His Sex," *Jet*, June 25, 1953, 26.

66. "Shake Dancer Postpones Sex Change for Face Lifting," *Jet*, August 6, 1953, 19.

67. Roderick Ferguson, *Aberrations in Black: Toward a Queer of Color Critique* (Minneapolis: University of Minnesota Press, 2004), 1.

68. Bhabha, *Location of Culture*, 123.

69. "Tax Snag Halts Male Dancer's Trip for Sex Change," *Jet*, October 15, 1953, 19.

70. Bhabha, *Location of Culture*, 123.

71. Ferguson, *Aberrations in Black*, 1–2.

72. Ibid., 2.

73. "'Double-Sexed' Defendant Makes No Hit with Jury," *Chicago Daily Defender*, April 4, 1957.

74. "Other Side of the News," *Pittsburgh Courier*, May 29, 1954, 29.

75. "'Double-Sexed' Defendant."

76. Judith Butler, *Gender Trouble: Feminism and the Subversion of Identity* (New York: Routledge, 1990), 9.

77. "Brutality 'Twist,'" *Chicago Daily Defender*, October 13, 1969.

78. Toni Anthony, "'Betty' Brown Charges Police Attacked 'Him,'" *Chicago Daily Defender*, October 13, 1969.

79. Barrett, *Blackness and Value*, 21.

80. Ferguson, *Aberrations in Black*, 1.

81. Ibid.

82. Serlin, *Replaceable You*, 139–40.

83. "Mississippi Woman Poses as Man for 8 Years," *Jet*, July 29, 1954, 7.

84. "The Woman Who Lived as a Man for 15 Years," *Ebony*, November 10, 1954, 93.

85. Eric A. Stanley, "Fugitive Flesh: Gender Self-Determination, Queer Abolition, and Trans Resistance," in *Captive Genders: Trans Embodiment and the Prison Industrial Complex*, ed. Eric A. Stanley and Nat Smith (Oakland, Calif.: AK Press, 2011), 4.

86. "Woman Who Lived as a Man," 93.

87. Ibid., 95.

88. Sarah Haley, *No Mercy Here: Gender, Punishment, and the Making of Jim Crow Modernity* (Chapel Hill: University of North Carolina Press, 2016), 6.

89. Ibid.

90. "Woman Who Lived as a Man," 93.

91. Ibid., 94.

92. Ibid., 97.

93. Ibid., 94.

94. Spillers, "Interstices," 163.

95. *Oxford English Dictionary Online* (Oxford University Press), s.v. "restive," http://www.oed.com/view/Entry/163973?redirectedFrom=restive.

96. "Woman Who Lived as a Man," 96.

97. Elizabeth Freeman, *Time Binds: Queer Temporalities, Queer Histories* (Durham, N.C.: Duke University Press, 2010), 60.

98. "Woman Who Lived as a Man," 98.

99. See, e.g., Prosser, *Second Skins*; Judith Halberstam, *In a Queer Time and Place: Transgender Bodies, Subcultural Lives* (New York: New York University Press, 2005); Gayle Salamon, *Assuming a Body: Transgender and Rhetorics of Materiality* (New York: Columbia University Press, 2010); and Dean Spade, *Normal Life: Administrative Violence, Critical Trans Politics, and the Limits of Law* (Durham, N.C.: Duke University Press, 2015).

5. DeVine's Cut

1. *The Brandon Teena Story*, directed by Susan Muska and Gréta Ólafs-dottir (1998; Docurama, 2000), DVD; *Boys Don't Cry*, directed by Kimberly Peirce (1999; 20th Century Fox Home Entertainment, 2000), DVD.

2. J. Jack Halberstam, *In a Queer Time and Place: Transgender Bodies, Subcultural Lives* (New York: New York University Press, 2005), 23.

3. Jennifer Devere Brody, "Boyz Do Cry: Screening History's White Lies," *Screen* 43, no. 1 (2002): 92.

4. Shana Agid, "The Disappearance of Phillip DeVine," screen-printed poster, Rind Press, October 26, 2007, https://rindpress.com/2007/10/26/the-disappearance-of-phillip-devine/.

5. "The Truth behind *Boys Don't Cry*," 20/20, ABC News, February 10, 2000, video, www.dailymotion.com/video/x2vw29e.

6. Halberstam, *In a Queer Time and Place*, 25.

7. Kevin Abourezk, "Teena Brandon Case Gave Rise to Transgendered Movement," *Lincoln Journal Star*, December 28, 2003.

8. I have written more extensively about the "symptom," as it pertains to media coverage of issues of race and sexuality, in "On the Question of 'Who's Out in Hip Hop,'" *Souls: A Critical Journal of Black Politics, Culture, and Society* 16, no. 3 (2014): 283–302.

9. For more on the politics of visibility and inclusion vis-à-vis hate-crimes law, see Dean Spade, *Administrative Violence, Critical Trans Politics, and the Limits of Law* (Brooklyn: South End Press, 2011).

10. Aphrodite Jones, *All S/he Wanted: The True Story of "Brandon Teena"* (New York: Pocket Books, 1996), 316.

11. David M. Jones, "Hegemonic Whiteness and the Humboldt Murders: *Boys Don't Cry*, Historical Memory, and the Ghostly Presence of Phillip DeVine," in *Coming Out to the Mainstream: New Queer Cinema in the 21st Century*, ed.

JoAnne C. Juett and David M. Jones (Newcastle upon Tyne: Cambridge Scholars, 2010), 177.

12. See, e.g., Halberstam, *In a Queer Time and Place*; Amy Villarejo, *Lesbian Rule: Cultural Criticism and the Value of Desire* (Durham, N.C.: Duke University Press, 2003); Jay Prosser, *Second Skins: The Body Narratives of Transsexuality* (New York: Columbia University Press, 1998); and the "Reports and Debates" section on Kimberly Peirce's *Boys Don't Cry* (1999) for *Screen* journal, 2001–2002. Among the several articles published in *Screen*, Brody's "Boyz Do Cry" is the only essay to discuss DeVine's palpable absence in Peirce's film.

13. Jones, "Hegemonic Whiteness and the Humboldt Murders," 213.

14. Frantz Fanon, *Black Skin, White Masks*, trans. Charles Lan Markmann (New York: Grove Press, 1967), 120.

15. Katherine McKittrick, *Demonic Grounds: Black Women and the Cartographies of Struggle* (Minneapolis: University of Minnesota Press, 2006), 5.

16. Hortense Spillers, *Black, White, and in Color: Essays on American Literature and Culture* (Chicago: University of Chicago Press, 2003), 205.

17. Muska and Ólafsdottir, *Brandon Teena Story*.

18. David Marriott, *Haunted Life: Visual Culture and Black Modernity* (New Brunswick, N.J.: Rutgers University Press, 2007), 1–2.

19. Jones, *All S/he Wanted*, 9.

20. See Ruth Wilson Gilmore's definition of racism in *Golden Gulag: Prisons, Surplus, Crisis, and Opposition in Globalizing California* (Berkeley: University of California Press, 2007), 28, which I draw heavily upon and am indebted to in describing the conditions that give rise to the emergence of secular martyrs consecrated by political movements.

21. See, e.g., Christina Sharpe, *Monstrous Intimacies: Making Post-slavery Subjects* (Durham, N.C.: Duke University Press, 2009), 4; as well as Saidiya V. Hartman, *Scenes of Subjection: Terror, Slavery, and Self-Making in Nineteenth-Century America* (New York: Oxford University Press, 1997).

22. See, e.g., Audre Lorde, *Zami: A New Spelling of My Name* (New York: Crossing Press, 1982); and Audre Lorde, *Sister Outsider: Essays and Speeches* (New York: Crossing Press, 1984).

23. Sylvia Wynter, "Towards the Sociogenic Principle: Fanon, Identity, the Puzzle of Conscious Experience, and What It Is Like to Be 'Black,'" in *National Identities and Sociopolitical Changes in Latin America,* ed. Mercedes F. Durán-Cogan and Antonio Gómez-Moriana (New York: Routledge, 2001), 60. Throughout her writings, Wynter often refers to "autopoiesis" as a formal praxis of the sociogenic principle, but I turn to Lorde's use of "biomythography" to foreground practices of living and dying and the urgent need for vocabulary—for new spellings—to describe those actions. Although I do not find Lorde's

and Wynter's concepts necessarily incompatible and would also include Saidiya Hartman's concept of "critical fabulation" among a constellation of terms that speak to these sets of concerns, I am particularly drawn to Lorde's emphasis on sensation and *Zami*'s articulation of the enmeshment of memory and fiction as a way to give life different meaning.

24. Katherine McKittrick, "Axis, Bold as Love: On Sylvia Wynter, Jimi Hendrix, and the Promise of Science," in *Sylvia Wynter: On Being Human as Praxis*, ed. Katherine McKittrick (Durham, N.C.: Duke University Press, 2015), 156 (emphasis in original).

25. Wynter, "Towards the Sociogenic Principle," 58.

26. In David Marriott's critique of Wynter's turn to "science," he contends that her elaboration of Fanon's articulation of "sociogeny," as that which, alongside ontogeny and phylogeny, would explain matters of being, has the effect of rendering sociogeny as "nothing but techne," wherein sociogenesis is posited as a purely methodological concern. David Marriott, "Inventions of Existence: Sylvia Wynter, Frantz Fanon, Sociogeny, and 'the Damned,'" *CR: The New Centennial Review* 11, no. 3 (2011): 81.

27. Lorde, *Zami*, 5. The reference to "dreams/myths/histories" is from an unnumbered page in *Zami* as well.

28. Elizabeth Alexander, "'Coming out Blackened and Whole': Fragmentation and Reintegration in Audre Lorde's *Zami* and *The Cancer Journals*," *American Literary History* 6, no. 4 (1994): 696. See also Mecca Jamilah Sullivan's dissertation, "Interstitial Voices: The Poetics of Difference in Afrodiasporic Women's Literature" (University of Pennsylvania, 2012), which attends to black women's formal in/ter/ventions as they provide new ways for understanding grammars of difference.

29. Sylvia Wynter, "Unsettling the Coloniality of Being/Power/Truth/Freedom: Towards the Human, after Man, Its Overrepresentation—an Argument," *CR: The New Centennial Review* 3, no. 3 (2003): 257–337.

30. Marriott, "Inventions of Existence," 53–54.

31. Orlando Patterson, *Slavery and Social Death: A Comparative Study* (Cambridge, Mass.: Harvard University Press, 1985); Jared Sexton, "The Social Life of Social Death: On Afro-pessimism and Black Optimism," *In Tensions* 5 (2011): 1–47; Eric Stanley, "Near Life, Queer Death: Overkill and Ontological Capture," *Social Text* 29, no. 2 (2011): 1–19.

32. Christina Sharpe, *In the Wake: On Blackness and Being* (Durham, N.C.: Duke University Press, 2016), 5.

33. Achille Mbembe, *On the Postcolony* (Berkeley: University of California Press, 2001), 197.

34. Alexander G. Weheliye, *Habeas Viscus: Racializing Assemblages, Biopolitics, and Black Feminist Theories of the Human* (Durham, N.C.: Duke University Press, 2014).

35. Frantz Fanon, *Black Skin, White Masks* (New York: Grove Press, 1967), 229.

36. Information about the impact of the earthquake may be found in U.S. Geological Survey, "Historic Earthquakes: San Fernando, California," abridged from Carl W. Stover and Jerry L. Coffman, "Seismicity of the United States, 1568–1989 (Revised)," U.S. Geological Survey Professional Paper 1527 (Washington: United States Government Printing Office, 1993), accessed December 15, 2015, http://earthquake.usgs.gov/earthquakes/states/events/1971_02_09 .php.

37. See, e.g., "Center for Disease Control and Prevention's DES Update," Centers for Disease Control and Prevention, accessed December 16, 2015, at http://www.cdc.gov/des/consumers/download/do3_update.pdf.

38. See, e.g., "DES History," Center for Disease Control and Prevention, accessed December 16, 2015, at http://www.cdc.gov/des/consumers/about/ history.html; and "Selected Item from the FDA Drug Bulletin—November 1971: Diethylstilbestrol Contraindicated in Pregnancy," *California Medicine* 116, no. 2 (1972): 85–86. DES has also been linked with transgender identification. In a presentation to the International Behavioral Development Symposium in 2005, Scott P. Kerlin reported that more than 30 percent of his sample of five hundred "members of the DES Sons International Network" identified as trans or gender-variant in some way. Though Kerlin does not claim causality, his research has been taken up in various strands of medical research to indicate a need for further research that explores whether transness, described in the medical literature as "gender-related disorders," is a potential outcome of prenatal DES and other endocrine-disrupting chemical (EDC) exposures. See, e.g., Ernie Hood, "Are EDCs Blurring Issues of Gender?," *Environmental Health Perspectives* 113, no. 10 (2005): A670–77.

39. Mel Chen, *Animacies: Biopolitics, Racial Mattering, and Queer Affect* (Durham, N.C.: Duke University Press, 2012).

40. Jared Sexton, "Unbearable Blackness," *Cultural Critique* 90 (2015): 167.

41. Jones, *All S/he Wanted,* 196. Unless otherwise noted, all information about Phillip's life is drawn from this source.

42. The specificity of which leg is confirmed in a description of DeVine in John Gregory Dunne, "The Humboldt Murders," January 13, 1997, *New Yorker,* http://www.newyorker.com/magazine/1997/01/13/the-humboldt-murders.

43. Fanon, *Black Skin, White Masks,* 111–12.

44. In *Black Skin, White Masks,* Fanon writes about and within the (film's) interval: "The crippled veteran of the Pacific war says to my brother, 'Resign yourself to your color the way I got used to my stump; we're both victims.' Nevertheless with all my strength I refuse to accept that amputation. I feel in myself a soul as immense as the world, truly a soul as deep as the deepest of rivers, my chest has the power to expand without limit" (ibid., 140). Kara Keeling discusses this moment in some depth, arguing that "Fanon's refusal to accept the film's delimitations of his existence is also an insistence, however fleeting, on the (im)possibility of a different perception when confronted by the film's images," and therefore, to reject the "humility of the cripple" is to deny the temporality of the interval, which is also the *now,* as the inevitable accumulation of the past. Kara Keeling, *The Witch's Flight: The Cinematic, the Black Femme, and the Image of Common Sense* (Durham, N.C.: Duke University Press, 2007), 39–40.

45. Uri McMillan, *Embodied Avatars: Genealogies of Black Feminist Art and Performance* (New York: New York University Press, 2015), 76.

46. See, e.g., the Meditation Trust for a description of the use of transcendental meditation: http://www.meditationtrust.com/.

47. Nikki Giovani, "Nikki-Rosa" (1969), in *The Black Woman: An Anthology,* ed. Toni Cade Bambara (New York: Washington Square Press, 1970), 11.

48. Dorothy E. Roberts, "Welfare and the Problem of Black Citizenship" (1996), University of Pennsylvania Law School, Faculty Scholarship Paper 1283, http://scholarship.law.upenn.edu/faculty_scholarship/1283.

49. See, e.g., Susan W. Blank and Barbara B. Blum, "A Brief History of Work Expectations for Welfare Mothers," *Welfare to Work* 7, no. 1 (1997): 28–38.

50. Martin Gilens, "How the Poor Became Black: The Racialization of American Poverty in the Mass Media," *Race and the Politics of Welfare Reform,* ed. Joe Soss, Sanford F. Schram, and Richard C. Fording (Ann Arbor: University of Michigan Press, 2003), 117.

51. Chris Burbach, "Mother of 3 Victims First to Testify in Slaying Trial," *Omaha World Herald News,* February 22, 1995.

52. Jones, "Hegemonic Whiteness and the Humboldt Murders," 211.

53. Dunne, "Humboldt Murders."

54. Sherley Williams, "Tell Martha Not to Moan," in Bambara, *Black Woman,* 48.

55. Burbach, "Mothers of 3 Victims."

56. Audre Lorde, *The Black Unicorn: Poems* (New York: Norton, 1978), 31. My argument here is deeply indebted to Wynter's work, particularly her essay "Unsettling the Coloniality." See also Denise Ferreira da Silva's meticulous study

on race and the production of space, *Toward a Global Idea of Race* (Minneapolis: University of Minnesota Press, 2007).

57. Dionne Brand, *A Map to the Door of No Return* (Toronto: Vintage Canada, 2002), 4–5.

58. Sonia Sanchez, "haiku poem: 1 year after 9/11," in *Morning Haiku* (Boston: Beacon Press, 2010), 95.

59. Fred Moten, "Black Op," *PMLA* 123, no. 5 (2008): 1745.

60. Brand, *Map to the Door of No Return*, 51.

61. "11 Major Misconceptions about the Black Lives Matter Movement," Black Lives Matter, http://blacklivesmatter.com/11-major-misconceptions-about-the-black-lives-matter-movement/.

62. Sexton, "Unbearable Blackness," 162.

63. Akiba Solomon, "CeCe McDonald: Attacked for Her Identity, Incarcerated for Surviving," *Ebony,* May 4, 2012, http://www.ebony.com/news-views/cece-mcdonald-bias-attack/#axzz3zqFbUFRQ. See also "The Trial of CeCe McDonald," American Independent Institute, accessed February 6, 2016, http://americanindependent.com/216037/the-trial-of-cece-mcdonald.

64. Lisa Marie Cacho, *Social Death: Racialized Rightlessness and the Criminalization of the Unprotected* (New York: New York University Press, 2012), 7. Also see Michelle Alexander, *The New Jim Crow: Mass Incarceration in the Age of Colorblindness* (New York: New Press, 2010); Gilmore, *Golden Gulag*; and Dennis Childs, *Slaves of the State: Black Incarceration from the Chain Gang to the Penitentiary* (Minneapolis: University of Minnesota Press, 2015).

65. Stanley, "Near Life, Queer Death," 1.

66. Sexton, "Social Life of Social Death," 23, 28–29.

67. L. H. Stallings, *Funk the Erotic: Transaesthetics and Black Sexual Cultures* (Urbana-Champaign: University of Illinois Press, 2015), 6, 207. Here, I relate "trans-world identity" to Stallings's larger project of sexual creativity and imagination, as well as to her deployment of the term as a way to articulate personhood away from (or perhaps in spite of) a public.

68. CeCe McDonald, quoted in Omise'Eke Natasha Tinsley, "'Go beyond Our Natural Selves': Letters from Minnesota Correctional Facility–St. Cloud; The Prison Letters of CeCe McDonald," *TSQ: Transgender Studies Quarterly* 4, no. 2 (2017): 252.

69. Ibid., 254.

70. Édouard Glissant, *Caribbean Discourse: Selected Essays,* Trans. J. Michael Dash (Charlottesville: University Press of Virginia / Caraf Books, 1989), 69 (emphasis in original).

INDEX

Page numbers in italics refer to figures.

Abbott, Lyman, 111
Abdur-Rahman, Aliyyah, 68, 76
abjection, 104–6, 121, 123, 130, 134, 192
abolitionists, 58, 62, 69, 72, 75, 77–78, 80, 82, 85–86, 90–91, 95, 108, 111, 226n7
Aborigines Protection Society, 91
about-to-die images, 153, 156
Adams, George C., 162
Advocate.com, viii, xii, 146
Africa, 39, 91, 93, 95, 120, 224n100. *See also individual countries*
African Aid Society, 91
Afro-American, The, 149–51
Afromodernism, 7, 104, 106–7, 106–8, 135–36
Afropessimism, 196
afterimages, xii
Agamben, Giorgio, 185

Agid, Shana: "The Disappearance of Phillip DeVine," 178–79, *179*
Aid to Families with Dependent Children (AFDC), 188–89
Alabama, 28; Montgomery, 20–22, *22,* 36, 41, 102; Selma, 102
Alabama Platform, 28
Alexander, Charles, 117
Alexander, Elizabeth, 184
Alexander, Michelle, 196
American-Anglo Ambulance Corps, 41
American Crystal Sugar Co., 147
American Gynecological Association, 41
American Journal of the Medical Sciences, 32
American Medical Association (AMA), 41, 44; Code of Medical Ethics, 28–29. See also *Journal of the American Medical Association*

Anarcha, 12, 17–18, 20–31, 36–37, 42–43, 53, 59

anatamopoiesis, 108–9, 111, 119, 136

Anderson, Reuben, 146, 150

Andrade, Heather Russell, 226n7

Anthony, Toni, 164

antiblackness, xi, 13, 26, 95, 105, 135, 142, 157, 181–82, 184, 187, 195

antidiscrimination law, xii

anti-Semitism, 26

antitransness, viii–ix, xi, 13, 181, 185, 195–96

archive, of this book, 7

Argentina, 147–48, 234n27

Armstead, Mary D. *See* Davis, Clarissa (Mary D. Armstead)

Asia, 39, 152. *See also individual countries*

Atlanta University, 118

Atlantic Monthly, 112

autopbiography, 119

autopoiesis, 239n23

Avon Books, 101–2, 225n2

bare life, 185

Barker-Benfield, G. J., 42

Barrett, Lindon, 18, 107, 152, 166

bathroom bills, x–xi

Bay, Mia, 94

Becker, Hermann, 44

being/power/truth/freedom, 96, 208n15

Belgium, 38

Bell, Sean, xii–xiii, *xiii,* 195

Bender, George, *49*

Benjamin, Walter, viii

Benton, Michael, 184

Betsey, 12, 17–18, 21–25, 29–31, 36, 42–43, 50, 53, 59

Bey, Yasiin: *Black on Both Sides,* xii, xiv

Bhabha, Homi, ix, 157, 160–61, 166

Bible, 31, 52, 190; John, 52

biomythography, 183–84, 187, 195, 239n23

biopolitics, ix, xiv, 12, 27–28, 40, 104, 109, 185

Black, Georgia, 13, 143–45, 151–57, 162

black art: relation to black personhood, 112–14

Blackett, R. J. M., 85, 91, 93, 95

Black Lives Matter (BLM), x, xii, xiii, 186, 195–97

Black Loyalists, 90, 224n100

black modernity, 12, 135

blackness, 15, 89–91, 93–94, 95–97, 109, 137, 167, 209n25, 223n85, 231n92, 231n98, 236n58; accounting and, viii, 12; art/literature, 111–19; black alienation, ix; black feminism, 7, 103, 195; colonialism and, ix, 141, 181, 187; death and, vii–ix, xiv, 7, 13–14, 101, 152–56, 175, 177–85, 192–97, 235n56; disability and, 27, 43, 186–89; gender and, xi, 1–4, 12–13, 17–53, 56–78, 83–84, 101, 103–8, 113, 119–36, 141–46, 149–58, 166, 169, 186, 188, 219n22, 222n76, 226n7, 226n9, 228n46; ontology and, 82–83; as "problem," 13, 65, 95, 102–4, 120, 125, 227n21; queerness and, 134, 178, 184–86, 195; relation

to transness, x, xiv, 5–11, 14, 20,
53, 57–59, 135–36, 174–75,
183–84, 189, 197–98, 206n15;
the wake and, 156, 185. *See also*
Black Lives Matter (BLM); Black
Trans Lives Matter (BTML)
Black Power movement, 9
black press, 13, 140–75, 235n56.
*See also individual publications
and journalists*
Black Trans Lives Matter (BTML),
184, 195, 197
Bland, Sandra, 195
Bloody Sunday, 102
Bontemps, Arna, 102, 225n2
Boyd, Rekia, 195
Boys Don't Cry, 177–78, 239n12
Braden, Spruille, 147, 234n27
Bradley, Rizvanna, 10–11
Brand, Dionne, 9, 194
Brandon Teena Story, The, 177
Brent, Linda. *See* Jacobs, Harriet
(Linda Brent)
British and Foreign Freedman's Aid
Society, 95
British Association for the
Advancement of Science, 93
BrocKINGton, xi
Brockington, Blake, x–xiv
Brödel, Max, 20, 44–48, *48*
Brody, Jennifer Devere, 178, 239n12
Brooks, Daphne, 2, 4, 75, 82
Brown, Ava Betty, 13, 143–45, 157,
161–66, 175
Brown, Bill, 6
Brown, Carlett, 13, 143–45, 157–
61, 164, 166, 175
Brown, John, 226n7
Brown, Josephine, 75; *Biography of
an American Bondman,* 77–78

Brown, Kimberly Juanita, xii
Brown, Mike, xii–xiii, *xiii*
Brown, Wells (Josephine's father),
75
Browne, Simone, 224n116
Brown v. Board of Education, 233n18
Bruce, Dickson, 118
Brunner, Christoph, 9
Bush, George W., 180
Butler, Judith, 52, 83, 162, 174,
235n55

Cacho, Lisa Marie, 196
Caesar, Julius, 93–94
cakewalk, 2, 4
California: Oxnard, 146–48; Sylmar,
186
camp, 4
Canada, 49, 223n85
Cannady, Mr., 223n85
capitalism, 85, 144, 160–61, 178;
racial, viii, 6, 114, 115, 181
Capri, Kandis, viii
Carby, Hazel, 67, 220n39
carceral gendering, 169
carceral logics, 62, 64, 149, 169,
180, 196–97
Caribbean, 1–2, 5, 9–10, 84, 93,
95, 131, 140. *See also individual
countries*
Carroll, Rebecca, 109
Chaney, Michael, 96
Charles, Ezzard, 151
Charles, Gladys, 151
Chen, Mel, 186
Chicago Defender, 118, 140, 161,
163, 165
Child, Lydia Maria, 67, 218n10
Childs, Dennis, 196
Chile, 56

Christianity, 31, 33, 42, 91, 95, 109; Catholicism, 113. *See also* Bible

citizenship, xii, 103, 124, 158

civil rights movement, 9, 142; Long Civil Rights Movement, 143, 233n18

Civil War (U.S.), 37–38, 41, 91, 95–96

Clay, Edward Williams: *Life in Philadelphia,* 62

Cobb, Jasmine, 62, 70, 90

Cody, John, 45

Cohen, Cathy, x

Cold War, 9, 13, 140, 142–43, 160–61

Colebrooke, Claire, 5

Colebrooke, Henry, 55, 80

Collège de France, 39, 214n52

Collins, Eliza, 76

Collins, Patricia Hills, 122

colonialism, 31, 40, 42, 92, 96, 111, 184, 189, 208n15; blackness and, ix, 141, 181, 187; British, 55, 84, 95, 224n100; decolonialism, 13, 160, 162, 166; European, 32, 39, 70; French, 1, 95; mimicry and, 157; settler, 56, 73; state of emergency and, ix; U.S., 160–61. *See also* imperialism

colonization movement (Black/African), 91–92

Colored American, The, 115–16, *116*

color line, 4, 12–13, 65, 104, 108, 114

commodities: fungibility of, 56, 62, 89; race and, 59, 66, 219n22

communism, 144, 152, 156, 235n44

Compton Cafeteria riot, 180

contract law, 55, 80, 218n2

Cornell University Library: Human Sexuality Collection, 1

countermythology, 143–44, 151

Countess de F, 38

Cox, Laverne, vii–x

Craft, Alfred, 90

Craft, Brougham, 90

Craft, Charles Estlin Phillips, 90

Craft, Ellen (William Johnson), 57–59, 67, 70, 74–86, *87,* 89–90, 95–96, 223n85, 224n100, 224n116

Craft, William, 59, 70, 74, 87, 89, 92–93, 224n100, 224n116; *Running a Thousand Miles for Freedom,* 12, 58, 66–67, 75–86, 90–91, 94–96, 223n85

Crawfund, Mr., 92–94

Crimson and Gray, 118

critical fabulation, 239n23

Crosby, Ranice, 45

cross-dressing, 1, 12, 57–59, 63–64, 69–70, 74, 219n12

Crystal Palace, 86–87, *87*

Cullen, Thomas S., 45, *46; Cancer of the Uterus,* 44

Currah, Paisley, 8

Curran, Andrew, 23

daguerreotypes, 39–40

Dahomean Committee, 91

Dahomey, 91–93, 95

Davis, Clarissa (Mary D. Armstead), 57

Davis, Jordan, xii–xiii, *xiii,* 195

death, x, xii, 21, 26–27, 41, 44–45, 48, 55, 112, 123, 126, 150, 236n57; black and trans, vii–ix, xiv, 7, 13–14, 101, 152–56, 175,

177–85, 192–97, 235n56; of mothers, 125–26, 129–35; slavery and, 23, 69, 71–72, 120, 222n76; slow, viii–ix, 120; social, 107, 185, 196. *See also* suicide

Declaration of Independence, 160

Deleuze, Gilles, 120, 150

Denmark, 140–41, 158; Copenhagen, 158, 162

Denmark–Norway, 56

Derrida, Jacques, 10, 83

desegregation, 152

DeVine, Aisha (Phyllis), 186–88, 190

DeVine, Edith, 186, 188

DeVine, Paul, III, 186, 188–90

DeVine, Paul, Jr., 186, 188–89

DeVine, Paul, Sr., 186, 188

DeVine, Phillip, 13–14, 177–98, 239n12, 241n41

Diallo, Amadou, xii–xiii, *xiii*

diaspora, 4–5, 8, 13, 85, 90, 185

diethylstilbestrol (DES), 186, 241n38

disability, 7, 27, 37, 43, 59, 70, 80–84, 178, 186–87, 189, 242n44

disability culture, 43

disability theory, 7

disgust, 26–27, 213n37

documentary film, xi, 7, 177, 206n15

Dominguez, Tamara, vii–viii

Donlon, Charles, 148

double consciousness, 8, 94, 106

"doubly trans-," 8

Douglass, Frederick, 85; *North Star,* 86

Doyle, Laura, 104

Dr. Henry, 21

Du Bois, W. E. B., 4, 65, 118, 208n8, 227n21, 228n46; "Criteria for Negro Art," 112–14; *Darkwater,* 231n92; on double consciousness, 8, 33, 135, 226n7; on manhood rights, 12, 102–4, 119; *Souls of Black Folk,* 12, 102–4, 106–9, 112–16, *116,* 119, 121–29, 136, 209n25, 226n7, 228n40; "The Study of the Negro Problems," 103

East India Company, 223n85

Ebony, 146, 151–57, 166–74, 196, 236n58

Edwards, Erica, 115

Ellis, Havelock, 4, 19, 208n8

Ellis, Nadia, 4

Ellison, Ralph: *Invisible Man,* 143–44, 174

Ellison, Treva, x

elsewhere and elsewhen, 5

Elworth, James, 181, 190, 195

emancipation, 9, 62, 103, 124, 126

England, 38, 55, 91, 94, 96, 118, 223n85; Liverpool, 84–85; London, 4, 37, 86–87, 90, 224n100; Surrey, 89. *See also* Great Britain; United Kingdom

enumeration, viii, 224n116

Essence.com, 146

Ethiopia, 188

ethnology, 82, 85, 92, 94–96, 224n116; black, 94

Eugénie de Montijo, Empress, 38

Europe, 2, 6, 20, 27, 32, 38, 41, 72, 92–93, 96, 134, 158, 161, 234n27; European colonialism, 39, 70, 95. *See also individual countries*

Fanon, Frantz, 108, 181–83, 185, 198, 227n21, 240n26; *Black Skin, White Masks,* vii, ix, xiv, 6–9, 104–6, 187, 242n44; *A Dying Colonialism,* 111

Farmer, William, 86, 89

Farrakhan, Louis (Calypso Gene), 140

Farred, Grant, 119

Farriss, Nancy, 6

fascism, ix, 144, 147–48, 234n27

"female" within, 13, 101–36, 186

femininity, 20, 25, 27, 33, 36, 42, 45, 59, 129, 132, 149, 172

feminism, 52; black, 7, 103, 195; labor critique, 166–67

Ferguson, Roderick, 160–61, 166

Ferrell, Jonathan, 195

First Pan-African Conference, 4

Fisk University, 102, 122

Fleetwood, Nicole, 70–71

flesh, 5, 69, 72, 74, 83, 144, 150, 185; as genealogy of transness, 57, 62, 64–66; ungendering and, 11–12, 17–53, 135

Food and Drug Administration, 186

Ford, Ezell, vii–viii, *viii*

Foucault, Michel, 33, 39–40, 109, 145, 208n15, 214n52

France, 1, 39, 56, 214n52; French colonialism, 95; Paris, 4, 20, 37–38, 41

Franco-Prussian War, 41

Franklin, John Hope, 101–2, 225n2

Freedmen's Bureau (Bureau for the Relief of Freedom and Refugees), 124–25

freedom, viii, 12, 15, 109, 124, 152, 161, 223n85; death and, 14, 155–56, 183; fungibility and, 55–97;

gender and, 103, 128, 131, 141–43, 160, 226n7. *See also* being/power/truth/freedom; unfreedom

Freeman, Elizabeth, 174

Freud, Sigmund, 51

Fugitive Slave Act, 64, 83–84

fugitivity, 174; fungibility and, 12, 53, 55–97, 172

fungibility, 6, 18, 22–23, 50, 119, 126, 172; fugitivity and, 12, 53, 55–97, 172

Garibaldi, Giuseppe, 38

Garner, Eric, xii–xiii, *xiii,* 195

Garrison, William Lloyd, 75, 86

gender. *See* racialized gender

Georgia, 57, 89; Altamaha, 127; Macon, 74, 76

Germany, 31; Bonn, 158

Gilman, Sander, 19

Gilmore, Ruth Wilson, 196, 239n20

Giovanni, Nikki: "Nikki-Rosa," 188

Glissant, Édouard, 9–10, 197

Glymph, Thavolia, 222n76

Goldsby, Jacqueline, 115

Gondek, Hans-Dieter, 51

Gooding-Williams, Robert, 112

Gordon, Lewis R., 227n21

Gould, Philip, 108

grammar, 1, 6, 11–12, 17, 40, 41, 55–56, 101, 121, 181, 195, 240n28; of criminality, 182, 192; of suffering, 18, 48, 50, 211n5

Grandma, vii

Grant, Oscar, xii–xiii, *xiii*

Great Britain, 37, 85, 92–94, 96; abolitionist movement, 84, 86, 95; British colonialism, 55, 76, 84, 90–91, 95, 223n86, 224n100;

British law, 55. *See also* England;
    Scotland; United Kingdom
Great Dismal Swamp, 72–73
Great Exhibition of All Nations, 86
Great Moments series, 50–51; *Great
    Moments in Medicine, 49*; *Great
    Moments in Pharmacy,* 49
Green, Kai M., x
grievable life, 156, 235n55
Guattari, Félix, 9
Guyana, 2
gynecology: racial suffering as
    foundation, 12, 17–53, 211n11

Haiti, x, 56, 95
Halberstam, Jack, 177–78
Haley, Sarah, 169, 211n9
Half-Century Magazine, 118
Hall, Jacqueline Dowd, 223n18
Hamburger, Christian, 158
Hamilton, Duchess of, 38
Hammonds, Evelynn, 43
Haritaworn, Jin, xii
Harlan, Louis R., 111, 228n34
Harris, Seale, 22–26, *22,* 28–29, 33,
    37–38, 46, 51
Hartman, Saidiya, 1–2, 19, 56, 67,
    68, 103, 120, 145, 239n23
Haslem, Robert, 59, 62
hate crime law, xii, 180
Hate Crimes Sentencing
    Enhancement Act (HCSEA), 180
Hate Crime Statistics Act, 180
Hemphill, Essex, 177
Henson, Josiah, 85
heteronormativity, 36
heteropatriarchy, 78, 193
heterosexuality, 40, 129, 141,
    236n58; compulsory, 181;
    heterosexual matrix, 121

Hicks, Clarence, 146
Hicks Anderson, Lucy, 13, 143–51,
    162, 175
Hinduism, 55
Holland, Sharon, 156, 235n56
Holloway, Karla F. C., 139, 152
homophobia, 8, 181, 196
homosexuality, *159,* 208n8
Horn, August, 44
House Bill 2 (HB2), x–xi
Howell, Joel, 49–50, 217n119
Hunt, Dr.: *Physical and Mental
    Character of the Negro,* 92–94

identity politics, 4, 69
Illinois: Chicago, 161, 162, 171
imperialism, 40, 42, 56, 85, 141,
    157; British, 84, 95, 223n86;
    European, 39, 95; U.S., 13,
    142, 152, 161. *See also*
    colonialism
"impersonation" discourse, 1, 145,
    158, 160, 164
India, 55
intersex conditions, 158, 186
Ireland: Dublin, 37
"Is She Is, or Is She Ain't?," 140
Ivy, Nicole, 40, 211n1

Jacobs, Harriet (Linda Brent), 53,
    220n39; *Incidents in the Life of a
    Slave Girl,* 12, 57–59, 66–74,
    218n10, 220n36
Jamaica, 140
Japan, 152
Jefferson Medical College, 41
Jet, 151, 158–61, 164, 166–67
Jim Crow, 13, 141–42, 144, 156,
    196, 228n40
Job Corps, 190–91

Johns Hopkins, 46; Department of Art as Applied to Medicine, 44

Johnson, Ike, 191

Johnson, James Weldon, 226n7; *Along This Way,* 115, 117–18; *Autobiography of an Ex-Colored Man,* 4, 12, 102, 106–7, 109, 112, 115–20, 122, 130–36; *Fifty Years and Other Poems,* 119–20

Johnson, Lyndon B., 188

Johnson, Marsha P., 145

Johnson, William. *See* Craft, Ellen (William Johnson)

Johnson Publishing Company, 151, 167

Jones, Aphrodite: *All S/he Wanted,* 177, 180–82, 187–88, 190–92

Jones, David M., 181

Jones, Mary (Peter Sewally), 57–66, 219n11, 219n18, 219n22

Jones, Rush, 28–29

Jorgensen, Christine, 13, 139–42, 144–45, 157–58, 160–162, 166, 174–85, 178, 232n3

journalism, 7, 76, 139–75, 196; photojournalism, 153–54. *See also* black press; *individual publications and journalists*

Journal of the American Medical Association, 141

Judaism, 26, 42

Kafka, Franz: "In the Penal Colony," 52

Katz, Jonathan Ned, 60, 63, 219n11

Katz, Tamar, 129

Kay, Jackie: *Trumpet,* 134

Keeling, Kara, ix, xiv, 242n44

Kelly, Howard, 20; *Medical Gynecology,* 20, 45–48; *Operative Gynecology,* 44

Kerlin, Scott P., 241n38

Korean War, 152

Koskovich, Gerard, 207n2

Kristeva, Julia, 105–6

Kucich, John J., 72

Ku Klux Klan, 180

Kuppers, Petra, 23, 43

Lambert, Anna Mae, 182, 193–94

Lambert, Lisa, 13, 177–78, 182, 192–94

Lancashire Cotton Famine, 91

Landrum, Lenny, 192–93

Leopold I, 38

liberalism, 103, 140, 178

Liberator, The, 75, 77, 86

Linen, James A., 148

lithography, 60, 62–63

looking after versus looking for, xiv

Lorde, Audre, xii, 183, 193–94; *Zami,* 184, 239n23, 240n27

Lotter, John, 177

Louis Napoleon III, Emperor, 38

Lucy, 12–13, 17–18, 21–25, 28–31, 36, 42–43, 50, 53, 59

Lugones, Maria, 31

Lyell, Charles: *Antiquity of Man,* 92–93

lynching, 134, 193, 231n98

Mabie, Hamilton W., 111

Malcolm X, 102; *Autobiography of Malcolm X,* 111

mammy, figure of, 119–21, 126–30, 134

manhood rights, 12, 103, 119, 135, 226n7

Manichean darkness, 31, 161

Man-Monster, The, 60–62

Marable, Manning, 228n40

Marassa, Damien-Adia, 10–11

Marriott, David, 9, 104, 182–84, 240n26

Martin, Eugene, 158

Martin, Trayvon, xii–xiii, *xiii*

Marxism, 180

Maryland, 189; Baltimore, 64, 78, 82

masculinity, 59, 102–3, 106, 119, 127–28, 133, 135, 149, 169, 181, 226n7

masochism, 120–21, 126

Maulhardt, Jeffrey: *Oxnard,* 146

Mayer, Peter, 101–2

Mbembe, Achille, 18, 42, 185

McBride, Renisha, 195

McCaskill, Barbara, 57, 78, 84, 89, 96

McClurg, A. C., 112

McDonald, CeCe, 195–97

McDonnell, Mr., 86

McGregor, Deborah Kuhn, 27, 50–51, 211n11

McHarris, James / Annie Lee Grant, 143, 166

McIntire, Gary, 236n58

McKittrick, Katherine, viii, 73, 182–83

McMillan, Uri, 89, 187

McRee, Amy, 36

medical experimentation, 17–53

medical illustrations, 7, 20, 31–35, 44–53

medical instruments, 18–19, 24–25, 29–36, 39, 43, 45–46, *46,* 50

medical plantation, 23, 40

Medical Society of the District of Columbia, 41

memorials, 41–43, 177–78, 200

methodology, of book, 6–11

Metzl, Jonathan, 49–50

Mexico, x, 56

Meyerowitz, Joanne, 141

Middle Passage, 10

Miller, William Ian, 26

mimicry, *71,* 104, 157, 160–62, 164

Mirzoeff, Nicholas, 143

miscegenation, 76, 89

Mississippi: Kosciusko, 166–67, 169, 171

Miss Major, 145

Mock, Janet: *Redefining Realness,* xiv

modernism, 127, 129; Afromodernism, 7, 104, 106–8, 135–36

Modern Pharmacy, 49

Monae, Janelle: "Hell You Talmbout (Say Their Names)," 195

Monroe, Amber, viii

Moore, Lisa Jean, 8

Morgan, Jennifer, 42, 103

Morrison, Toni, 142

Moten, Fred, 5, 57, 137, 194

motherhood, 21, 36, 42–43, 67, 76, 153, 182, 186–90, 194; death and, 125–26, 129–35; racialized gender and, 12–13, 101, 103–8, 129–35. *See also* "female" within

Mothering across Continents, x

Movement for Black Lives. *See* Black Lives Matter (BLM)

Moynihan report, 121

Mrs. A. F., 36

Muñoz, José Esteban, 7

Murray, James, *154*

Muska, Susan: *The Brandon Teena Story,* 177

Musser, Amber, 120–21
Mussolini, Benito, 234n27

Namaste, Viviane, 142–43
National Anti-slavery Standard, 90
National Association for the
   Advancement of Colored People:
   The Crisis, 117
National Era, 86
Nation of Islam, 140
near life, 196
Nebraska, 193; Falls City, 191–92;
   Humboldt, 13–14, 177–78, 180,
   183, 192, 195
necropolitics, ix, xiv, 40, 180
nègre, 23
Negro Star, 118
Nélaton, Auguste, 38
Nero, Charles, 129
Netherlands, 56
New York Academy of Medicine, 17,
   19, 24, 42
New York Age, 117
New York City, 20, 35, 37, 41, 58,
   60, 109, 117, 140
*New-York Medical Gazette and
   Journal of Health,* 35
Ngai, Sianne, 213n37
Nicaragua, 117
Nigeria: Lagos, 91
Nissen, Marvin Thomas, 177, 180–
   81, 187, 190, 193
nonbeing, 5, 48, 73, 105–6, 108,
   121
Norcom, James, 70
North Carolina: Charlotte, x, *xiii*;
   Edenton, 72; Smithfield, viii. *See
   also* Snaky Swamp
North Star, 86
Nyong'o, Tavia, 8–9, 60, 63, 65

Occidentalism, 40
Ockham School, 89–90
Ojanuga, Durrenda, 19
Ólafsdottir, Gréta: *The Brandon
   Teena Story,* 177
ontology, xiv, 39, 48, 52, 74, 194,
   226n9; gender and, 90; race and,
   27–28, 56, 82–83, 96
Operation Plumbbob, 161
Outlook, 109–11, 109–12, 228n34

Page, Enoch, viii
Parke-Davis, 48–49
passing, 57–58, 69–71, 75, 77–84,
   151, 156, 167, 172, 236n58. *See
   also* cross-dressing; fugitivity;
   fungibility
patriarchy, 103, 105, 108, 126;
   heteropatriarchy, 78, 193
Peirce, Kimberly: *Boys Don't Cry,*
   177–78, 239n12
Pennsylvania, 90; Philadelphia, 41,
   62, 72
Pennsylvania Freeman, 90, 117
People's Gay Caucus, 236n58
Perón, Juan Domingo, 147, 234n27
Phillips and Sampson, 220n36
pickup notices, 7, 58, 64–65, *65*
Piola, Erika, 62
plantation visuality, 33
Plantinga, Alvin, 196
poetry, 7, 102, 112, 119
polyvalent mobility, 31, 214n52
pornotroping, 34, 46, 214n63
Portugal, 56
Powers, Hiram: *Greek Slave,* 86–88,
   88
prisons, ix, 58, 64, 146, 148, 150–
   51, 158, 167, 169–70, *170,* 174,
   196–97

Progressive Era, 112, 124
property: racially gendered, xi, 56, 58, 64, 80, 89, 103–4, 125, 129
Prosser, Jay, 132, 233n9
psychoanalysis, 66, 121, 180. *See also* abjection
Punch, 86, *88*

queer and trans of color critique, 7
queerness, x, 120, 127, 129, 180; antiqueer violence, 8, 181, 196; blackness and, 134, 178, 184–86, 195; queer performance, 1, 4–5

racialized gender, ix–xi, 2, 208n8, 214n49, 214n52, 223n85, 224n116, 226n8, 228n46; anatamopoiesis and, 108–9; carceral gendering, 169; commodities and, 59, 66, 219n22; definition, viii; flesh and, 5, 12–13, 17–53, 211n11; fugitivity and, 55–97; manhood rights, 12, 103, 119, 135, 226n7; medicine and, 13, 17–53; motherhood and, 12–13, 101, 103–8, 129–35; ontology and, 27–28, 56, 82–83, 96; property and, xi, 56, 58, 64, 80, 89, 103–4, 125, 129; racial capitalism, viii, 6, 114, 115, 181; sex and, 4, 11–12, 17–53, 62, 74, 97, 126, 135; slavery and, 12, 17–53, 103–4, 120, 126, 130–31, 135, 211n1, 222n76, 226n9; as theory of history, 8; transatlantic litera-ture and, 13, 101–36; trans martyrdom and, 13–14, 177–98; transsexuality and, 13, 139–75. *See also* antiblackness; blackness; color line; patriarchy; transness; transsexuality; ungendering; whiteness
racial real, 13, 104, 108, 112–13, 115, 228n46
racial science, 19; producing sex and gender, 40–41
racism, 13, 23, 114, 128, 152, 196, 214n52, 231n98, 235n55; definition, 239n20; scientific racism, 208n8. *See also* anti-blackness; Jim Crow; Ku Klux Klan; slavery; white supremacy
raw life, 185
Reconstruction, 12, 65, 104, 107, 122–25
Redmond, Shana, 117
Report of the British Association for the Advancement of Science, 93
restive, 166, 169, 172, 174
Rhoades, Troy, 9
Rhythm (record label), 140
Richardson, Matt, viii, 134
Riges Hospital, 158
Riggs, Marlon: *Tongues Untied,* 161
Roberts, Monica, 146
Roberts, Neil, 8
Roberts, Robin, vii
Robinson, Jackie, 152
Rooks, Noliwe, 123
Roper, Moses, 85
Rosenberg, Julius and Ethel, 236n57
Ross, Marlon, 113, 226n8

Saint Helena, 223n85
Saint Kitts, 2
Samuels, Ellen, 83–84
Sanchez, Sonia, 194
#Say Her/Their Name(s), 195
Scarry, Elaine, 33

Schmitz, Dean, 196

Schwartz, Marie Jenkins, 22–23

Scotland: Edinburgh, 37

Scott, Darieck, 121, 134

Sedgwick, Eve Kosofsky, 129

Semenya, Caster, 219n22

Serlin, David, 139–40, 142, 166

Sewally, Peter. *See* Jones, Mary (Peter Sewally)

sex, 2, 5, 70, 140, 151, 153, 156, 158–62, 171; race and, 4, 11–12, 17–53, 62, 74, 97, 126, 135. *See also* intersex conditions; transsexuality

sexology, 19, 23, 66, 132, 208n8

Sexton, Jared, 195–96

sexuality, 1, 43, 152, 193, 243n67; race and, 4–5, 13, 58, 62–64, 66–68, 76, 86, 104, 111, 119–21, 129, 143, 214n63, 238n8. *See also* heterosexuality; homosexuality

sexual violence, 19, 76, 128, 172, 182

sex work, 59, 63–64, 161

Sharpe, Christina, 12, 15, 69, 156, 185, 210n45

Sierra Leone, 90, 93, 95

Silva, Denise Ferreira da, 227n26

Sims, J. Marion, 218n2; medical experimentation by, 12, 17–53, 49, 59, 74, 135, 211n1, 213n37, 214n49; *The Story of My Life,* 20–27, 38–39; *Uterine Surgery,* 38

Sir Lady Java, 145

Skidmore, Emily, 141

slavery, viii, 9, 115, 218n2, 223n86, 224n116; afterlives of, 10, 125, 135, 172, 196, 210n36; death and, 23, 69, 71–72, 120, 155, 222n76; fugitivity and, 7, 12, 55–97, 169, 172; fungibility and, 19–53, 55–56; racialized gender and, 103–4, 120, 126, 130–31, 135, 211n1, 222n76, 226n9; slavery-to-freedom plot, 108–9. *See also* emancipation; Middle Passage

Slavery Abolition Act, 223n85

Smith, James P., 76

Smith, Valerie, 67

Snaky Swamp, 69, 71–73

social death, 107, 185, 196

socialism, 144, 234n27

Solomon, Akiba, 196

Somerville, Siobhan, 131, 133, 208n8

Sontag, Susan, 153

South Africa, x

South Carolina, 42; Charleston, x; Columbia, 41

South Sudan, x

Spain, 56

Speaking Sex exhibit, 1

Spillers, Hortense, xi, 10–11, 66, 182; on flesh, 17–19, 34, 53; on gender, 12–13, 19, 55–57, 83, 101, 103, 106, 108, 119, 121, 129, 143, 172, 186; on pornotroping, 214n63

Sri Lanka, 223n85

SS *Cambria,* 84

Stallings, L. H., 11, 26, 99, 136, 196, 243n67

Stanley, Eric, 167, 196

Stanley-Jones, Aiyana, 195

Starcke, Viggo, 162

state of emergence, ix

state of emergency, vii–ix

Sterling, Dorothy, 91, 95

Still, William, 57

Still Black: A Portrait of Black Transmen, 206n15
still life, 185, 196–98
Stoler, Ann Laura, 214n52
Stone Butch Blues, 209n25
Stonewall Rebellion, 164, 180
Stowe, Harriet Beecher, 220n39; *Dred,* 72; *Uncle Tom's Cabin,* 67
Stryker, Susan, 8, 139–40, 232n3
substitution, 13, 22–23, 42, 104
suicide, xii, 182
Sullivan, Mecca Jamilah, 240n28
Summers, Martin, 226n8
Sun Ra, 198
super vivere, 193
supplementarity, 83–84, 187
Symonds, John Addington, 4
synecdoche, 13, 104

Teena, Brandon, 178, 180–81, 193; Brandon archive, 13, 177, 182, 186, 191–92, 194, 197
temporal drag, 174
Tenniel, Joseph: "The Virginian Slave," 86, *88*
thanatopolitics, 111
Thayer and Eldridge, 220n36
theft, 12, 48, 55–56, 58–59, 63, 74, 219n12
thing theory, 6
Thom, Robert, 48, 52; *J. Marion Sims,* 20, 49–53, *49*
Thomas, Greg, 40
Thompkins, Kyla Wazana, 66
Thompson, Amelia, 86, 89
Thompson, Miss, 86
Thompson, Mrs., 86
Thrasher, Max Bennett, 111, 228n36

Three Negro Classics, 12, 101–36. *See also* Du Bois, W. E. B.: *Souls of Black Folk*; Johnson, James Weldon: *Autobiography of an Ex-Colored Man*; Washington, Booker T.: *Up from Slavery*
Till, Emmett, xii–xiii, *xiii*
Time magazine, 147–48, 234n27
Tisdel, Leslie, 191–94
Tom Joyner Morning Show, 145
tranifesting, x
transaesthetics, 99, 136
"transgender bathroom bill." *See* House Bill 2 (HB2)
Transgender Day of Remembrance/Resistance, xii, 184
transitivity, 5–12, 14, 18, 21, 53, 56–58, 64, 69, 75, 135–36, 152, 172, 174, 183, 185
Trans Lives Matter (TLM), x, 7, 184, 195, 197
transness: DES and, 241n38; relation to blackness, x, xiv, 5–10, 5–11, 14, 20, 53, 57–59, 135–36, 174–75, 183–84, 189, 197–98, 206n15; relation to transgender, 8
transparency thesis of modernity, 227n26
transphobia, viii–ix, xi, 13, 181, 185, 195–96
transsexuality, 11, 13, 139–40, 140–44, 150, 157, 160, 162, 166, 174–75, 232n3; transsexual autobiography, 132, 233n9
transsexual real, 175
trans studies, xiv, 7, 175
transubstantiation, 6, 19, 83–85, 92, 94, 104, 111

transversality, 5, 8–11, 18, 21, 26, 57–58, 69, 73, 136, 143, 172, 185
trans-world identity, 196, 243n67
Tubman, Harriet, 57
20/20, 178

Underground Railroad, 57, 75, 82
unfreedom, 62, 141–42, 155, 160
ungendering, 11, 19, 33, 44, 56–57, 56–59, 63, 67, 69–70, 74, 90, 135
United Kingdom, 56, 75–76, 84, 140, 218n10. *See also* England; Great Britain
Uruguay, 56
U.S. Department of Labor, 190

Venezuela, 56
vesticovagina fistula (VVF), 17–38, 43, 211n11, 213n37, 214n49
Virginia, 57, 65, 73, 78, 82, 86, *88*
virtualities, 150
visual culture studies, 7
von Miller, Ferdinand Freiherr, 41
Voting Rights Act, 102, 233n18

wake: blackness and, 156, 185
Walcott, Rinaldo, 154–55, 236n60
Walker, Elisha, viii
Wall, Cheryl, 112, 114
Wall, L. L., 19
Wallace-Sanders, Kimberly, 120
Wanzo, Rebecca, 42–43, 213n37
Warner, Anne Bradford, 72
War on Poverty, 188
Washington, Booker T., 226n7, 228n36, 228n40; *Up from Slavery,* 12, 102, 106–7, 109–16, 119, 121–22, 124–26, 129–31, 135

Washington, Harriet, 24, 48, 50
Washington, D.C., 191
Waters, Mary Ann, 58–59, 64–65, *65*
Watts Rebellion, 102
Webb, Alvin Chick, 140
Weems, Maria Ann (Jo Wright), 57
Weheliye, Alexander, 53, 135, 185, 228n46
Wells Brown, William, 75–78, 82, 86–87, *87*
Wescott, Mr., 21, 23
We've Been Around—Lucy Hicks Anderson, 146
White, Barbara, 50
whiteness, 7, 111, 117–20, 124, 152–53, 156, 178, 187, 189–90, 223n85, 231n98, 236n58; colonialism and, 1, 161; fugitive slave narratives and, 57–59, 62, 67–70, 72, 75–86, 89, 93–97; gender and, 19, 21, 23, 27, 32–33, 37, 40, 46, 50–51, 67–70, 72, 75–96, 89, 97, 103–4, 125–33, 141–42, 193, 222n76; hegemonic, 181; performance and, 1–2; U.S. versus British, 95–96
white supremacy, 132, 142, 161, 181. *See also* Ku Klux Klan
Wilderson, Frank, 48, 82–83, 104, 211n5
Williams, Sherley, 191
Wilson, Sondra Kathryn, 117
Woman's Hospital, 37, 41
Women's Missionary Society, 153
Woodard, Vincent, 65
Work Incentive Program (WIN), 189
World Health Organization, 211n11

World War II, 9, 13, 143, 154;
    Treaty of San Francisco, 152
Woubshet, Dagmawi, viii
Wright, Jo. *See* Weems, Maria Ann
    (Jo Wright)
Wright, Richard: *Native Son,* 104
Wynter, Sylvia, xi, 7, 53, 73, 96,
    104–6, 182, 185, 208n15,
211n47, 239n23, 240n26,
    242n56

Yugoslavia, 158

Zelizer, Barbara
Ziegler, Kortney Ryan: *Still Black,*
    206n15

C. Riley Snorton is associate professor of Africana studies and feminist, gender, and sexuality studies at Cornell University and visiting associate professor of American studies and ethnicity at the University of Southern California. He is the author of *Nobody Is Supposed to Know: Black Sexuality on the Down Low* (Minnesota, 2014).